THE ARMY OF ALEXANDER THE GREAT

Richard Taylor

Helion & Company

Helion & Company Limited
Unit 8 Amherst Business Centre
Budbrooke Road
Warwick
CV34 5WE
England
Tel. 01926 499 619
Email: info@helion.co.uk
Website: www.helion.co.uk
Twitter: @helionbooks
Visit our blog https://helionbooks.wordpress.com/

Published by Helion & Company 2025
Designed and typeset by Mach 3 Solutions (www.mach3solutions.co.uk)
Cover designed by Paul Hewitt, Battlefield Design (www.battlefield-design.co.uk)

Text © Richard Taylor 2025
All photographs and illustrations by the author unless individually credited
Colour artwork by Renato Dalmaso © Helion & Company 2025

Maps by Richard Taylor © Helion & Company 2025

Every reasonable effort has been made to trace copyright holders and to obtain their permission for the use of copyright material. The author and publisher apologize for any errors or omissions in this work and would be grateful if notified of any corrections that should be incorporated in future reprints or editions of this book.

ISBN 978-1-804517-70-3

British Library Cataloguing-in-Publication Data.
A catalogue record for this book is available from the British Library.

All rights reserved. No part of this publication may be reproduced, stored in a retrieval system, or transmitted, in any form, or by any means, electronic, mechanical, photocopying, recording or otherwise, without the express written consent of Helion & Company Limited.

For details of other military history titles published by Helion & Company Limited contact the above address or visit our website: http://www.helion.co.uk.

We always welcome receiving book proposals from prospective authors.

Contents

1	Introduction	5
2	The Campaigns of Alexander	18
3	The Macedonian Cavalry	28
4	The Macedonian Infantry	44
5	Subjects, Allies and Mercenaries	76
6	The Imperial Army	104
7	Command and Operations	122
8	Serving in the Army	139
9	Minor Actions and Sieges	150
10	The Major Battles	166

Notes to colour plates	208
Further Reading	213
Bibliography	216

1
Introduction

Scope and Sources

The army with which Alexander (Alexandros), known as 'the Great' (356–323 BCE – all dates in this book are BCE, unless stated otherwise) conquered the Persian Empire, was in large part the creation of his father, Philip (Philippos) II. It was Philip who, succeeding to the Macedonian throne in 359, brought the kingdom up from a position of weakness, beset on all sides by enemies and without an effective army, and made it the most powerful state in Greece. His achievement involved numerous reforms and improvements to the functioning of the Macedonian kingdom and was greatly aided by the fortuitous discovery of large silver mines, but it was largely driven by his creation of a new Macedonian army, based around a well-trained and well-equipped force of heavy infantry. Macedon had a long tradition of effective cavalry, with the land-owning nobility of the kingdom providing a modestly sized but effective cavalry force, but it had traditionally lacked effective heavy infantry, which would have allowed it to stand up against the hoplite (heavily armoured citizen militia) forces of the Greek cities to the south. Macedonian infantry traditionally fought as lightly-armed skirmishers, dependent on the javelin and using hit-and-run tactics. Such forces could be numerous, and effective enough when skirmishing in rough terrain, but they lacked the steadiness required to stand up in pitched battle against hoplites. Philip changed this by organising and equipping a Macedonian phalanx – a force of native heavy infantry capable of fighting in the main line of battle. This phalanx was not simply a copy of the hoplite phalanxes of the Greek cities to the south; it was differently equipped, with a long *sarissa*, or pike, taking the place of the shorter Greek spear, and it was also highly drilled and trained, contrasting with the tradition of amateurism that had always been the norm in the south (although during the fourth century there was a trend in much of Greece toward forming at least a core force of well trained professional infantry). With this new model army, formed around the new phalanx, Philip was able, over a period of 20 years, to defeat Macedon's immediate neighbours, consolidate and expand the kingdom's borders, and bring under his control many of the Greek cities and colonies dotted around the north shore of the Aegean. He then turned south and, by defeating Athens and

THE ARMY OF ALEXANDER THE GREAT

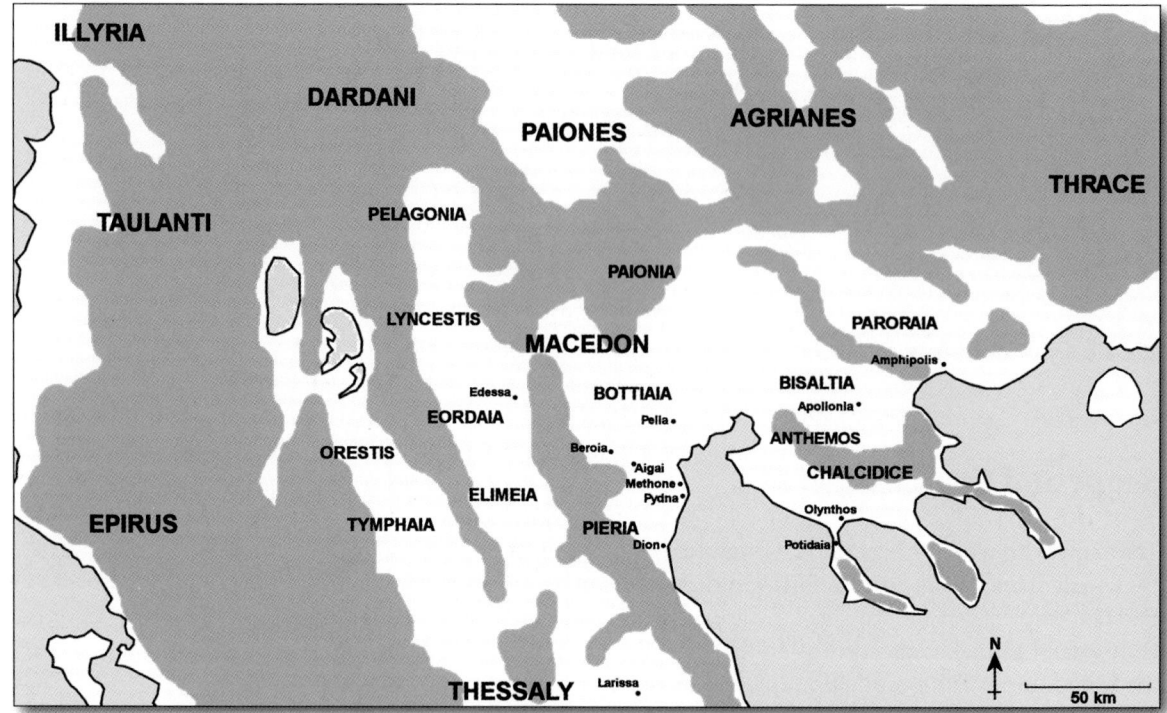

The Kingdom of Macedon and surrounding regions in the late fourth century BCE.

Thebes at the Battle of Chaironeia (338), made himself the master of Greece, forcing all the Greek cities except the Spartans, who stubbornly refused to take part, to join the Hellenic League (often called the League of Corinth by modern historians), with the express purpose of carrying out the long-planned scheme to invade and conquer the Persian Empire, or at least part of it.

Persia was the sole superpower of this period in the Mediterranean and Near Eastern world; from the Persian homeland in what is now Iran, a succession of highly effective kings had, during the sixth and fifth centuries, extended Persian control over a vast empire stretching from India in the east to Egypt and the shores of the Mediterranean in the west. In Asia Minor (modern Turkey), the Persian Empire came up against the Greek colonies of the Ionian coast, and the Persian desire to control the frontiers of its empire clashed with the Greek desire for political independence. Two major Persian invasions of Greece were defeated in the early fifth century; subsequently, the Persians took a more hands-off approach, using diplomacy, bribery and proxy forces (usually Spartans) to protect their interests without again attempting to conquer Greece. Yet from the late fifth century, the Empire was in a state of constant turmoil and decline, with major rebellions, particularly in Egypt, sapping its strength and the energies of Philip (along with many Greek thinkers who wished to see the Greek cities stop fighting each other and instead fight an external enemy and win vast tracts of land and treasures), after his subjugation of Greece, were directed toward organising an invasion of the Persian Empire.

The advance force of this invasion was already active in Asia Minor, establishing a bridgehead, when Philip was assassinated by a disaffected

Macedonian officer. He was succeeded by his 20-year-old son Alexander. Along with the kingdom and the army, Alexander inherited the plan to conquer the Persian Empire, a plan which he was to put into spectacularly successful effect over the next 13 years. It is possible that Philip's intention had not been to conquer the whole of the Persian Empire but merely to carve out new territories for Greek expansion in Asia Minor, but Alexander's ambitions were (or became, as success followed success) far grander, and led him, and the Macedonian army he commanded, all the way to the frontiers of India, with Alexander himself replacing the Persian Darius (Dareios) III as 'King of Kings', in control of the entire Persian Empire. Alexander and the Macedonian army remained undefeated on the battlefield throughout this campaign of conquest, and ironically, Alexander's only defeat was at the hands of his own army, which ultimately refused to march further into India, forcing Alexander to turn back and return to Babylon, where he died, probably of disease, possibly of poison, in 323, aged 33.

It is this army – initially created by Philip and commanded with such spectacular success by Alexander – that forms the subject of this book. The origins of the army under Philip must be described in order to understand the success of Alexander, as the army was never Alexander's alone, and in particular, the nature of the Macedonian phalanx which Philip created will form a large part of the subject matter of Chapter 4. Alexander's army was also not simply the national army of Macedon, which only formed its core. The native Macedonian units – chiefly the infantry of the phalanx and the Hypaspists, along with the Companion cavalry and various smaller auxiliary units – were supplemented by allied, subject or mercenary forces. Philip and Alexander recruited forces from their 'barbarian' neighbours, the Thracians, Illyrians and related peoples of the southern Balkans, and from Greek states further south, particularly the Thessalian cavalry from Macedon's southern neighbour. A large force of infantry was also supplied by the cities of the League (though, as we will see, its role in Alexander's campaigns is consistently downplayed in our sources), and mercenaries were also recruited to provide additional forces of light infantry and cavalry. This Macedonian-Allied army served up to the point where Darius was overthrown, and Alexander replaced him. Thereafter, many of the Greek units were sent home and Alexander recruited increasingly from his new Asian subjects, with forces at first mostly of cavalry and ultimately large forces of infantry being drawn from such sources. It is convenient, therefore, to consider Alexander's army in three parts: the native Macedonian forces, the allied and mercenary Greeks and Balkan peoples, and the Asian subjects. Of these, most is known about the native Macedonians, many of whom stayed with Alexander throughout the campaign. But it is important to remember that the 'big three' of this core Macedonian army (phalanx, Hypaspists, Companions) only ever formed around half (at most) of the total field army available to Alexander.

As to the sources of information available for the army of Alexander, historical sources broadly fall into three categories – contemporary documentary evidence (true primary evidence), contemporary or later historical accounts (literary or secondary evidence), and survivals and discoveries of contemporary depictions of military equipment, or of that equipment itself (usually, only those parts of it that were made of metal, since organic materials have mostly decomposed to dust in the intervening 23 centuries).[1]

The army of Alexander is unusually badly served by this last category, archaeological evidence. Although there exist many sculptural depictions of Alexander himself, these naturally tell us very little about the army he commanded. Depictions of soldiers of the army are exceedingly few, and none certainly contemporary. The best, which should be the most useful, is the 'Alexander Sarcophagus', not, in fact, the sarcophagus of Alexander, but of one of his client rulers, created about a decade after Alexander's death. This monument is decorated with carved depictions of soldiers of Alexander's army, but as we shall see, it poses as many questions as it answers due to uncertainties about exactly which soldiers from which units are depicted, or indeed if any are depicted accurately at all, as it may be that artistic conventions were foremost in the mind of the sculptor, rather than strict adherence to details of uniforms or equipment. Equally tantalising is the 'Alexander Mosaic', a Roman mosaic copy from Pompeii, of a contemporary Greek painting of Alexander and Darius and their forces locked in battle (though which battle is also open to debate). This mosaic contains a fine depiction of the central figures, Alexander and Darius, though sadly, the section of the mosaic containing most of the Macedonians following Alexander has been heavily damaged. Surviving parts of the mosaic tell us rather more about the Persian army than they do about the Macedonian. To these two depictions can be added other artistic evidence, including coin images (obviously limited by their small size) and tomb paintings, though most of the latter date from after the period of Alexander; nevertheless, given the paucity of direct contemporary evidence, we must use such depictions on occasion, with caution. Most useful should be the most remarkable discovery of all, the tomb of Philip II himself, confidently identified as such by its discoverer (though not everyone is convinced by the identification). Although some military equipment has been found in and around the tomb (and other related high-status tombs in the area), the tomb of a king does not necessarily tell us much about the appearance and equipment (and, of course, nothing at all about the organisation) of the rank and file of the army. Wall paintings associated with the tomb, while of enormous artistic value and importance, also do not depict military scenes. As to other survivals of actual military equipment, again, pickings are perhaps surprisingly slim. We know quite a lot about the equipment of Greek armies from the southern states, thanks to the twin boons of numerous artistic depictions, in the form of painted vases, and of survivals of actual pieces of equipment, due sometimes to the early practice of burying equipment with the dead, but mostly from the more common tradition of dedicating captured equipment at one of the great religious centres of Greece, chiefly Olympia. By the reign of Alexander, however, these practices had largely died out; vase paintings no longer appear (at least, not ones depicting contemporary equipment), there

---

1 For a discussion of the sources, see Baynham (2003) and the relevant chapters (Part III) of Ogden (2024).

INTRODUCTION

The 'Alexander Sarcophagus', discovered in Sidon and now in the Istanbul Archaeological Museum (Osman Hamdi Bey and T. Reinach, *Une nécropole royale à Sidon: fouilles: Plate XXV*)

are few, if any, finds of dedicated equipment, and the few surviving tomb paintings go only some way to making up the shortfall. Actual equipment from Alexander's reign (or even Philip's, aside from that found in the royal tombs) is almost entirely unknown. Such items of equipment as have been discovered can only ever be tentatively identified as belonging to any part of Alexander's army, and often their exact identification is uncertain. More such equipment (particularly shields and helmets) survives from the three centuries or so after Alexander (the Hellenistic age), and as with other forms

The 'Alexander Mosaic', a Roman copy of a Hellenistic original, found in the House of the Faun, Pompeii, now in the Naples Archaeological Museum (Photographer: Berthold Werner, Public Domain)

of evidence, we must sometimes, with caution, use this to inform our view of Alexander's army.

As a result of these issues, direct archaeological evidence for the army is tantalisingly limited and difficult to interpret, and we must often rely instead on the written sources. Direct contemporary documentary evidence for Alexander's army is, however, even more limited than the archaeological evidence. During the Hellenistic period, those Successors of Alexander who established their power base in Egypt (the Ptolemaic dynasty) used papyrus for many official records, which the dry climate of Egypt has sometimes preserved to this day. Such documents are, however, almost completely absent for Alexander's reign itself. Greeks preferred to inscribe official texts on stone, and there are some survivals of such epigraphic evidence, as it is called, but they tell us little about the army. Instead, we are very heavily reliant on the literary evidence – the various histories of Alexander written by historians in antiquity. Here too, there are tantalising gaps – several contemporaries of Alexander are known to have written detailed accounts of his campaigns, including two officers in his army, Aristoboulos and Ptolemy (Ptolemaios, the same Ptolemy who made himself Pharaoh of Egypt after Alexander's death), and the official court historian, Callisthenes (at least up to the point where he fell out with Alexander and was executed, or died in captivity, according to different accounts). However, although at least some of these accounts were known and read for several hundred years after Alexander, none have survived to the present day. Instead, we must rely on the works of later historians, all of them writing under either the Roman Republic or later Empire, and all separated in time from Alexander by at least three centuries. Of these later accounts, the most important are the 'big four': Diodorus of Sicily, Quintus Curtius, Plutarch, and Arrian.

Diodorus (Diodoros) wrote his account of Alexander in the first century as part of his monumental 'Library of History', an account of the Greek and Roman worlds from earliest times up to his own day. Diodorus does not come across as an especially skilled historian, often being content to take a single source (an earlier written account) for each section of his history and embellish it a little with some stock phrases or his own imagination. He did, however, have access to earlier sources now lost to us, and in the case of Alexander, this was a now lost history by an author called Cleitarchos, written at the end of the fourth century. This original source, along with a variety of other contemporary or near-contemporary accounts, make up what is termed today the 'Vulgate' tradition about Alexander. This same source, or group of sources, was also used in the first century CE by Quintus Curtius Rufus, a Roman historian who wrote a full account of the campaigns of Alexander, of which all but the first two books have survived. Curtius was perhaps a more careful historian than Diodorus, though when it comes to technical details of Alexander's army, his work has the drawback of being written in Latin, meaning that some technical terms have been obscured by the process of translation. Also writing in the first century CE was Plutarch (Ploutarchos), a prolific writer of improving, historically-based literature who wrote a series of biographies of important figures of the Greek and Roman world. Plutarch's brief account of the life of Alexander is useful for some details, but Plutarch was writing quick character sketches with a moral purpose, and technical details of armies, deployments and equipment were of little interest to him. In contrast, is the last but not least of the 'big four', Arrian (full name Lucius Flavius Arrianus), who was a Roman governor, military commander and historian living in the second century CE and an admirer both of Alexander and of the earlier Greek historian and military theorist, Xenophon. Arrian, too, wrote a history, in Greek, of Alexander, calling it the *Anabasis of Alexander*, taking the name from Xenophon's earlier *Anabasis* ('Expedition'), an account of the march of the Ten Thousand mercenaries at the close of the fourth century. For his main sources, Arrian used the now lost, and even in his own day less well known, accounts of Ptolemy and Aristoboulos. As such – with access to excellent sources and with an interest in and knowledge of military matters – Arrian is by far the most important and useful of the Alexander historians whose work survives from antiquity, and his account forms the most reliable source for modern accounts of Alexander's life and times (including this one). However, Arrian, too, has his weaknesses; in particular, he shows an unfortunate tendency to repeat technical terms or unit names he found in his sources without explaining their meaning (perhaps because he did not understand them himself) or to skate over technical military matters which it would be helpful to have more clearly elucidated. It is also the case that sometimes the accounts conflict and Arrian was no more able to establish the truth than we are. As Arrian himself says, with a note of some despair:

> Not even those whose narratives are entirely trustworthy and who actually accompanied Alexander at that time agree in their accounts of events which were public and within their own knowledge. (Arr. *Anab*. 4.14.3)

On technical military matters, we also have a tradition of Hellenistic military manuals, composed, in the case of Asclepiodotus (Asclepiodotos), the earliest that has survived, late in the Hellenistic period or, in the case of Aelian (Ailianos) and Arrian, the same man as the historian of Alexander, under the Roman Empire but based on earlier examples. These authors together are generally referred to as 'the Tacticians', and their manuals provide detailed technical specifications – unit names and numbers, equipment, drill commands – for an idealised Hellenistic army based around a Macedonian phalanx. This type of phalanx was invented by Philip and used by Alexander, and the writers of these manuals were confident that they were describing a military organisation that would have been known to Alexander. So, it may well be that we can apply many of these technical details to Alexander's army, even though the earliest surviving manual dates from two centuries after Alexander's time. But we must do so with caution, since while there was undoubtedly continuity of military practice throughout the Hellenistic period, there was also development and change, and we cannot be sure that details preserved in the Tacticians are directly applicable to Alexander's army. Also available are the collections of 'stratagems', clever military tricks and tactics, collections of which were popular under the Roman Empire, and of which two examples, those of Polyaenus (Polyainos) and Frontinus, have survived. These naturally contain many references to the stratagems of Alexander and Philip, some of which are of value, though these collections were by their nature gathered uncritically, and many of the tricks described are either too vague or too commonplace to be of great use for technical military matters.[2]

Though the account of Arrian forms the most important basis for any account of Alexander's army, it still leaves many gaps in our understanding. Some aspects of the army remain hopelessly obscure or completely unknown to us today, and around a few core controversies (such as the identity of the 'Asthetairoi', the equipment of the Hypaspists, and the organisation of the Hipparchies, all of which will be encountered in the following pages), a large but inconclusive literature has developed, as modern historians argue their various interpretations to and fro. There is much more we do not know about the army of Alexander than we do know, and even what we think we know is all too often based on scant or uncertain evidence. In this book, I will acknowledge these controversies and the lack of clear evidence for many interpretations; however, I expect that readers of this book are looking for an account of the army of Alexander, even if it may only be one among several possible interpretations, rather than picking through the details of modern scholarly debate. As such, what follows will be my personal interpretation of the army. I will not engage in detailed analysis or comparison of other modern views, which will, however, be referenced in the footnotes and can be followed up by interested readers through the works listed in the bibliography. Nor will I always consider all the possible interpretations of the ancient evidence, instead selecting the one that I consider most likely (though on some of the controversies, I will delve into more detail of the varying possibilities). Again, readers can seek out other views using the bibliography. Some of the problems of Alexander's army are unresolvable, and in such cases, I will simply set out various possibilities. Readers troubled by such uncertainties or dismayed at the frequency with which the words 'perhaps', 'possibly' and 'we do not know' appear in this account might do better to limit their interests to other better-documented periods of history.

The Size of the Army

The core of the army of Alexander was formed from the Macedonian contingents themselves, those of the national Macedonian army first created by Philip. These can be divided into five groups: the Companion cavalry, the Hypaspists (infantry guard), the bulk of the phalanx (Pezhetairoi and Asthetairoi), other Macedonian cavalry, and Macedonian light infantry. At the outset, it is worth commenting on some of the difficulties inherent in studying these various units (and the others that made up the army of Alexander). The most basic information that any historian might want about an army is its order of battle, that is, the identity and strength of the various

---

2   For the Tacticians, see Rance and Sekunda (2017).

units of which the army is composed. However, this basic information is almost completely lacking in this case. The historical accounts name various units, and on occasion (chiefly, the major battles) will sometimes provide a list of unit names along with their deployment position in the line, but they never provide the combination of unit name and identity with strength in the consistent fashion which the modern historian would like. As a result, we have to piece together orders of battle from scattered references, which frequently are not mutually compatible.

Even the most basic information – such as the size of Alexander's invasion army at its initial crossing of the Hellespont – remains uncertain, as various sources (or references in later accounts to such sources) give divergent figures. According to Arrian (Arr. *Anab.* 1.11.3), basing his account on that of Ptolemy, on Alexander's march to the Hellespont, 'his infantry including light troops and archers numbered not much above 30,000, his cavalry over 5,000'. The second-century Greek statesman and historian Polybius (Polybios) wrote a criticism of the official account of Alexander's campaigns by Callisthenes, noting that Callisthenes 'says that he [Alexander] crossed into Asia with 40,000 infantry and 4,500 cavalry' (Pol. 12.19.1). Plutarch (in one of his moralising works about Alexander), provides some more options: Alexander invaded Asia 'relying only on the 30,000 foot and 4,000 cavalry which were his; for, according to Aristoboulos, that was the full extent of their number. But King Ptolemy puts them at 30,000 foot and 5,000 horse, Anaximenes at 43,000 foot, 5,500 horse.' (Plut. *De Alex.* 1.3 (327 D-E)). Diodorus also gets in on the act and performs the unusual trick of disagreeing with himself. Noting that Alexander, on crossing to Asia, 'made an accurate count of his accompanying forces', he then gives the details: 'There were found to be, of infantry, 12,000 Macedonians, 7,000 allies, and 5,000 mercenaries, all of whom were under the command of Parmenion. Odrysians, Triballians, and Illyrians accompanied him to the number of 7,000; and of archers and the so-called Agrianians 1,000, making up a total of 30,000 foot soldiers. Of cavalry there were 1,800 Macedonians, commanded by Philotas son of Parmenion; 1,800 Thessalians, commanded by Callas son of Harpalus; 600 from the rest of Greece under the command of Erigyius; and 900 Thracians, scouts and Paeonians with Cassander in command, making a total of 4,500 cavalry' (Diod. 17.17.3–4). The totals of the infantry figures Diodorus gives, in fact, add up to 32,000, and the cavalry to 5,100 (presumably Diodorus forgot to include the 600 Greeks among the cavalry and rounded down the number of infantry).

These figures can be reconciled with the application of a little ingenuity, and doing so is a favourite pastime of modern historians of Alexander. In particular, the greatest discrepancy (about 30,000 infantry or about 40,000) is likely to arise from the inclusion or exclusion in the total of the advance force, which numbered about 10,000 (Polyaenus 5.44.4). However, these figures are for a single army at a single point in time before any losses had been suffered in siege or battle, before any detached forces had been sent for garrison or independent duty, and before any reinforcements were received. Obtaining reliable figures at this point should be easy, yet even so, there is confusion. For the later years of Alexander's reign, the picture is vastly more complicated, and despite the valiant efforts of modern historians to collect references to reinforcements (always incomplete in our sources) and to estimate losses and attrition, it remains very doubtful that we can obtain a really accurate order of battle for any point in Alexander's campaigns, even for the major pitched battles where we sometimes have more detailed lists of units present.

Furthermore, the army with which Alexander crossed to Asia was not the whole of the Macedonian army – Diodorus (Diod. 17.17.5) tells us that 12,000 infantry and 1,500 cavalry were left behind in Macedon with the Regent, Antipater (Antipatros), some of whom may well later have been sent to Asia as reinforcements. Over the course of such a long campaign, the army would also have been constantly changing in size. Aside from attrition from battle and disease and detachment to garrisons or as settlers in the new city foundations, Greek armies were always recruited by age classes so that each year, a proportion of the men would have reached retirement age (usually 60) and a number back home in Macedon would have come of age (at 20) and become eligible for service. Although some men remained with Alexander past retirement age, there must also have been flows of manpower to and from the army, which are mostly unrecorded, or only patchily recorded, in our sources. Combined with this is the fact that in any army the notional (paper) strength of the units was probably rarely in agreement with their actual strength.

As such, any sort of precision about numbers and sizes of units is impossible to achieve, and the precise size of units, though a favourite topic of the military historian, is by no means the most useful thing it is possible to know about an army. We are not, of course, totally in the dark; that Alexander's army at the invasion of Asia contained about 30,000 infantry (40,000 including the advance force) and about 5,000 cavalry is uncontroversial, and the size of some individual units – such as the 1,800 Companions and 1,800 Thessalians – seem also precise and plausible enough to be true, provided that we do not imagine that these units retained precisely these strengths throughout the campaign (we cannot, for example, be certain that the Companions still had this exact strength at Gaugamela three years later). In the course of this book, I will devote less effort to establishing unit strengths than is usual in works of this kind. I will, however, suggest orders of battle at each of the main battles in the relevant chapters since these provide fixed points for which more detailed information is usually available.

Note on Reconstructions

This book contains two major types of reconstructions; the pictorial reconstructions of the various soldiers of Alexander's army, and (in Chapter 10) written reconstructions of each of the major battles. Some words perhaps need to be said in defence of such reconstructions. Chapter 10 opens with some thoughts on the thorny question of the validity of reconstructing battles; I am generally suspicious of attempts to reconstruct any ancient battle with any degree of certainty, but attempting to understand more clearly the accounts of our sources seems a worthwhile activity, provided the resulting accounts, and the diagrams accompanying them, are understood as only one possible version of what may have happened on each of these fateful days.

As to the pictorial reconstructions, we are forced, given the sparse nature of the evidence discussed above, to apply a certain amount of artistic licence to any such depictions, to take particular examples of dress or equipment that may survive only through chance as more typical than they really were, and to extrapolate certain details backwards or forwards from periods with more surviving evidence. I cannot pretend that any of the depictions will precisely match how these men actually appeared in antiquity, but I hope that they will nevertheless convey something of the spirit of the appearance of the various warriors discussed.

A few words are also called for on the question of uniformity in ancient armies in general, and Alexander's army in particular. There certainly were some items of uniform equipment and dress, which we will encounter in the course of this book, and where equipment was supplied centrally rather than being provided by each individual soldier (as had been the norm in Greek armies), we can expect it to have been of a standard pattern. However, I am generally more doubtful either that unit uniforms existed (in the form we are familiar with from more modern armies, that is, clothing of particular colours for particular units) or, more importantly perhaps, that it is possible to identify depictions in art as relating to particular units. Even where equipment was centrally supplied, clothing (which for a Greek typically meant a tunic, *chiton*, and a cloak, *chlamys*) would most probably still have been provided by the individual. There were exceptions, and there is good evidence that a few elite units (such as the Hypaspists in Alexander's army and the Peltasts of Antigonid armies) were uniformly dressed. The later Greek writer Athenaeus preserves a record of the ceremony at Susa following the army's return from the Indian campaign:

> Inside, all round it [Alexander's tent], stood first of all five hundred Persians, Applebearers, with bright clothing of purple and quince-yellow; after them bow men to the number of a thousand, some dressed in flame-colour, others in crimson; but many, too, had mantles of dark blue. At the head of these stood five hundred Argyraspides, Macedonians... Outside the tent the elephant agema was posted nearby in a circle with full equipment, also a thousand Macedonians in Macedonian clothing, next ten thousand Persians, and the large body, amounting to five hundred, who wore the purple; for Alexander had granted them the privilege of wearing this garment... On one occasion Alexander actually wrote to the cities in Ionia, and first of all the Chians, directing them to dispatch purple dye to him. For he wanted to dress all his friends in garments dyed with sea-purple. (Athenaeus, 12.539e-f; cf. Polyaen. 4.3.24)

The use of purple as an indication of high status is well known throughout antiquity, and purple clothing often appears in depictions of soldiers around the time of Alexander (for example, on the Alexander Sarcophagus). The passage above suggests both a degree of uniformity and a variety of colours employed in clothing, and depending on how we understand 'Macedonian

An 'Alexander tetradrachm', a coin depicting Heracles (with a strong resemblance to Alexander), minted by Alexander's general Seleucus at the Persian capital Susa, now in the Metropolitan Museum, New York. (Metropolitan Museum)

clothing' (*Makedonikas stolas*), we might also expect the Argyraspides at least to be uniformly clothed. However, such artistic depictions as we have (thanks to the Macedonian practice of decorating tombs with elaborate and realistic wall paintings and the Hellenistic practice of painting a depiction of the deceased on tombstones) tend to be striking for their very lack of uniformity, with a large range of clothing colours depicted even on a single monument. I am generally of the view that while some units did have uniforms, most did not, and ancient armies in general, and Greek and Macedonian ones in particular, would be notable for their lack of uniformity.[3]

Note on Personal and Geographical Names

It is usual to use anglicised or Latinised versions of Greek personal names, such as Alexander (for Alexandros) or Philip (for Philippos). I have followed this practice for the more familiar names, though the first time such names appear, I will usually also give a direct transliteration of the Greek form of the name. For more unfamiliar names, I will instead just use a transliteration. There remains a grey area of names with a familiar English form (such as Ptolemy for Ptolemaios), where I will use whichever form comes naturally (to me). The same principle applies to names of geographical places and regions, where I will use either the Latinised or modern English form if well-known and familiar (such as Issus for Issos), otherwise a transliteration of the Greek. No system of transliteration of names is perfect, and total consistency is impossible. For technical terms such as unit names or the names of sub-units, I will generally use a transliteration of the Greek form rather than a translation (so, 'Pezhetairoi' not 'Foot Companions', and *ilai* and *taxeis* not 'squadrons' and 'battalions'), but will indicate the common translated or anglicised form where it first occurs. There are some exceptions, such as the Companion cavalry, where the English form, which I will use, is more familiar to English speakers than the Greek. In transliterating, I prefer 'c' (always a hard 'c') for kappa, rather than 'k' (this avoids awkward forms like 'Kilikia' for Cilicia), and otherwise will follow the usual practice, such as representing solitary upsilon as 'y' (so 'Polybios' rather than 'Polubios'). Long 'ē' (eta) and long 'ō' (omega) are marked only when doing so helps with pronunciation.

---

3 See English (2009) pp.55–9; Karunanithy (2013) pp.40–63; pp.81–99 on cavalry dress and equipment and pp.241–50 for colours. Sekunda (1984) makes the case for uniformity of clothing, and Juhel (2009) also for uniformity of equipment.

Abbreviations

The following abbreviations are used:
Ael. *Tact.* = Aelian, *Tactics*
Arr. *Anab.* = Arrian, *Anabasis of Alexander*
Arr. *Ind.* = Arrian, *Indica*
Arr. *Tact.* = Arrian, *Art of Tactics*
Asclep. = Asclepiodotus, *Tactics*
Diod. = Diodorus Siculus, *Library of History*
Just. = Justin, *Epitome of Pompeius Trogus*
Plut. *Alex.* = Plutarch, *Life of Alexander*
Plut. *Philop.* = Plutarch, *Life of Philopoemen*
Pol. = Polybius, *Histories*
Polyaen. = Polyaenus, *Stratagems*
QC = Quintus Curtius Rufus, *Histories of Alexander the Great*
Xen. *Anab.* = Xenophon, *Anabasis*
Xen. *Hell.* = Xenophon, *Hellenica*

FrGrHist = Jacoby, *Die Fragmente der griechischen Historiker*

2

The Campaigns of Alexander

The bulk of this book will consist of an analysis of the organisation and equipment of the various parts of Alexander's army, and of the major engagements in which it fought, but it will be helpful to set this account in context with a brief overview of the campaigns of Alexander. As these campaigns, and the life of Alexander in general, are covered in detail in numerous modern histories (which are still being published at an astonishing rate), I will not go into any great detail in this section, which is intended only to set the various more technical matters discussed below in their historical context. I will also not attempt to narrate the earlier campaigns of Philip, largely because they are so much less well known than those of Alexander. Only Diodorus wrote an account of Philip's career that has survived in anything more than scattered fragments and for much of Philip's reign, although there are some valuable contemporary written documents, chiefly the speeches of Philip's political opponent, Demosthenes of Athens, we know no more than the barest outline.[1]

The creation of the army of Alexander began with the accession to the throne of Macedon of his father, Philip II, in 359. Philip put in train a series of social, economic and military reforms, which must have continued throughout his reign. We should not imagine the army we meet under Alexander springing fully formed from Philip's head in the first year of his reign, and much of what was created by Philip in his early years may well have changed significantly by the accession of Alexander some 20 years later. Philip's first task was to protect his kingdom from its various Greek and 'barbarian' (non-Greek) enemies, something he achieved through a combination of diplomacy, military victory, and bribery. This was made possible by the creation of a disciplined, professional, centralised Macedonian army, formed of three main components. First was the Companion cavalry – the 'Companions' (*hetairoi* in Greek) of a Macedonian king were originally his close attendants and supporters, drawn, in the style of a Homeric warlord, both from the independently wealthy nobility or aristocracy of

---

1   Biographies of Alexander are too numerous to list here; a good sample would include Tarn (1948), Lane Fox (1973), Hammond (1989c), Green (1991), Cartledge (2005), Goldsworthy (2021). Philip II's career is well covered by Worthington (2008) and Goldsworthy (2021).

THE CAMPAIGNS OF ALEXANDER

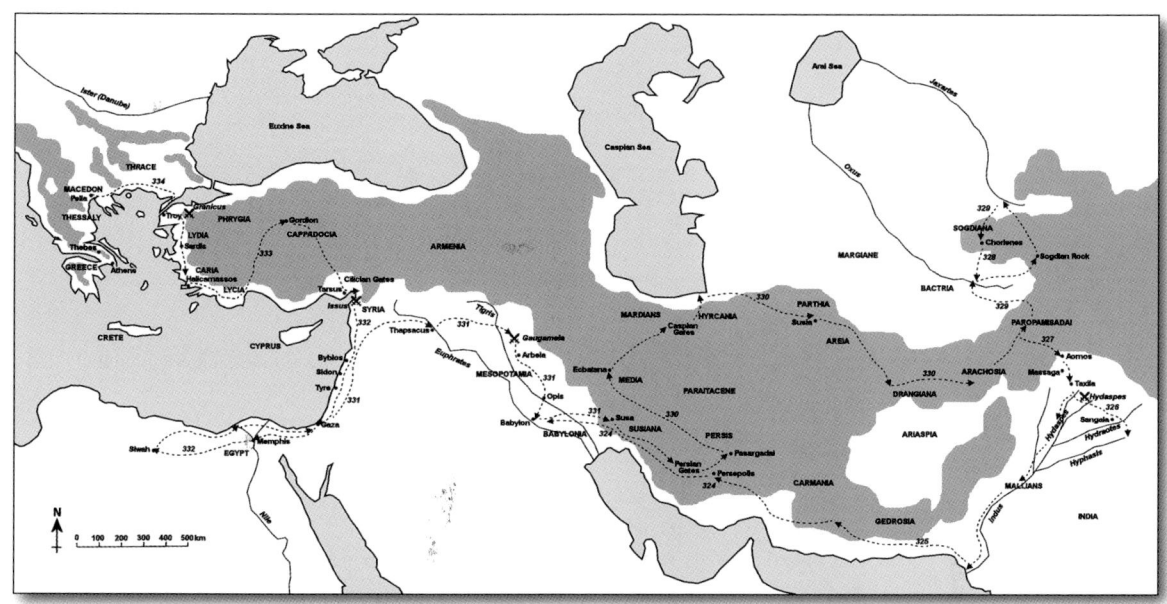

The campaigns of Alexander the Great, 334–323 BCE.

the kingdom, and from outsiders (chiefly Greeks) that the king bound to himself with gifts of land and treasure, and with promises of advancement in return for loyal and effective service. These Companions formed the nucleus of a Macedonian king's power, and from them he drew his governors and the commanders of his army. They also formed the core of the Macedonian army, fighting on horseback as an elite heavy cavalry. Philip, as he acquired power, wealth and land during his campaigns, was able to greatly expand the numbers of the Companions, from a few hundred to several thousand, and formalised their organisation as a cavalry unit. It is sometimes necessary to distinguish between the Companions, the supporters and followers of the king, and the Companion cavalry, the cavalry unit of the army. However, in practice, the same men would, in many cases, have formed both.

As noted earlier, Macedon had long lacked a useful force of heavy infantry. One of Philip's predecessors – perhaps Alexander I in the fifth century – had formed a small guard unit of infantry, perhaps equipped identically to the hoplite infantry of southern Greece – with a large shield, short spear, and variable amounts of bronze, leather or linen armour. Bronze helmets and perhaps bronze greaves (shin guards) were widely worn, and body armour may also have been worn in the early period, though in the rest of Greece body armour became increasingly uncommon during the fifth and fourth centuries. This small infantry guard was called the Pezhetairoi ('Foot Companions'), and it served alongside the Companion cavalry. Beyond this, Macedon had traditionally fielded only large but often ineffective forces of lightly equipped javelin-armed skirmishers, which were of little use in pitched battle. Philip changed this by taking the mass of infantry and training them to fight as heavy infantry, forming a distinctive Macedonian phalanx armed with the long *sarissa* or pike, as will be discussed in greater detail in Chapter 4. This new phalanx may have had an identifying name from the outset, though if so, it is unknown to us. However, at some point, Philip (or

The remains of House of Dionysos in the palace at Pella, the Macedonian capital. (Carole Raddato, CC BY-SA 2.0)

perhaps Alexander himself) extended the name Pezhetairoi to the phalanx as a whole, renaming the original guard as 'Hypaspists'. 'Hypaspists' translates literally as 'Shield Bearers', though the sense is of 'bearers of the shields of the King or the Companions', their personal attendants, rather than 'men equipped with shields'.[2]

This gave Macedon an army capable of standing up to and defeating any of the hoplite militias of southern Greece, and this national army was supplemented, as funds became available, with large forces of mercenaries, creating a largely professional army capable of campaigning all year round (Greek armies traditionally only undertook short campaigns during the summer season), and acquiring considerable technical expertise in matters such as siege warfare. With this army, Philip absorbed many of the neighbouring states into the kingdom, either by formally annexing their land or, more usually, by forming a close alliance which required the subject state to provide men, usually in the form of complete fully formed units, for the Macedonian army. Greek resistance to this expansion, led by Athens, was finally crushed at the Battle of Chaironeia (338). Philip then began to turn his attention toward the conquest of the Persian Empire at the head of the newly formed Hellenic League (League of Corinth), an alliance of Greek states.

However, it was Philip's son Alexander who was, in due course, to undertake this campaign. Following Philip's assassination, Alexander quickly established his own authority within the kingdom and over the less enthusiastic members of the Hellenic League. Desiring to safeguard Macedon's borders before he headed east, Alexander led a campaign against the Balkan peoples living to the north of Macedon, as far as the river Danube.

---

2   For an overview of Philip's reforms, see Billows (2018), pp.103–140.

While he was absent on this campaign, Athens and Thebes both rebelled against Macedonian control, relying on Alexander's youth and inexperience or even his hoped-for death on campaign against the barbarians. But they miscalculated badly, as Alexander marched rapidly back south and laid siege to Thebes (in 335). The city was swiftly captured and was made an example of, through its ruthless sack and destruction, to encourage the other members of the League.

His kingdom now secure, Alexander turned to the invasion of the Persian Empire. Leaving one of Philip's loyal adherents, Antipatros, as Regent in Macedon, along with around half the Macedonian army, Alexander, with the other half along with large mercenary and allied League forces, crossed the Hellespont into Asia, where he joined forces with Philip's advance force, which had suffered defeat at the hands of the Persians in the interim. The local Persian satraps (governors and commanders) were advised by the Greek commander Memnon (Macedonian hegemony over Greece was not universally popular, and at least as many Greeks fought against Alexander as fought for him) to withdraw before Alexander's advance until supply problems and the vast distances to be covered had weakened his army. But the Persians were unwilling to abandon their territories and instead determined to make a fight of it, offering pitched battle at the River Granicus (Granicos) (334). Here, Alexander, relieved no doubt to be able to lead his reliable, well-trained army into battle rather than chase an elusive enemy across Asia Minor, aggressively attacked across the river. Initial setbacks were swiftly followed by success as the Persian cavalry were driven from the banks. A large force of Greek mercenaries in Persian service, which should have been stationed on the riverbank but which were instead wastefully deployed further back, were then surrounded and massacred by the Macedonians in another attempt to instil loyalty through fear.

The defeat of the local Persian satraps left Alexander free to campaign against the Persian-controlled or Greek cities of the coastal regions of Asia Minor. Having failed to defeat the invaders on land, the Persians switched their strategy to using their powerful navy to raid the Aegean coasts while fomenting opposition to Macedonian control within Greece. Alexander had dismissed his navy early in the campaign, believing it to be incapable of standing up to the Persian fleet, so he now needed to reduce the Persian naval bases from the land. Some cities came over to Alexander voluntarily, but others required lengthy sieges, particularly Halicarnassos, which put up the toughest resistance.

It took a year of sieges and campaigning to gain control of the Ionian coast and central Asia Minor. Alexander's route took him deep into the interior to the city of Gordion, where he received a large group of reinforcements, after which Alexander was able to turn his attention east, marching down to the Cilician coast, aiming to invade Syria. By this time, Darius had gathered a large army, representing the full military capability of the western regions of the Empire, and was marching from Syria into Cilicia to oppose the invaders. The two armies missed each other in the mountain passes, allowing the Persians to march down to the coastal road behind Alexander. Nothing daunted, Alexander swiftly turned back, marched back up the coast

The harbour of Bodrum, Turkey – ancient Halicarnassos. (Shadowgate, CC BY 2.0)

to where the Persian army had established a defensive position on a river near Issus (Issos), and inflicted a crushing defeat on them (333). Darius and the remnants of the army fled back into Mesopotamia, leaving Alexander to continue his march down the Phoenician coast, capturing or winning over the major cities and naval bases as he went. The toughest nut to crack was the city of Tyre (Tyros), lying on an island just off shore, which Alexander first tried to reach by building a mole from the shore before eventually taking the city (and massacring its inhabitants) with the aid of ships from other Phoenician cities, that had defected from the Persian fleet.

Alexander now continued his march around the Mediterranean coast, undertaking another difficult siege at Gaza, then marching on into Egypt, where the population, long resentful of Persian rule and only recently brought back into the Empire after a long period of rebellion, greeted him as a liberator. In Egypt, Alexander made the most famous and successful of his many city foundations, the city at the mouth of the Nile that bears his name to this day. He also took time for a desert trip to the famous oracle at Siwa, where he received a presumably satisfactory response to his question to the god. Now, Alexander was free to march east again to complete his conquest of the Persian heartland. This was not an objective that had been clearly articulated by Philip, and there were those in the army, notably Alexander's second in command, Parmenion, who advised him to be content with what had already been won. Alexander, however, was incapable of being content, and he led his army across Mesopotamia, where they were confronted at Gaugamela by another, possibly even larger, Persian army raised by Darius

The ancient city of Tyre. Coloured lithograph by Louis Haghe, after David Roberts, 1843. (Wellcome Collection)

(331). As at Issus, the outcome was total defeat for the Persians and the end of any large-scale Persian resistance, though local forces continued to oppose the invaders for another four years. Alexander failed to capture Darius himself but was able to march into Babylon, the greatest city of the Empire, and then Susa, the Persian winter capital, largely unopposed. Darius, for his part, was murdered by some of his officers, leaving Alexander to replace him as King of Kings in 330.

The initial objective of the invasion, the conquest of the Persian Empire, was now complete, and Alexander was able to send home many of the Greek allied forces that had accompanied him, though many Greeks remained in the army, with varying degrees of enthusiasm, and some were settled into the numerous city foundations which Alexander dotted across the eastern satrapies (provinces) of his new Empire. From this point, Alexander began to recruit local Asian forces from the territories he conquered, leaving only the core Macedonian forces unchanged (though there were organisational changes too, as will be discussed in more detail in later chapters).

The following years were taken up with relentless, bloody campaigning to suppress all local opposition to his rule in the eastern regions of the Empire – areas that are now Iran, Afghanistan and Pakistan. Local forces were engaged and defeated, strongholds (notably the Sogdian Rock) were captured, new satraps were appointed, and new cities were founded. The campaign was carried beyond the boundaries of the Persian Empire, as Alexander sought to pacify the frontier with the Scythians (steppe nomads to the northeast) by campaigns across the river Jaxartes (329). This period also saw Alexander

Persepolis, capital of the Achaemenid (Persian) Empire. (Carole Raddato, CC BY-SA 2.0)

increasingly embrace the customs and dress of his conquered subjects, as well as employing them in his army. This caused growing resentment among the Macedonian soldiers, who would have preferred the subject peoples to remain firmly in their place. Stresses and tensions arose between the 'Orientalising' elements and the Macedonian traditionalists, and between the younger men who had advanced their careers wholly under Alexander and the older men who had served under Philip. These tensions broke out in a succession of plots, alleged plots and murders. First, Parmenion himself was implicated, by way of his son Philotas, commander of the Companion cavalry, in a plot against Alexander, and both were swiftly done away with. Alexander's attempts to introduce Persian court etiquette, particularly the practice of *proskynesis* (obeisance), provoked further controversy, and on this Alexander fell out with his official historian, Callisthenes. Finally, in a drunken brawl arising during one of the many heavy drinking sessions in which the court indulged, Cleitos the Black, replacement commander of the Companions, who had saved Alexander's life at the Granicus, was murdered by Alexander's own hand. Cleitos had (in the accounts that come down to us at least) expressed the unspoken thoughts of many in the army – resentment of Alexander's orientalising and the feeling that Philip, the old guard of senior commanders, and the army itself, did not get the credit they deserved for Alexander's success. Alexander was undoubtedly popular with the army, as any commander with such a record of success would be. However, the divisions and resentments expressed by Cleitos were to continue throughout Alexander's reign and, indeed, afterwards. Few in the army, or even among the officers and nobility, bought into Alexander's relentless drive for continued conquest and still less to his apparent desire to treat conquered Asian peoples as anything other than subject barbarians.

The Swat Valley in the Hindu Kush mountains, modern Pakistan. (Farhan3aslam2, CC BY-SA 4.0)

For the present, however, Alexander restored discipline, and with the eastern satrapies pacified (for now – once Alexander's back was turned, many broke out in further rebellion), the march continued east, across the Hindu Kush mountains and into India (327). What Alexander's objectives were, if indeed he had any, remains controversial. Possibly, he sought the 'outer ocean', which Greek geographical knowledge of the time told him surrounded the Persian Empire to the east, though surely his new subjects could quickly have put him right on that score. Possibly, he hoped that India itself, disunited and under the precarious rule of a fading empire, would fall as readily as Persia had. Possibly, he had no clear idea what he wanted but was unwilling or unable to turn back. Whatever the case may be, the army pressed on, winning over the divided local rulers or defeating them in battle, culminating in perhaps the hardest-fought of Alexander's battles, that on the river Hydaspes (326), where Alexander defeated the local Indian king Poros, whose army was equipped with numerous war elephants, the first encounter in battle between Greeks and these animals. The elephants made a deep impression (in every sense) on the Macedonians, and the prospect of armies ahead equipped with thousands more such beasts, together with the monsoon weather, nostalgia for the homeland, the exhaustion of long campaigning, and the grievances that had been simmering for so long, led the army to finally refuse to march further and demand to be taken home.

Alexander was forced to comply, with great reluctance – his only defeat thus being suffered at the hands of his own army. The army marched south down the Indus to the sea, massacring any recalcitrant local inhabitants as they went, then marched back across the desert lands of Gedrosia, along the Indian Ocean coast of the Empire (325). This march proved the hardest of the whole campaign, the enemies being natural rather than human – heat, and lack of water and supplies – and the army and its long train of

THE ARMY OF ALEXANDER THE GREAT

The Tomb of Cyrus the Great, Pasargadae, Iran. The tomb was restored in antiquity by Aristoboulos, the historian of Alexander. (Matson collection, Library of Congress)

The reconstructed walls of Babylon, Iraq. (Osama Sarm, CC BY-SA 4.0)

followers suffered heavy losses from thirst, hunger and natural disasters such as flash floods. Alexander arrived back in the heart of his new Empire to find, as could be expected after so long an absence, various degrees of misrule and rebellion, which had to be violently suppressed. He also set about formalising the transition from a national Macedonian army to an Imperial one, parading a phalanx recruited from young Asian men and enrolling Asians in the ranks of the Companion cavalry. This led to a further mutiny from the Macedonian contingents. This time, Alexander suppressed the mutineers rather than acceding to their wishes. However, his days were now numbered, and in 323, in Babylon, Alexander died, aged 33, leaving no heir. His Empire swiftly broke apart as his senior generals attempted to carve out dominions of their own, using the Macedonian elements of the army (from which Asians were now rigidly excluded) as pawns in their power struggles. Twenty years of interminable warfare were needed for a return to some equilibrium, as three major kingdoms (that of Ptolemy in Egypt, Seleucos in Syria, and eventually Antigonos in Macedon itself) were established, ushering in the Hellenistic age.

3

The Macedonian Cavalry

The Companion cavalry

Identity

The Companion Cavalry (*Hetairoi,* or *Hippeis tōn Hetairōn*, Cavalry of the Companions in full) were the foremost and arguably the most important unit in the Macedonian army. Their name indicates that they were at least notionally all drawn from the Companions of the King. This means they were made up of two types of men (with considerable overlap between the two groups).

First, were the traditional aristocracy of Macedon, the rich men of the kingdom (rich in land, since ownership of land was always the main source of wealth in antiquity). Questions of land ownership in Macedon remain somewhat obscure. It may be that, in theory, all land within the kingdom belonged to the king and could be disposed of at will to his followers, though it is likely that there was also private land ownership independent of royal power. Whatever the case in theory, in practice, there were certainly wealthy, landed men and families whose lands were passed on between generations and who had independent wealth from such lands. This Macedonian nobility had formed the most important of the Companions of the King from time immemorial, since Macedon had retained a Homeric style of kingship. The wealthiest and most important men of the kingdom were counted amongst the King's Companions, and from them, the king would draw the commanders of his armies, the governors of his provinces, and, in greater numbers, his force of cavalry. But in addition to such wealthy, independently powerful men, the king had it in his power to count among his Companions any man, including non-Macedonians, who caught his attention for worth or excellence in any field. Such men might come to the Macedonian court from elsewhere in the Greek (or non-Greek) world and might be given grants of royal land to set them up independently in Macedon, along with gifts of goods or cash to cement their loyalty. The need to attract men with such gifts of land or treasure was one of the driving forces of Macedonian imperialism since a king who could not attract, reward and retain followers would quickly lose power. These two groups – the more

THE MACEDONIAN CAVALRY

Alexander in combat, detail from the Alexander Sarcophagus. (Osman Hamdi Bey and T. Reinach, *Une nécropole royale à Sidon: fouilles: Plate XXX*)

or less wealthy aristocracy and the king's favourites – together made up the Companions of the King.[1]

Greek writers often made no distinction between the Companions, this body of nobles and followers, and the Companion cavalry, the force of cavalry we are examining here, calling both simply *hetairoi*. However, it is usually clear enough from the context which is meant, and occasionally Arrian, for example, will refer to 'the cavalry of the Companions' (e.g. Arr. *Anab*. 3.11.8). The Companion cavalry would all have been Companions of the King, though not every Companion would be serving in the Companion cavalry, since many would have had separate commands within the army, or might have been employed elsewhere as governors, diplomats or other officials, or might simply have been left behind in Macedon for any number of reasons. For convenience, I will usually refer to the military unit simply as 'the Companions', and on those occasions where the body of men rather than the body of cavalry is meant, will say so.

The strength of the Companions early in Philip's reign, and under his predecessors, was probably a few hundred men, but as part of his expansion of the power of the kingdom, Philip dramatically increased their numbers, allowing Alexander to field the 1,800 men described by Diodorus (17.17.4) as being in the invasion army, to which must be added at least a few hundred who were employed outside the cavalry or left with Antipatros in Macedon. This was made possible by Philip's acquisition of large tracts of land at the expense of Macedon's neighbours, and in particular of those Greek cities on and around the northern Aegean coast; such lands, as 'spear won territory', could be gifted by the king to his followers, which allowed both an expansion in the numbers of horse-raising aristocrats, who could then serve as cavalry, and also the creation of a body whose position and loyalty was owed entirely

---

1 King (2010); Anson (2008); Hammond (1989b) pp.152–165; Lane-Fox (2011).

to the king. This made the Companions (in both senses) both more numerous and more dependable – the traditional Macedonian aristocracy having a history of unruliness that contributed to the Macedonian monarchy's chronic problem of assassination and usurpation.[2]

Organisation

Because we do not know how many, if any, of the Companions were left behind in Macedon, we cannot draw any conclusions about the organisation or size of the Companions as a whole. This section will, therefore, consider only those who formed a part of the army of Alexander (which may indeed have been all of them).

Arrian gives a description of the deployment of the Companions at Gaugamela (331). They were led by the *ilē basilikē*, 'Royal Squadron', under Cleitos, followed by seven further *ilai* (squadrons), each under a named commander, and with the Companions as a whole under the command of Philotas, son of Parmenion (Arr. *Anab.* 3.11.8). If we take this organisation as the normal one throughout the early part of the campaign at least, then each of the eight *ilai* would have contained an average of 225 men (using the 1,800 total from Diodorus discussed above). Alternatively, the Royal Squadron might have been larger (as the leading squadron of the Thessalian cavalry was, see Chapter 5), so another permutation would be seven 200-man regular *ilai* (we often see Companions operating in multiples of 200, e.g. Arr. *Anab.* 1.18.1; 4.17.3; 4.22.1), with a 400-man Royal Squadron. Whatever the case, we can be sure that the precise strength of each squadron would not have remained static throughout the campaign, given losses, sickness and so forth, nor that it would always have been some notional exact number determined by the shape of the formation, so it is safest to say simply that squadrons would have averaged about 200 men.

Arrian (Arr. *Anab.* 3.16.11) states that the *ilai* were not subdivided into sub-units, *lochoi,* before the reforms of 331 (see Chapter 6), so there may have been no smaller subdivision of the *ilai*. However, Arrian also refers once (Arr. *Anab.* 3.18.5) to a *tetrarchia* of cavalry but gives no indication of what he means by this. This is after the reform of 331, so the *tetrarchia* too may not have existed before this time, but it may also be that the *tetrarchia* was an existing unit – one quarter of an *ilē* (by comparison with the arrangement in the infantry described by Asclepiodotus 2.10, where a *tetrarchia* is one quarter of a *syntagma* or *syntaxiarchia*). If so, a *tetrarchia* would contain around 50 men.

Arrian lists the *ilai* by the name of the commander at Gaugamela, but earlier in the campaign, geographic designations are used, along with the names of the commanders. Only a selection of squadrons are so identified, however, with most being grouped as 'the Companions' generally. The known squadron designations can be summarised as follows:

---

2   Millett (2010), Sawada (2010), Lane-Fox (2011).

Arr. *Anab*. 1.2.5 (campaign versus the Triballians, 335)
'Cavalry of Upper Macedonia' under Philotas
Bottiaia cavalry, under Heracleides
Amphipolis cavalry, under Sopolis

Arr. *Anab*. 1.12.7 (Granicus, 334)
Companions as a whole, under Philotas
Apollonia *ilē*, under Socrates

Arr. *Anab*. 2.9.3 (Issus, 333)
Anthemos *ilē*, under Peroides
Leugaian *ilē* ('so called'), under Pantordanos

Arr *Anab*. 3.11.8 (Gaugamela, 331)
Companions as a whole, under Philotas
Royal Squadron (*basilikē ilē*), under Cleitos
Ilē of Glaucias
Ilē of Aristo
Ilē of Sopolis
Ilē of Heracleides
Ilē of Demetrios
Ilē of Meleagros
Ilē of Hegelochos (also 'Royal' in the manuscripts of Arrian, in error).

Some of these commanders are consistent between the early campaigns and Gaugamela (Sopolis and Heracleides), while others have changed. Clearly, commanders could be replaced (due to promotion, demotion, detached duty or death), and the *ilē*, when it was not referred to by its geographic title, would be known by the name of the current commander (a similar practice was followed in the infantry, see below). It is likely that every squadron did have a geographical name, although not all are recorded. These names were those of the region from which the squadron was recruited. Many of the names are known to be of regions of the kingdom recently conquered from the Thracians or Greeks where the king would have had 'spear-won land' available to grant to his followers, who would then have been recruited to serve in the cavalry. The exception is the 'Leugaian' *ilē*, the location of which is not known (and probably not known to Arrian either, since he designates it 'so-called'). Perhaps this was from a region which had been longer under Macedonian control, in which case we can compare it with the 'cavalry of Upper Macedonia' under Philotas in Arr. *Anab*. 1.2.5; 'Upper Macedonia' being the interior, upland regions of Macedon that Philip brought under his control early in his reign. These then may represent several squadrons similar to the Leugaian, bearing their traditional names.

After Gaugamela, as part of the changes to the army that marked the completion of the initial objective of the campaign (the defeat of the Persian Empire) and the transition to the second stage (the establishment of

Alexander's Empire), the organisation of the cavalry underwent a series of changes – these will be considered in Chapter 6.[3]

Equipment and Dress

For the equipment of the Companions, we have a few scraps of information in the literary sources, chiefly concerned with the offensive weaponry, and archaeology can tell us a little more – mainly depictions in ancient art since very little in the way of equipment that can be directly linked to the Companions has survived. That said, we can make some general points about the appearance of the Companions, based chiefly on depictions of cavalry on the Alexander Mosaic and the Alexander Sarcophagus, and also on a number of later Hellenistic tomb paintings which can be cautiously applied to the earlier period.

The Companions were a force of landed nobles who most likely provided their own equipment. This would have consisted of a tunic and cloak, the tunic being worn tucked up into a belt and the cloak clasped around the neck and draped over the left shoulder. The tunics depicted on the mosaic (worn by Alexander) and sarcophagus have long sleeves, so this may have been the normal form, although long sleeves may also be an indication of Persian influence and applicable later in the campaign. The colour of the tunic was perhaps at the whim of the individual, though again, mosaic and sarcophagus alike show purple tunics, so this might have been the preferred colour (purple dye was the most expensive and is usually a sign of status). Tunic colour might have varied with the specific unit, with purple reserved for the Royal Squadron, but we have no direct evidence that this was the case. While Companions might initially have supplied their own cloaks, in their own choice of colours, Diodorus tells us that after the death of Darius, Alexander 'distributed to his companions cloaks with purple borders and dressed the horses in Persian harness' (Diod. 17.77.5). As usual, we cannot know for sure if this meant to his closest companions or to the Companion cavalry but at any rate, figures on Macedonian tombs are depicted with yellow cloaks with purple borders, which suggests that this became the uniform of all the Companions, and also confirms these as reliable sources of colour information.[4]

Headgear would have consisted of a choice of items – the characteristic and distinctive Macedonian hat was the *kausia*, resembling a beret, probably made of rolled felt, and usually depicted in white, off-white, grey, light brown or purple. This hat was common to Macedonian infantry and cavalry alike and probably standard campaign wear, for occasions outside of active combat when a metal helmet was not required. Also available was the traditional Greek *petasos*, a sun hat with a wide brim and shallow crown, often worn tied to the head to prevent it from blowing off, which would also have been a campaign hat. In combat, depictions on the sarcophagus and elsewhere suggest that the Boeotian style of bronze helmet was preferred (as had been recommended by Xenophon, Xen. *Hipp.* 12.3). This helmet was itself

---

3   Brunt (1963).
4   Sekunda (1984).

A Companion cavalryman, detail from the Alexander Sarcophagus, Istanbul Archaeological Museum. (Osman Hamdi Bey and T. Reinach, *Une nécropole royale à Sidon: fouilles: Plate XXX*)

an adaptation into bronze of a *petasos*-style hat, and it gave good all-round vision without the restrictions imposed by traditional infantry helmets with their cheek pieces and low brows. These may well have been uniform wear for the Companions in Alexander's day. However, depictions of cavalry from Philip's reign suggest other types of helmets, such as the Phrygian were also worn. The helmet would also have been the place to display indications of rank. Traditionally, Greeks indicated rank with helmet plumes or feathers, and a figure on the mosaic with a silvered wreath around his helmet may be wearing a similar badge of rank.[5]

Tactically, the Companions functioned as heavy cavalry (see below), and as such, they will generally have been armoured. The sarcophagus depicts cavalry both with and without armour – partly this is due to the fact that some of the men are hunting, and so are not in full combat gear, but also because the wearing of armour may have been optional. Curtius (4.13.25) reports that Alexander rarely wore armour and then only at the request of his friends. The armour worn would have been of two types; most common was the so-called (by modern writers) 'tube and yoke' style of organic armour, common also to

---

5   Sekunda (1984), Karunanithy (2013) pp.86–90. Juhel (2017a) for infantry rank insignia.

THE ARMY OF ALEXANDER THE GREAT

A Companion cavalryman, detail from the Alexander Sarcophagus, Istanbul Archaeological Museum. (Osman Hamdi Bey and T. Reinach, *Une nécropole royale à Sidon: fouilles*: Plate XXX)

the infantry. This type of armour is sometimes termed 'the linothorax' (linen cuirass), though this word does not appear as a noun in the ancient sources. At least some armour of this style may have been made from layers of quilted or perhaps glued linen, but it could also have been made from leather; no doubt there was a mix of styles and materials. Metal reinforcements in the form of scales or plates could also, on occasion, be attached to armour of this sort. This type of armour had become common for infantry during the fifth century and was no doubt also widely worn by cavalry. In terms of colour, vase paintings, with their very limited colour palette, tend to show it white, which could represent pale linen, whitened leather, or any other pale colour. The Alexander Sarcophagus and other later depictions, such as the Agios Athanasios tomb paintings, show such armour highly coloured, with purple being a preferred colour – again, perhaps an indication of an elite unit (like the Companions). As well as organic armour, depictions sometimes show metal armour of the 'muscled cuirass' style. Bronze body armour had been popular for infantry before the fifth century, when it was largely replaced by more organic materials or, in the fourth century, by no armour at all. Cavalry, being wealthy and able to afford the best, may have retained metal armour more widely, in this case, in the later naturalistic 'muscled' style. Such armour naturally had drawbacks in terms of coolness, weight and flexibility. Along the bottom edge of all such armour, protecting the lower stomach and groin, were one or two rows of flaps or *pteruges* ('feathers'), which would have offered some protection while still allowing flexibility. In the case of organic armour, these *pteruges* were integral to the armour itself.[6]

---

6   Karunanithy (2013) pp.90–3; Aldrete, Bartell and Aldrete (2013) for the 'linothorax', though details of the reconstruction are controversial.

THE MACEDONIAN CAVALRY

Macedonian cavalryman, from the 'Judgement Tomb', Lefkadia, Greece. He wears a yellow cloak with purple border over a red tunic and white 'linothorax' with red panels. (Egisto Sani, CC BY-SA 2.0)

In common with all Greek cavalry of this period, shields do not appear to have been carried. Xenophon had instead recommended armour for the left arm, but there is no evidence that this was widely adopted, the cavalryman instead relying on parrying or striking first with his own weapons. On their feet, the Companions will have worn *krepides*, calf-length leather boots with open toes and strapwork heels, which made them both tough and relatively cool in hot climates. In colder conditions, socks could be worn. There were also enclosed styles of boot made from sheet leather, sometimes with openings for the toes.[7]

The main offensive weapon of the Companion was his *xyston* or *dory* (his spear, or more properly, as a cavalryman, his lance). As is usual in Greek writers, we do not see strict usage of technical terms for weapons, with different words being used interchangeably, even in the same passage. The clearest example of this is the fight in which Alexander was engaged at the Granicus where Arrian (Arr. *Anab*. 1.15.6–8) uses both *xyston* and *dory* in quick succession to describe the spear wielded by Alexander and his men. However, in another passage (Arr. *Anab*. 1.15.5), Arrian made a clear distinction between the 'cornel-wood *xyston*' of the Macedonians and the *palta* (javelins) of the Persians, with the Macedonian weapon offering an

---

7   Karunanithy (2013) pp.84–6.

THE ARMY OF ALEXANDER THE GREAT

Alexander in action, detail from the Alexander Mosaic, Naples Archaeological Museum. (PD)

A boeotian helmet found in the Tigris and now in the Ashmolean Museum, Oxford. (Ashmolean Museum)

advantage. So, it seems fair to conclude that *xyston* is the more technically accurate term, and *dory* is just a generalisation for any shafted weapon. Cornel wood, the wood of the Cornelian cherry, *Cornus mas*, was favoured for spear shafts because of its strength. Although, as we will see, it was probably too heavy – heavy enough to sink in water – for really long shafts like those of the infantry sarissa. There seems no reason to suppose that the spear of the Companions was usually called a sarissa (the name of the infantry weapon), still less that it had the same dimensions as the infantry weapon (see below), but Greek terminology is sufficiently imprecise, and *sarisa* is a Macedonian dialect word for long spear, so it may have occasionally been called that. There was also a cavalry unit specifically called 'sarrisa-carriers' (see below).[8]

The Alexander Mosaic depicts Alexander wielding such a lance, and it appears very long, although it is not possible to measure the precise length since the rear portion of the weapon is missing. We might estimate the length at about three metres. A similar weapon is borne by a Macedonian cavalryman in the Kinch tomb painting. In this case, we can see the full length of the weapon, that it is held about one-third of the way along its length, and that the rear end (as well as the front) carries a blade – this could be useful if the weapon was broken, allowing it to be reversed and the rear end used. Spear heads have been discovered in Macedonian tombs (including in the royal tombs at Vergina), and have been confidently identified as belonging to particular weapons (published dimensions and weights then frequently appear in accounts of Macedonian armies), but all such identifications are necessarily speculative. In the absence of the survival of the wooden shafts, we cannot tell how long any such weapon was, and we have no firm basis for matching any particular spear head with any particular weapon (this problem applies particularly to the infantry sarissa). As such, I do not feel that confidently assigning quantitative measures to the size or shape of the blades is justified. We can only say that in painted or mosaic depictions, these blades appear to be quite large, and diamond or leaf shaped.[9]

As a secondary weapon (when the lance broke, or for close-quarters fighting), the Companion carried a sword. Greek swords were of two main types, the *xiphos*, with a tapered, leaf-shaped blade, and the *kopis*, with a curved blade with a single cutting edge, weighted toward the end of the blade. As usual, Greek writers were not meticulous in distinguishing between these weapons, and *machaira* (generic 'sword'), could also be used for both. The *kopis* was specifically a cavalry weapon, designed for cutting and slashing rather than thrusting, and was evidently fearsome in battle – Arrian describes Cleitos using his *kopis* to sever the arm of the Persian commander Spithridates with a single blow in the fighting at the Granicus (Arr. *Anab.* 1.15.8).[10]

---

8   Manti, P.A. (1983), Markle (1977) and (1978), argues for a 'cavalry sarissa'.
9   Andronikos (1970), (1989).
10 Karunanithy (2013) pp.137–44 on swords.

A mosaic from Pella depicting a lion hunt. Note the *petasos* hat and curved *kopis* sword. (Julianna Lees, CC BY-SA 2.0)

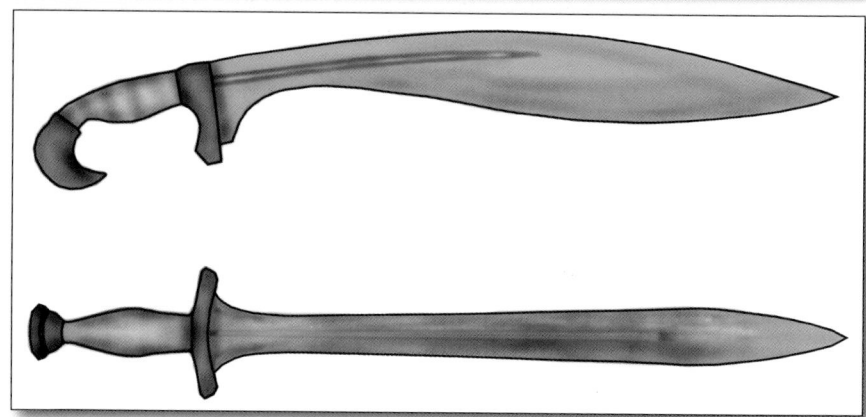

Greek swords; the curved kopis and straight xiphos.

Drill and Tactics

The Companions were heavy cavalry, and as such were intended to charge at and defeat in hand-to-hand combat enemy formations of infantry or cavalry. Whether this actually involved charging into full contact, horses slamming into horses and men, is a broad and more controversial topic, and one best left for another time. My own view is that they did not, though there could be a deal of pushing and shoving in a closely fought, static contest – as at the Granicus, vividly described by Arrian:

> Though the fighting was on horseback, it was more like an infantry battle, horse entangled with horse, man with man in the struggle, the Macedonians trying to push the Persians once and for all from the bank and force them onto the level ground, the Persians trying to bar their landing and thrust them back again into the river. Arr. *Anab.* 1.15.4

Ancient authors frequently make this distinction between infantry fighting, close quarters and hand-to-hand, and normal cavalry fighting, which was supposed to be more mobile and tentative, with advances, manoeuvres and retreats, rather than lines closing and becoming locked together in combat – unless one was trying to force and one to oppose a river crossing.[11]

None of the accounts of Alexander's campaigns specifies the formation in which the Companions fought, but the Tacticians describe the wedge formation and note that it was adopted by the Macedonians or even specifically by Philip II (Asclep. 7.4; Ael. *Tact*. 19, Arr. *Tact*. 16.4). The usual assumption – which seems reasonable – is therefore that Alexander's cavalry would have fought in wedge, the advantage of which was that it aided manoeuvrability, as the officers stationed at the apex of the wedge could set the direction of the formation, which could then follow them 'like a flight of cranes', rather than the slower and more complex wheeling manoeuvres required of traditional Greek and Persian square or rectangular formations. Note that the use of 'wedge', *embolos* or *embolon*, or 'wedge-shaped', *emboloeides*, is somewhat inconsistent in Arrian (and other writers). The cavalry formation of Arrian (Arr. *Tact*. 16.1; 16.6) is different from the infantry marching formation (Arr. *Tact*. 29.5), and from the deep or columnar formation used by the Thebans at Mantineia (Arr. *Tact*. 11.2). In the *Anabasis of Alexander*, Arrian never refers to a Macedonian cavalry wedge but does mention an infantry formation (Arr. *Anab*. 1.6.3), a Persian cavalry formation at Granicus, (Arr. *Anab*. 1.15.7), and a combined arms Macedonian formation at Gaugamela (Arr. *Anab*. 3.14.2) – causing some confusion in accounts of those battles (see Chapter 10).

The wedges described by the Tacticians are fairly small formations, the *ilē* of their day being the smallest unit of the cavalry, some 50 men strong, rather than the 200-man squadrons of Alexander's time. It is not clear whether the Companions would have formed in huge 200-man wedges or would be subdivided into smaller units, with each in wedge. Asclepiodotus (7.6–9) describes two types of rhombus (diamond-shaped) formations, though he does not describe the wedge in detail. Each held 49 or 61 men, depending on whether each rank held one more man or two more men than the previous rank. A wedge of 200 men, using the two more men per rank layout, would need to be some 14 ranks deep, which is possible, although the Tacticians observe (for example, Asclep 7.4) that depth greater than eight ranks was useless to a cavalry formation. If the *tetrarchia*, containing around 50 men, did pre-date the 331 reforms, this could be the unit from which the wedge was formed, which would provide a better match with the Tacticians.[12]

The intervals (spacing between files) of cavalry are not clearly given by the Tacticians. The implication is that the 'natural' spacing of the infantry – that is, four cubits or two metres between each man – was also used for cavalry, with the option of closing up to one-metre spacing, which would be equivalent to the boot-to-boot spacing used by more recent heavy cavalry formations. Between each squadron, gaps as wide as the formation itself had to be left, according to the account of Polybius, when discussing Alexander's army at Issus (Pol. 12.18.3), so that the overall frontage of a cavalry formation

---

11 Greek horsemanship in battle, Willekes (2015); horses, Karunanithy (2013) pp.64–78.
12 Sekunda (2010) pp.452–3 and Sekunda (1984) p.14.

THE ARMY OF ALEXANDER THE GREAT

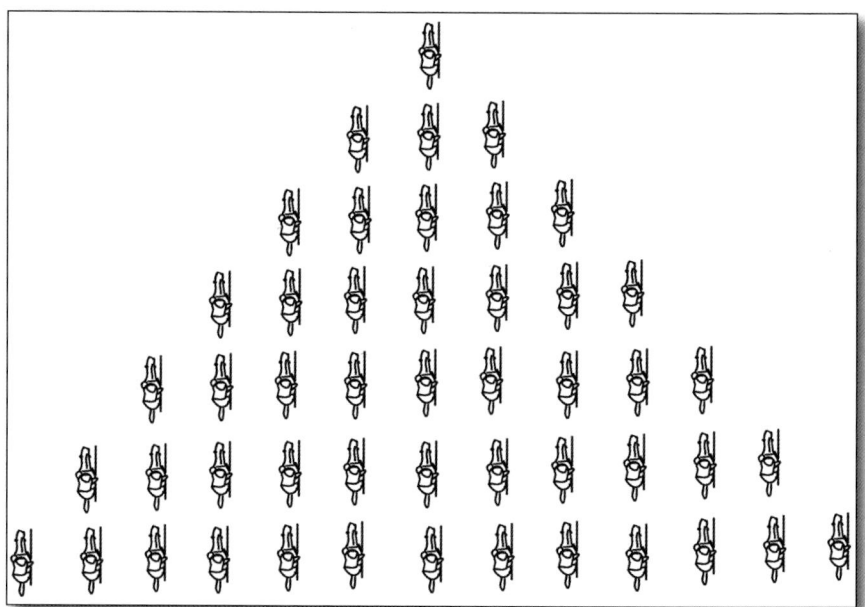

A *tetrarchia* of cavalry in wedge formation.

would be double that obtained by dividing the number of men by the number of ranks and multiplying by the file interval (modified appropriately for the different rank strengths of a wedge).

Prodromoi or *Sarissophoroi*

Identity

In his listing of the army at the crossing into Asia, Diodorus breaks down the cavalry force into its national contingents. He lists 1,800 Macedonians (the Companions), 1,800 Thessalians, 600 other Greeks, and 900 'Thracians, *prodromoi* and Paionians'. *Prodromoi* is a Greek word meaning literally 'front runners' and is usually translated into English as 'scouts'. In the usual fashion of ancient texts, the word is used in various ways – sometimes in a broad sense, where it describes a particular type of soldier or function, and sometimes in a narrower sense, where it describes a particular unit. In English, we can use upper and lower case letters to indicate the difference (so '*prodromoi*' or 'Prodromoi'), but written Greek of this period did not have that option (and historians were perhaps not always aware of the distinction). As a result, when we encounter *prodromoi* in the texts of Arrian or Diodorus, we cannot be certain if what is meant are scouts in general (that is, fast moving, lightly equipped cavalry used to scout ahead of the main army) or Scouts in particular, a given named unit. Diodorus' text has been taken to mean '900 Prodromoi, who were Thracians, and Paionians', but could equally mean '900 Thracian light cavalry and Paionians'. Adding to the difficulties, it has been suggested that the text of this passage is corrupt in the surviving manuscript, and an 'and' (*kai*) has dropped out, so that what Diodorus actually meant was '900 Thracians, and Prodromoi, and Paionians'.

Certainly, in the text of Arrian, when *prodromoi* are referred to, it is usually without any ethnic designation (such as 'Thracian'), which usually indicates that Macedonians are meant (this being the default ethnicity in Alexander's army). This does mean that on any given occasion, we might not know if a force of *prodromoi* really is the Macedonian Prodromoi Cavalry, or whether they are Thracian or some other type of light cavalry scouts. In practice, most of the references to *prodromoi* in the text can, from the context and lack of any ethnic designation, be identified with some certainty as the Prodromoi, and so probably as Macedonians.[13]

It is not clear precisely who these men are – most Macedonian cavalry, as we have seen, were recruited to the Companions, but there may have been a class, perhaps set apart by lesser wealth or by region, who were instead recruited to the Prodromoi. As a general rule, Greek recruitment tended to link ethnic origin with a particular military function, so that Greek citizens were heavy infantry, Cretans were archers, Thracians were javelin-men, and so forth. These Macedonian light cavalry might have come from more recently conquered and absorbed parts of the kingdom, perhaps meaning they were ethnically Thracian for all that they were now inhabitants of the Macedonian kingdom. Certainty on this point is impossible, however.

To complicate the identity of the Prodromoi, our sources sometimes also use the name *sarissophoroi*, 'sarissa-carriers', the sarissa usually being the long pike used by the infantry of the Macedonian phalanx. When the word *sarissophoroi* occurs in other authors, describing the armies of the Hellenistic period, it always refers to infantry of the phalanx. As 'sarissa' appears to be a Macedonian dialect word for any long spear, these cavalry could simply have been armed with spears that were long, but not necessarily as long as or identical in design to the infantry sarissa. Translating *sarissophoroi* as 'lancers' captures the meaning well enough. Of course, the Companions also had long spears; perhaps the *xyston* of the Companions was shorter than the sarissa of the Sarissophoroi, which perhaps also needed to be wielded, like its infantry equivalent, in two hands. There is nothing conclusive in the name alone, however, to lead us to these conclusions, nor do we know if *sarissophoroi* was an official unit name, or a nickname, or a functional descriptor of the unit type (in the same way as the Pezhetairoi of the phalanx could also be called simply 'hoplites'). It is at any rate certain that the Prodromoi and the Sarissophoroi are the same unit; when Arrian describes the deployment at the Granicus, he says first that 'Next to Philotas [with the Companions and others] Amyntas son of Arrabaios was posted, with the Sarissophoroi, the Paionians, and Socrates' squadron [of the Companions]' (Arr. *Anab.* 1.14.1), and he later writes that Alexander led the attack and 'ordered the Prodromoi and the Paionians to plunge first into the stream, under command of Amyntas son of Arrabaios, with one battalion of the infantry and in advance Socrates' squadron.' (Arr. *Anab.* 1.14.6). Similarly, Arrian describes the deployment at Gaugamela: 'in front of the Agrianians and archers cavalry were stationed, consisting of the Prodromoi and the Paionians under the

---

13 Different interpretations of the Prodromoi: English (2009) pp.41–43; Sekunda (1984) pp.20–1.

command of Aretas and Ariston' (3.12.3), while Curtius notes that during the ensuing battle, Alexander 'sent Aretas, the leader of the lancers [*hastati*] called Sarisophoroi, against the Scythians.' (QC 4.15.13), so Sarissophoroi and Prodromoi are evidently alternative names for the same unit.

Organisation

Before the Granicus, Alexander sent forward a scouting force; 'Amyntas son of Arrabaios led them with the squadron of Companions from Apollonia … with four squadrons (*ilai*) of the so-called Prodromoi' (Arr. *Anab.* 1.12.7). At the Granicus itself as we saw above, the Prodromoi and the Paionians were ordered together into the stream, and Plutarch notes that Alexander 'plunged into the stream with thirteen *ilai* of horsemen' (Plut. Alex. 16.2). The Companions make up eight *ilai* and the Paionians one, leaving the Prodromoi with four. At the crossing of the Jaxartes in 329, four *ilai* of Sarissophoroi are sent over the river (Arr. Anab. 4.4.6). So, the Prodromoi/Sarissophoroi were evidently formed into four *ilai*, which (if the *ilai* were the same size as those of the Companions, 200 men each) would give a total of around 800 men. Most likely, they would also have adopted the same lower-level organisation as the Companions, with four *tetrarchiai* to each *ilē*.

Equipment and Dress

The name Sarissophoroi suggests the carrying of a sarissa, a lance perhaps longer than the regular *xyston* of the Companions. No certain depictions in art or discoveries in archaeology exist to give us a clearer picture of this lance, or of the rest of this unit's equipment. There is no particular reason either to suppose that the lance was wielded with two hands, as some later cavalry lances were, and in practice, there may be little difference between the sarissa of the Sarissophoroi and the *xyston* of the Companions and the reasons for the use of this particular name are unknown. My own guess is that the Sarissophoroi wielded spears similar in size and function to those of the Companions, and the name was a nickname acquired when these spears were first issued to what had previously been javelin-armed light cavalry. Depictions of cavalry with long spears (such as that on the Kinch tomb) can equally well be interpreted as Companions (or later in the Hellenistic period, as heavy cavalry equivalent to the Companions), the presence or absence of armour not being decisive in such cases (the Alexander Sarcophagus shows cavalry, presumably Companions, without body armour). We should at any rate expect these cavalry, as scouts, to be lightly equipped, perhaps with a helmet or possibly just with a hat, as was often the case with earlier Greek light cavalry, and only the long lance would be distinctive. The depiction of such a cavalryman in the plates is speculative, aiming to give only a broad idea of the type of equipment that might have been used.

Drill and Tactics

As with equipment, we are largely in the dark as to the tactical use of the Prodromoi. Presumably, in their role as scouts, they might have deployed in loose order and open formations (though, as we have seen, Companions could also be sent on scouting missions). Whether they formed in wedge

Watercolour reproduction of late fourth century BCE fresco, now lost, from a Macedonian tomb at Naousa, sometimes identified as a cavalryman of the Prodromoi. The tunic is red and blue over a cream long-sleeved tunic, with a red cloak. (K.F. Kinch, 1889)

formations, like the Companions, is unclear, but I think it likely that, as Macedonian cavalry, they did. At any rate, we can see that their tactical use in battle was much the same as the Companions – they were expected to charge enemy forces, especially enemy cavalry, not merely to skirmish with or delay them. Their weapon would, of course, make skirmishing tactics impossible. At the Granicus, they were first to attack into the river, at Issus they were similarly posted on Alexander's right, though their exploits are not recorded. At Gaugamela, Ariston's Paionians and Aretes' Prodromoi both made charges against the Scythians who were trying to ride around Alexander's right flank, eventually defeating them (Arr. *Anab*. 3.13.3 and 3.14.3). Arrian notes that the Scythians, 'riders and horses alike, were better protected by defensive armour', though due to problems in the text of Arrian and a possible mix-up between Ariston and Aretas, it is unclear if the comparison is with the Paionians and mercenaries or the Prodromoi. It remains likely that the Prodronoi were armed as light cavalry (in terms of the armour, or lack thereof) but functioned tactically as heavy cavalry in battle, along with their scouting role outside of pitched battle.

4

The Macedonian Infantry

Hypaspists

Identity

There was probably a Macedonian infantry guard, equivalent to the Companion cavalry, from at least the fifth century. This would be the unit described in the passage of Anaximenes, writer of a lost biography of Philip II, who related (as we can tell from later references in other sources) that an unspecified king called Alexander had first created a unit of Pezhetairoi (Foot Companions), and organised them into formal units (Anaximenes, *FrGrHist* 72 F 4). The identity of this Alexander has exercised scholars of Alexander the Great's army ever since. If it was Alexander III, the Great, then it seems odd that Philip II, the originator of the Macedonian phalanx, had never created such a force. However, Alexander II was a minor king, only ruling from 369–368, and seems unlikely to be the originator of any significant military reform. This leaves Alexander I, ruling from 498–454, with time and opportunity to create this force of infantry. However, the fact that Macedon seems to have been without reliable infantry throughout the fifth and early fourth centuries suggests that the unit was relatively small or that later rulers failed to maintain its standards of discipline, both of which are inherently likely and would explain Macedon's poor battlefield performance before Philip's reign. Confirmation of this comes from another surviving fragment of a lost history, this time by the historian Theopompus: 'Theopompus says that men, chosen as tallest and strongest, served as a bodyguard to the king and were called the Pezhetairoi' (Photius, Theopompus *FrGrHist* 115 F 348). Philip's political opponent, Demosthenes, noted in a speech that, 'As for his [Philip's] household forces and Pezhetairoi, they have indeed the name of admirable soldiers' (Demosthenes, *Olynthiac* 2.17). So, the Pezhetairoi were the infantry guard of the king, initially formed probably in the first half of the fifth century, but with a strength of perhaps just a few hundred men, at least until the time of Philip II's army reforms in the mid-fourth century.[1]

---

1 Sekunda (2010) pp.447–8, stressing the Achaemenid (Persian) origins of these arrangements; Bosworth (2010).

Philip will have used this force as the kernel of his new model army. As suggested by Theopompus, the members of the Pezhetairoi were not picked from the nobility (such men would have served in the Companion cavalry), nor were they recruited regionally like the mass of the infantry, which at the start of Philip's reign would still have been poorly organised and lightly equipped skirmishers. They were a select force chosen from the 'best' men of military age in the kingdom, by whichever criteria this was judged – height and strength are the qualities identified by Theopompus. Though we must be cautious in applying examples from later Macedonian history backwards in time, we can note that the equivalent unit in Antigonid Macedon in the third and second centuries, the peltasts, was 'selected for their strength and the vigour of their youth' (Livy 42.51.4). So, the Pezhetairoi were probably younger men, taller and stronger than average, and selected from throughout the kingdom to serve, on at least a semi-professional basis, as the king's bodyguard. Other Greek states, during the fifth century, were also taking steps to complement their militia infantry with small professional forces of picked men (*epilektoi*), so it would be unsurprising to find Macedon undertaking similar measures. However, given the political turmoil and instability and the lack of funds, this force in Macedon may have remained largely ineffective until Philip's reign. When Philip began to re-equip, reorganise and expand his infantry soon after taking the throne, this unit would have been the first to adopt the new equipment and the first to receive intensive new training, hence the high opinion of their quality expressed by Demosthenes.

At some point, the unit name Pezhetairoi was extended to a much larger proportion of the Macedonian infantry (see below), and a new name, 'Hypaspists' (*hypaspistai*, literally 'shield-bearers') was given to the original Pezhetairoi. No source tells us when this happened, but we can reasonably guess, given Demosthenes' references to Philip's guard as Pezhetairoi, that it was Alexander the Great himself who made this change at the outset of his reign before his invasion of Persia. The Hypaspists were to change name again later in Alexander's reign to the Argyraspides (Silver Shields), no doubt due to the distribution of expensive new equipment. The name 'Hypaspists' itself does not, however, refer to any particular type of equipment (see below) – a hypaspist was, in general Greek usage, an attendant to a wealthy, noble or royal figure, literally the carrier of his master's shield, and as an honorific title it indicated closeness to the king (like 'Companion'), not the soldier's own equipment. There also continued, under Alexander, to be a smaller group of seven bodyguards (*somataphylakes*), and such a group continued to exist under the name 'Hypaspists' under the later Antigonid kings.[2]

Arrian is the only one of our sources to use the name 'Hypaspists', Diodorus and Curtius prefer to paraphrase or translate to 'bodyguard'. Arrian, however, is somewhat careless in his use of the name, referring variously to Hypaspists of the Companions (Arr. *Anab* 1.14.2), Royal Hypaspists, or just Hypaspists. Arrian also refers to 'the *agema* and the Hypaspists' (for example, Arr. *Anab.*

---

2   For debates on the identity of the Hypaspists, Milns (1967), Milns (1971), Ellis (1975), Lock (1977), Hammond (1978), Anson (1981), Anson (1985), Hammond (1991), Hammon (1997a), Bosworth (1997). For their later career, Roisman (2012)

1.1.11), though the Agema ('Vanguard') was itself part of the Hypaspists – as Arr. *Anab*. 3.11.9 (Gaugamela) shows, 'the agema of the Hypaspists were stationed first next to the cavalry and then the rest of the Hypaspists'. At the Hydaspes, Arrian notes that 'next to the cavalry, [Alexander] marshalled from the infantry the Royal Hypaspists under Seleucus, then the Royal Agema, and next the rest of the Hypaspists' (Arr. *Anab*, 5.13.4). Arrian also throws in 'royal bodyguards and Hypaspists' (Arr. *Anab*. 3.17.2; cf. 4.3.2). The Royal Hypaspists were likely a separate body, distinct from the Agema and the ordinary Hypaspists, and much smaller in number. At Gaugamela, the Agema and the Hypaspists formed to the left of the Companions, in the front line, yet the Persian chariots that charged through the Companions were disposed of behind the lines by 'the grooms and the Royal Hypaspists' (Arr. *Anab*. 3.13.6). If the Royal Hypaspists were a select group of at most a few hundred men they could have been stationed separately behind the Companions and served as *hamippoi* for them (that is, as infantry runners who keep pace with and fight alongside the cavalry – one is depicted in the Alexander Mosaic, running alongside Alexander). The Royal Hypaspists, with their special role and proximity to the king and Companions, may have been the original bearers of the name 'Hypaspists'. When this name was extended to cover the whole of the Hypaspists (formerly Pezhetairoi), only the designation 'Royal' served to distinguish the original body, to the confusion of Arrian and of subsequent historians.[3]

Organisation

Given the above, and the curious fact that none of our sources state the strength of the Hypaspists, any account of Hypaspist organisation is necessarily speculative. Their strength is normally assumed to be 3,000 men, based on references in Arrian, who relates that Nearchus and Antiochus were 'the chiliarchs of the Hypaspists' (4.30.5), while at 5.23.7 Ptolemy is given a force including three chiliarchies of Hypaspists. A chiliarchy (*chiliarchia*) is a unit of 1,000 men, a well-established unit in Greek and Persian armies, and its commander is a chiliarch, (*chiliarchos*, the same word was also used for a high-ranking official of the Persian Empire). Furthermore, the Argyraspides, as the Hypaspists became known, had a long and varied career in the wars of Alexander's Successors following his death, and they were 3,000 strong (Diod. 19.28.1). So, it seems safe to assume that there were three chiliarchies of Hypaspists, of which one was the Agema, with the Royal Hypaspists a small unit separate from and additional to the other Hypaspists. At Gaugamela, the Hypaspists as a whole were commanded by Nicanor son of Parmenion (Arr. *Anab*. 3.11.9), while Diodorus (17.61.3) notes that Hephaistion commanded the 'bodyguards', which on this occasion probably means neither the seven-man Bodyguard nor any part of the regular Hypaspists, but rather the Royal Hypaspists.

This neat picture is somewhat muddied by the story told by Curtius (5.2.2–5) that in 331, as part of the same reform that Alexander made to

---

3   On Hypaspists and their various possible subdivisions, Milns (1971), Hammond (1997); Bosworth (1997). As *hamippoi*, Heckel (2012).

the Companions, there was a competition to award, as a prize for courage in action, the rank of chiliarch and command of a chiliarchy. As Curtius relates, 'this was the first time the Macedonian troops had been thus divided numerically, for previously there had been cohorts of 500, and command of them had not been granted as a prize of valour.' Cohort is the Latin term for a unit of about this size, which Curtius used as he was writing in Latin for a Roman audience. This story has aroused considerable doubt, for good reason, as it seems a most haphazard way to appoint senior commanders, and it is not clear which units were involved (the Hypaspists are usually assumed, but Curtius does not say so). Curtius also relates that eight chiliarchs were appointed, which means 8,000 men were involved and rules out the 3,000-strong Hypaspists as the object of the reform. Some modern writers instead guess that Curtius meant that eight *pentakosiarchoi* (the Greek name for commanders of 500 men) were appointed, but this is the opposite of what Curtius says. Given these problems, it is hard to lend much credence to this reported reform, but we should accept the possibility that prior to this date, the Hypaspists were indeed formed in units of 500, not of 1,000, men.[4]

We should also note that the evidence for the total strength of 3,000 also comes from late in Alexander's reign, and in the early years it may be that the Hypaspists were a smaller unit. Since membership of the Hypaspists was subject to physical and (we would hope) martial excellence, there need not have been any particular draft of reinforcements required to increase their strength. If Alexander desired to increase their numbers from 2,000 to 3,000, say, this could have been done by drafting in promising specimens from the main phalanx. This might have happened when the large reinforcement of 6,000 infantry and 500 cavalry reached Alexander at Susa, in 331 (Arr. *Anab* 3.16.10). As such, it could be that the familiar strength of 3,000 applies only to the later years of the campaign, and in the major battles up to Gaugamela they might have been only 2,000 strong. To this number should then be added the Royal Hypaspists, who are invariably omitted from orders of battle for Alexander's army and who were probably a few hundred strong.

Equipment and Dress

If the organisation of the Hypaspists is obscure and subject to some controversy, this is as nothing compared to the problem of their appearance, equipment and tactical role. No ancient author describes the equipment of the Hypaspists, even in the most general terms, and there is no ancient artistic depiction that can unequivocally be said to be of them, and no surviving artefacts definitely belonging to them. The equipment of the main phalanx (see below) is broadly agreed on by most (though perhaps wrongly, as we will see) as being the typical equipment of the Macedonian phalangite – helmet, light or no armour, the long sarissa or pike, and a small rimless shield or *pelta*. The Hypaspists are sometimes assumed to be similarly equipped, for the good reason that no ancient writer says they were not. However, there are infantry figures on the Alexander Sarcophagus armed (those who are

---

4 Sekunda (2010) p.455 is inclined to accept Curtius' story but does not address the difficulties. English (2009) pp.31–5 is suitably cautious.

THE ARMY OF ALEXANDER THE GREAT

Macedonian infantry, a detail from the Alexander Sarcophagus, Istanbul Archaeological Museum. (Osman Hamdi Bey and T. Reinach, *Une nécropole royale à Sidon: fouilles: Plate XXX*)

not 'heroically' naked) with helmets, armour and traditional Argive shields – a larger shield or *aspis*, up to about one metre in diameter, with a bowled shape surrounded by an offset rim. As we do not expect to find traditionally equipped hoplites in the main phalanx, and as the sarcophagus is presumed to depict Macedonian infantry, some have concluded that the men depicted are Hypaspists, and, therefore, that Hypaspists carried the same equipment as traditional Greek hoplites, which is to say, the large Argive shield and a short spear or *dory*, approximately two to three metres long.

I believe that both these theories are in error and that the equipment of the main phalanx is also misunderstood. The main reason for supposing that the sarcophagus figures cannot be phalangites – that they are carrying the Argive shield – is unsound. The theory is based on two assumptions: that the Argive shield could not be carried with a sarissa, since the sarissa requires two hands to wield it; and that the shield of the phalanx was significantly smaller than the typical Argive shield. Yet the sarcophagus itself depicts infantry equipped with Argive shields who have their left hands free, due to some different carrying arrangement than the normal two handles used by Greek hoplites (though no evidence exists of precisely what this different carrying arrangement was). On the sarcophagus, the men depicted are using their left hands to grab prisoners, but they could equally well be holding a sarissa. It seems, therefore, that there is no reason to suppose that the Argive shield and sarissa could not be used together. For comparison, we might note that at the end of the third century, when the Spartan army was re-equipped 'in the Macedonian fashion' with the sarissa, they are not said to have adopted new shields but rather to have changed the carrying arrangements of their shields, exactly as we would expect (Plut. *Cleom.* 11.2).[5]

As for the shield of the phalanx being a small *pelta*, this is based on the testimony of Asclepiodotus (and the other Tacticians). But Asclepiodotus was writing in the first century and describing the equipment of an army two centuries later than that of Alexander. His description might also be valid for Alexander's army, but we cannot simply assume that it is. What is more, Asclepiodotus says that 'of the shields (*aspides*) of the phalanx, the best is the Macedonian, bronze, of eight palms width, not too concave' (Asclep. 5.1). Clearly then, other types of shield, or other configurations and sizes of Macedonian shield, were available, of which the 'best' may have been that described, in Asclepiodotus' or his source's opinion. Depictions in art of

---

5 Supporting the identification of the Sarcophagus infantry as Pezhetairoi (or Asthetairoi), Sekunda and McBride (1984); Sekunda (2020) pp.457–8. Shield carrying arrangements, Taylor (2020) pp.46–65.

Macedonian and Greek infantry, a detail from the Alexander Sarcophagus, Istanbul Archaeological Museum. The tunics are red, under purple armour with yellow *pteruges*. (Osman Hamdi Bey and T. Reinach, *Une nécropole royale à Sidon: fouilles: Plate XXXV*)

Macedonian shields (identifiable as Macedonian by their distinctive pattern, and their lack of rim) from the late third and second centuries show large and very concave shields, presumably carried by the Macedonian phalanx. Importantly, Asclepiodotus himself (Asclep 1.2) says that the phalanx carries 'the largest size of shield', so Asclepiodotus is not internally consistent, and throughout he calls this shield an *aspis*, never a *pelta*. We also know from third- and second-century Macedonian inscriptions that the shield of the phalanx was called an *aspis* by the Macedonians themselves. There are, therefore, no grounds for assuming that the main phalanx carried a small shield. While the traditional Macedonian shield could, on occasion, be called a *pelta* (because it lacked a rim), we cannot make any clear distinction between the Macedonian phalanx (putatively with a small rimless *pelta*) and Greek hoplites (with a larger rimmed Argive *aspis*).[6]

There are also good reasons to suppose that the Hypaspists were not equipped like traditional hoplites. As is often noted, the Hypaspists were frequently selected for special missions such as storming cities, forced marches and seizing important terrain. While hoplites could perform such functions, they were not ideally suited to them, and centuries of Greek warfare had amply demonstrated that hoplites were at their weakest on difficult terrain or in circumstances requiring swift movement, and that the single greatest obstacle to their swiftness was precisely the large heavy Argive shield. The shield was a sufficient hindrance to speed that men running from battle would frequently cast away their shields, trading protection for speed. It seems, therefore, inherently unlikely that Alexander's fast strike force was equipped with the heaviest type of shield.

Instead, I think the clue to the Hypaspists' equipment lies in comparison with their successors in Hellenistic, and particularly Antigonid Macedonian, armies of the third and second centuries. The Antigonid army contained,

---

6   Shields, Liampi (1998), Taylor (2020) pp.46–65. For the common opinion that the Hypaspists carried the Argive aspis, see the references for Hypaspists above.

alongside the main phalanx, a unit equivalent to the Hypaspists – also 3,000 strong and specially selected from all the men of the kingdom. This unit was called the Peltasts, and it was most likely equipped like the peltasts described in the Tacticians, that is, with a small shield (*pelta*) and a spear that was long but shorter than the full-size sarissa. The origin of this type of equipment is sometimes attributed to the early fourth century Athenian general Iphicrates, with men so equipped being termed by modern historians 'Iphicratean peltasts', to distinguish them from the traditional peltasts of Classical Greece, who were lightly equipped javelin-armed skirmishers. It is not certain that Iphicrates' equipment reforms ever really took place, and heavier-armed peltasts with spears seem to have existed before Iphicrates, but the term is a convenient one to identify this type of armament. Men so equipped could have fought in the line of battle as part of the main phalanx. The spear was probably of a length that could be wielded with either one or both hands, but if held in two hands, it would be functionally equivalent to the sarissa of the main phalanx. But the Hypaspists (and the Antigonid Peltasts) were also used on occasions when using such a spear would make little sense, such as assaults on cities and quick marches over difficult ground. For such missions, the Hypaspists could doubtless be equipped either with shorter spears or javelins (or, indeed, with both). The javelin was the traditional infantry weapon of Macedon, and there would have been many men who were adept in its use, without the need for special training. As well as a long spear or javelins, the Hypaspists will have carried a sword, as all Macedonian infantry did. They also may have worn greaves (metal shin guards), though the wearing of greaves had largely fallen out of fashion in the rest of Greece at this period.[7]

The Hypaspists' peltast shield was smaller in size than the shields of the main phalanx, though details of its design are lacking. Probably, it was a small 'Macedonian' shield (one without a rim) and, in this case, of fairly flat construction. Its precise size is unknown – Asclepiodotus tells us that the best shield for the phalanx (of hoplites, in the main phalanx) was eight palms in width (about 60 cm), but that the hoplites had the largest shields and peltasts a smaller shield. But there is little or no artistic or archaeological evidence for shields smaller than 60 cm, and a number of Macedonian-pattern shields have been discovered that range in size from a little over 60 cm to 75 cm or more. Given the relatively small numerical size of the Hypaspists (and their Peltast successors) as a unit, it is possible that none of their shields have survived. It is also possible that about 60 cm (eight palms) was, in fact, the smallest size of shield used, that this was the shield of the Hypaspists, and that the main phalanx carried, as Asclepiodotus (1.2) says, larger shields (there will be more on this question below). As a smaller rimless shield, the shield of the Hypaspists could be called a *pelta*, as could larger shields of the Macedonian pattern, which were also rimless.[8]

---

7 'Iphicratean peltasts' – Sekunda (2007) pp.326–9.
8 Macedonians shields in general – Liampi (1998); hoplite and peltast shields, Taylor (2020) pp.46–65.

THE MACEDONIAN INFANTRY

A possible depiction of Peltast equipment, Roman fresco from the House of Menander, Pompeii. He wears a red tunic with blue border. (Falk2 – CC BY-SA 4.0)

The origins of this equipment take us back to the creation of the unit, the original Pezhetairoi, under Philip II. When Philip began his reforms of the Macedonian army, he would naturally have begun with his household troops, his infantry guard, who were already selected professionals used to being drilled and equipped at state expense. They will have received the earliest form of the new Macedonian equipment, and their training regime is described by Polyaenus:

> Philip accustomed the Macedonians to constant exercise, before they went to war: so that he would frequently make them march 300 stades [about 54 km], carrying with them their helmets, shields [*peltas*], greaves, and spears [*sarisas*]. Polyaenus 4.2.10

This equipment – with modifications no doubt, since there is no reason to suppose the equipment remained completely unchanged throughout Philip's reign – would eventually be rolled out to the whole Macedonian levy, becoming heavier as it was applied to the mass of the infantry, but the guards themselves, as special forces needed for difficult missions, will have retained the lighter version with smaller shield and a shorter sarissa.

This will also apply to the Royal Hypaspists (for the equipment of which there is no direct evidence). As they were intended to act as *hamippoi* alongside the cavalry, they will have been relatively lightly equipped for speed and certainly will not have carried the traditional Argive aspis. The smaller pattern of shield, a long spear, and no body armour are the most likely combination.

Drill and Tactics

The Hypaspists (excluding the Royal Hypaspists) will have fought as part of the phalanx in a pitched battle. Their drill and fighting methods in this role will have been very similar to those of the main phalanx (see the next section). When they were tasked with special missions, they would have fought in a looser, more open order and, depending on the terrain and task in hand, need not have adopted formal formations, being instead able to fight in dispersed and irregular formations, using their spears or javelins and swords.

The Royal Hypaspists acted as *hamippoi* to the Companions, infantry employed to run alongside cavalry, mingled in amongst them. Clearly, they could not cover long distances like this or move at top speed. However, there are tales, in Alexander's long pursuits of fleeing Persians, of remarkable feats of endurance from infantrymen running alongside cavalry (for example, QC 8.2.33–9). There are several occasions where such infantry, mixed in amongst cavalry in a more static fight, could tilt the balance decisively against enemy cavalry (for this was a tactic particularly useful in cavalry versus cavalry fights). Cavalry of this period, having no stirrups or built-up saddles, were fairly precariously seated, and infantry appearing among them could severely disadvantage them.[9]

Pezhetairoi and Asthetairoi

Identity

We have seen that Philip II created the Macedonian phalanx by equipping and training first his elite infantry unit and then the rest of the full Macedonian levy. This meant that a kingdom that at the start of his reign could muster only some 10,000 infantry of doubtful military value could at the start of Alexander's reign send 12,000 heavy infantry to Asia with Alexander while keeping the same number at home under Antipatros and still send out drafts of reinforcements to Alexander during his campaigns. Attempts to estimate the total number of phalanx infantry who served with Alexander throughout his campaign are fraught with difficulty; we do not have complete accounts of all the reinforcements sent out, losses suffered to battle or sickness, or numbers left in garrisons or detached forces. Even so, there must have been about 40,000 Macedonian infantry active across the period, at home and

---

9 Heckel (2012).

abroad, and Macedonians were to continue to campaign through Asia under Alexander's Successors and formed the core group of settlers from which the Hellenistic kingdoms were established.[10]

In the literary accounts of Alexander's reign, the mass of the heavy infantry are variously termed 'the phalanx' or 'the hoplites' – both generic terms indicating heavy, line-of-battle infantry. Arrian alone also uses two proper names for them, which he no doubt found in his sources, Ptolemy and Aristoboulos: Pezhetairoi ('Foot Companions') and Asthetairoi (the exact meaning of which is unclear). More myths and misconceptions have grown up around these two units (or single unit if we consider them as two parts of the phalanx as a whole) than any other part of Alexander's army, particularly when it comes to equipment (see below). An important point is the name Pezhetairoi itself. Some modern authors treat this word as if it means the same thing as 'phalangite' – a sarissa-armed member of the Macedonian phalanx. But it does not – it is a unit name, not a type of armament, and as we have seen, it was initially applied to the infantry guard, and only later (perhaps under Alexander) was the name extended to the main phalanx and even then not to all of it. So far as we know, no phalanx unit after Alexander was called Pezhetairoi. The word crops up in a couple of late and doubtful contexts, but Hellenistic kingdoms gave their phalanx units different names, the best known of which is the Chalcaspides, 'Bronze Shields', of the Antigonid kingdom.

So, the Pezhetairoi were originally the guard unit of the Macedonian army, which Philip would have used as the basis for the reforms that eventually encompassed the entire Macedonian infantry. The details of the recruitment of the phalanx are somewhat unclear (see further in Chapter 8). Evidently, at least at the outset of the campaign, the phalanx battalions were recruited regionally. This was similar to the recruitment of the cavalry, but the regions involved were more likely to be large, traditional regions of the kingdom rather than newly settled areas. Arrian identifies the battalions only by their commander, but Diodorus (17.57.2) tells us that Coinos' battalion was from Elimiotis, Perdiccas's consisted of Orestai and Lyncestai, and Polyperchon's of Stymphaians. Elimiotis (also Elimeia) and Stymphaia (or Tymphaia) were regions of Upper Macedonia, the mountainous hinterland that came under central Macedonian control in the first decade of Philip's reign. Lyncestis and Orestis were similarly satellite kingdoms of Macedon, which had, before Philip, maintained independence.

We have more information about recruitment in Antigonid Macedon than in Philip's and Alexander's days, though similar arrangements were likely in place. Recruitment was by conscription based on households and by age group, as was normal practice in Greece. On reaching a given age, men would become eligible for service in the army and would be required to join their local unit and attend training or march off to campaign in wartime. It has been estimated that by the end of Philip's reign, Macedon

---

10 Some believe Macedon was impoverished by the flow of manpower to the east, Bosworth (1986); others believe that Macedon's population was well able to sustain the numbers, Hammond (1989b).

Late fourth-century Macedonian soldiers – shieldless cavalry in yellow/purple cloaks and purple armour, and shielded infantry with red or blue tunics, Agios Athanasios tomb, Thessaloniki, Greece (Egisto Sani, CC BY-SA 2.0)

could produce 3,000 new infantry recruits and 300 cavalry per year. What portion of the population was eligible for such service is not clear – it was normal practice in most Greek states for military service to be a privilege of a relatively wealthy portion of society; poorer men could volunteer or could serve as mercenaries, but this would often be as light infantry (particularly if they had to provide their own equipment). Service in the heavy infantry (the hoplites) was generally restricted to the better-off. In Macedon, the new arms devised by Philip were manufactured and distributed centrally, which means that there was no requirement for the men to provide their own kit. As such, we should expect that a larger proportion of society was able to serve in the phalanx. There was also no urban middle class in Macedon, or only a small one, and part of Philip's reforms, continued by Alexander in Asia, was to found and develop cities and move populations into them to develop this urban class, considered in Greek thought to be essential to the development of effective infantry and for a politically engaged population, capable of the full enjoyment of Greek cultural life. The usual characterisation of the Macedonian phalanx – that it consisted of the Macedonian peasantry – is true up to a point, given certain understandings of the term 'peasantry'. It was probably drawn from the bulk of the male population, except the wealthy who served in the cavalry, though increasingly, these would have been urban and land-owning men, at least in theory. There would also have been a class of men below the level (socially and economically) of those who served in the phalanx. This would have included the slaves who were ubiquitous in the Greek world, but also most likely a class of landless labourers, both rural

THE MACEDONIAN INFANTRY

Late fourth-century Macedonian soldiers in *chlamys* and *kausia*, Agios Athanasios tomb, Thessaloniki, Greece. Cloaks are red-brown with white borders. (PD)

labourers and artisans, the classes excluded from the hoplite class in the rest of Greece; it is likely that these did not form a part of the Macedonian phalanx either. The phalanx was thus drawn from a slightly socio-economically elevated group, land-holding farmers and later city-dwellers.[11]

Organisation

The size of the phalanx in Alexander's army is usually stated as 12,000 men, based on the description of Diodorus (17.17) of the muster near Troy at the start of the campaign: 'There were found to be, of infantry, twelve thousand Macedonians'. This number presumably includes the Hypaspists, generally reckoned to be 3,000 strong as we have seen, and as we know that there were six *taxeis* (battalions) of the phalanx (they are enumerated at several of the battles, and particularly at Gaugamela), the usual conclusion is that each *taxis* contained 1,500 men. For all that this is often stated as a solid fact, numerous caveats, as usual, apply. As with the rest of the army, we cannot be certain of the numbers of reinforcements received or losses to all causes, so we do not know how the numbers – either the total or the numbers in the constituent units – will have fluctuated up and down. At the least, we

---

11 Hatzopoulos (2001); Ellis (1976); size of yearly intake – Noguera Borel (2006) p.231.

must expect that, like all military units throughout history, actual strength was often well below paper strength. More fundamentally, the strength of 3,000 for the Hypaspists is based largely on later evidence (the strength of the Argyraspides in the wars of the Successors and the number of chiliarchies later in the campaign), and although it is possible that the Hypaspists were indeed 3,000 strong for much of the campaign, it is not a given that they were from the outset. We also do not know how many Macedonians, if any, were in the advance force of 10,000 men that Philip had sent across into Asia. The usual assumption is that these were all mercenaries or allied units, but if the force contained Macedonians, which Diodorus did not include in his total (which, as we saw earlier, is 10,000 men short of the total given by other historians), then it may be that one or more *taxeis* of the phalanx were included in this force, in which case the number of Macedonians in the initial invasion army may have been higher than 12,000, and the size of each *taxis* correspondingly higher also.

As a result of such uncertainties, I am more sceptical than most modern authors of the figure of 1,500 men for each phalanx *taxis*. Arrian lists the constituent *taxeis* of the phalanx, for example at Gaugamela (Arr. *Anab* 3.11.9), naming each *taxis* and identifying it by the name of its commander. *Taxis* is a generic Greek word for a large body of soldiers, usually infantry, and, on occasion, Arrian uses the word in this general sense. When describing the phalanx however, it is clear that he is using the word in a more technical sense – a *taxis* of the phalanx was a specific unit in the same way as an *ilē* of cavalry or a *chiliarchia* of Hypaspists was. The later Tacticians do not list a large unit called a *taxis* but the unit of equivalent size would be that made up of two *chiliarchiai*; as Asclepiodotus describes it, 'two *chiliarchiai* were formerly called a *keras* and a *telos*, but later it was called a *merarchia*' (Asclep 2.10 – Asclepiodotus offers no clue when he means by 'formerly' and 'later'). However, there is an obvious problem, as a unit made up of two *chiliarchiai* would be 2,000 men strong, not 1,500, and there is no unit in the Tacticians that consisted of 1,500 men. According to the usual interpretation, Alexander's *taxeis* of 1,500 would have each contained three *pentakosiarchai* (or *lochoi*, as they are sometimes designated by modern authors), each 500 strong (compare this with the Hypaspist organisation discussed above). This is a possibility; however, in the Tacticians, all the various subdivisions of the phalanx are based on powers of two (so units have 64, 128, 256, 512 men and so on), and each larger unit is made up of exactly two constituent units. It is possible that this preference for even numbers is more a product of the fact that the Tacticians, increasingly distant in time from the active service of phalanx-based armies, were more concerned with theoretical neatness and round numbers than with actual practice, but there was good reason to base a phalanx on multiples of two, since the various evolutions of the phalanx – doubling and halving in order to adopt formations of differing depths, widths and densities – could be much more easily accomplished with even numbers of subunits than with odd. This point cannot be pushed too far as we can see that the Hypapists, at least later in the campaign, probably had three units each of 1,000 men, but I think it is at least likely that the main phalanx of Alexander followed the principles of the Tacticians, and that each *taxis* consisted of 2,000 men. There is at least enough uncertainty in the numbers given by Diodorus to allow for this possibility (he misses out all of the advance force, and his infantry total is 2,000 men short of his unit listing), and so to render unsafe the usual assumption of 1,500-man *taxeis*, given that there is no other evidence for units of this size. The fact that Antipatros was left with 12,000 men, which probably did not include any Hypaspists, as they were specifically the king's guard, lends some support to the idea since this suggests that the phalanx was divided into two equal halves of 12,000. If this theory is correct, then the main phalanx was formed from six 2,000-man *taxeis*, and the phalanx itself was 12,000 strong, to which the Hypaspists were additional.[12]

In addition, there is the question of the 3,000 Macedonian infantry reinforcements that joined the army at Gordion in 333 (after Granicus and before Issus, Arr. *Anab*. 1.29.4). These are usually assumed to more or less compensate for losses to battle and sickness, but not to garrisons, since Macedonians were not used for permanent garrisons at this stage, mercenaries being preferred for this role. The totals – 9,000 Pezhetairoi/Asthetairoi, 3,000 Hypaspists – are assumed to remain unchanged between Granicus, Issus and Gaugamela. However, such a large reinforcement is not balanced by any losses we know of, so it is also possible that the size of the phalanx increased to approximately 12,000 men with these reinforcements. Exactly how they would be incorporated into the *taxeis* we do not know, but the *taxeis* may have been understrength at the Granicus. In the orders of battle for the major battles in Chapter 10, I will assume a phalanx of 12,000 phalangites in addition to the Hypaspists from Issus onwards, but I will also note the traditional numbers.

The whole of the phalanx with Alexander was designated by two names – Pezhetairoi and Asthetairoi. We cannot tell whether those left behind in Macedon were also designated by these names or by some other title. The name Pezhetairoi (Foot Companions) we are already familiar with as the original name of Philip's guard. The name Asthetairoi is more enigmatic, and various proposals have been made. Editors of Arrian's text (the name appears only in Arrian) used to assume that the name was an error for Pezhetairoi and edited it out. However, it has now long been accepted that this was a mistake, despite which innumerable modern writers still mentally edit out the Asthetairoi, referring exclusively to Pezhetairoi and mentioning the Asthetairoi, if at all, as if they were a subset of the Pezhetairoi. The meaning of the name is unclear. The prefix 'Ast-' is presumably a contraction of something (in Greek), and suggested translations have included 'Star-', 'City-', 'Best-', or 'Closest-' Companions. The first *taxis* to be identified as belonging to the Asthetairoi is that of Coinos at the siege of Tyre (Arr. *Anab*. 2.23.2); subsequently, it appears that half of Alexander's phalanx – three *taxeis* at least – are Asthetairoi. In 327, Alexander formed a task force of 'the Hypaspists, all the Companion cavalry not detailed with Hephaistion [that is, half of them], and the *taxeis* of the so-called Asthetairoi' (Arr. *Anab*. 4.23.1). In 326,

---

12 For arguments in favour of the 2,000-man *taxis* see Ueda-Sarson (2001).

Perdiccas commanded the left wing with the Asthetairoi (Arr. *Anab*. 5.22.6). In 325, on the Indus, Alexander took 'half of the Hypaspists and the archers, [and] the *taxeis* of the so-called Asthetairoi' (Arr. *Anab*. 6.21.3). At the Opis mutiny, Alexander threatened to dismiss his Macedonians and recruit in their place 'Persian Pezhetairoi and Asthetairoi too' (Arr. *Anab*. 7.11.3). All of this suggests that the phalanx was split half-and-half between Pezhetairoi and Asthetairoi. It has been plausibly suggested (based on the example of Coinos' battalion, recruited from upland Elimiotis, and Perdiccas', from Orestis and Lyncestis, Diod. 17.57.2) that the Asthetairoi were specifically the infantry of Upper Macedonia, which was absorbed into the kingdom by Philip. It would make sense for Alexander to take with him the infantry of the newly absorbed regions, thus reducing the likelihood of separatist sentiments breaking out at home in his absence. The Asthetairoi also seem to be crack battalions, chosen for city assaults (like Coinos' at Tyre) and often selected by Alexander for rapid marches. Another possibility is that at the outset of the campaign, all *taxeis* of the phalanx were called Pezhetairoi, and specific units acquired the name Asthetairoi as a sort of battle honour or reward for good service. Given the nature of the evidence, we cannot be certain whether this is the case. Some passages of Arrian (for example, Arr. *Anab*. 1.28.3) do seem to suggest that early in the campaign, all units were Pezhetairoi, and Asthetairoi are not definitely attested before the siege of Tyre. So, it remains a possibility that the Asthetairoi designation was applied unit by unit in the course of the campaign. However, a comparison with the Antigonid army, where the phalanx was divided into two halves called respectively Chalcaspides (Bronze Shields) and Leukaspides (White Shields), offers some support for there having always been a distinction between the two in Alexander's army. It is also possible that these two parts of the phalanx had different equipment from each other (more on this below).[13]

We have very little information on the subunits of the *taxeis* in Alexander's army. The Tacticians provide a detailed breakdown of units down to the individual file of 16 men: *chiliarchia* of 1,024, *pentakosiarchia* of 512, *syntagma* (other names were also used) of 256, *taxis* of 128 (note the different usage of *taxis* here), *tetrarchia* of 64, *dilochia* of 32, and *lochos* (file) of 16. There is little trace of this organisation in Alexander's army, though we must assume that it, or something like it, was present. Twice, late in Alexander's reign, Arrian refers to '*ilai* and "hundreds" and *lochoi*' (Arr. *Anab*. 6.27.6), or '*lochoi* and "hundreds"' (7.24.4). 'Hundreds', *hekatostuas*, are not otherwise recorded, but if they were units of infantry (Arrian does not specify), they might be equivalent to the 128-man *taxis* of the Tacticians. The manoeuvre unit (the smallest independent unit which could be used for tactical manoeuvres) of the Hellenistic phalanx was the *syntagma*. In Alexander's army, we frequently hear of *taxeis* being separated and tasked with independent missions, but there is no account of the use of individual subunits. It is reasonable to assume, however, that they did exist and that the various evolutions of the phalanx in battle were based around these smaller units. We cannot, however, assume

---

13 Asthetairoi, Hammond (1989a) pp.148–151 (identity as Upper Macedonians); Hammond and Griffith (1979) pp.711–12; Bosworth (1973); Heckel (2009); English (2009) pp.25–7.

that the same names were used as those that were used by the Tacticians, given the obvious differences, so that while a unit of 256 men no doubt existed, we cannot state that it was called a *syntagma*. Only at the level of the file do we get a glimpse of the low-level organisation in Alexander's army. When Arrian describes Alexander's planned creation of a hybrid Persian-Macedonian phalanx (Arr. *Anab*, 7.23.3), we are told that each file was called a *dekados* (dekad), led by a *dekadarchos*, that the second man in the file received double pay (*dimoirites*), the third was a 'ten-stater-man' on increased pay but less than double, then 12 ordinary soldiers (Persians in this case), and finally a file closer, also a 'ten-stater-man'. The name 'dekad', literally 'ten', for the file of 16, suggests that this name was a survival from an earlier form of organisation – possibly from as far back as the original fifth-century Pezhetairoi, whose organisation may have reflected Persian organisation, which was based on multiples of 10. The same would apply to the 'hundreds'. We should also note that according to the Tacticians (including Arrian himself, *Tact*. 6, along with Asclep. 2.2 and Aelian *Tact*. 5), the *dimoirites* was so named as he was the 'half file leader', not 'on double pay'. This would mean that the correct designation of the junior officers would be a *dekadarchos* (file leader) commanding the file, a *dimoirites* (half-file leader) commanding the second half-file, and 'two ten-stater-men' acting as file closers to each of the half-files. This is not precisely what Arrian describes – he implies that all the Persians are grouped together – but the existing roles of the junior officers may have been altered for this experimental, hybrid phalanx.[14]

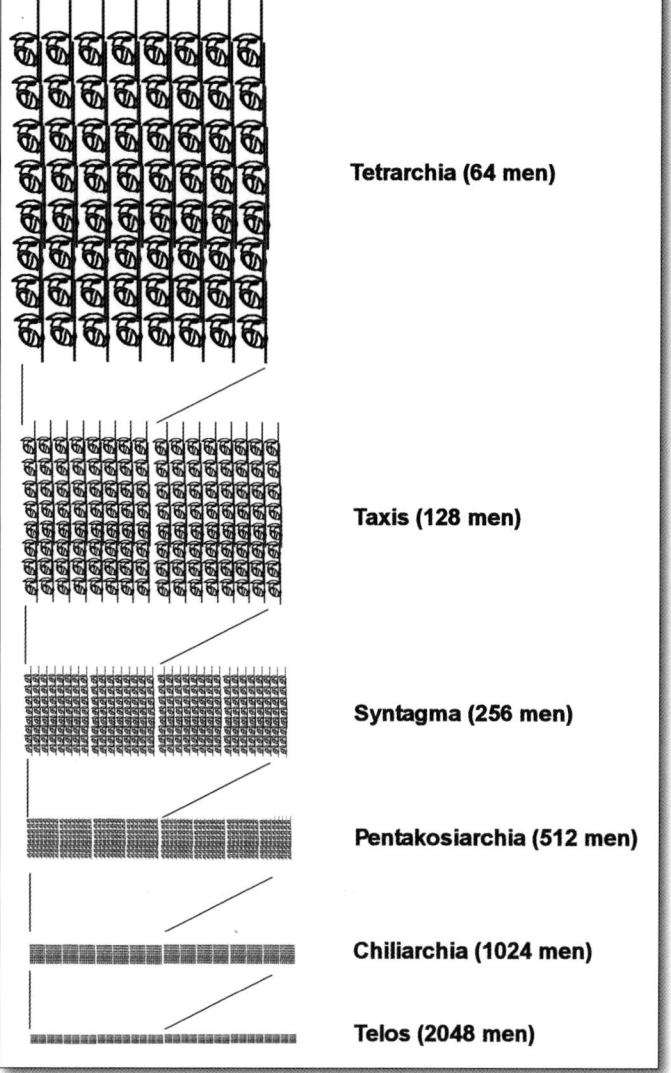

Phalanx organisation as described by Asclepiodotus (first century). The *telos* is equivalent to the *taxis* of Arrian

The *taxeis* themselves are generally identified by the name of their commander. This creates some difficulties, since when Arrian names a *taxis* by its commander it is not always clear if he means the permanent, on-paper commander, or the current acting commander. On occasions, he specifies clearly which he means – at Gaugamela, for example, the phalanx included the *taxis* 'of Amyntas son of Philip; this was led by Simmias, since Amyntas

---

14 Sekunda (2010), taking *hekatostuas* to be units of cavalry.

had been sent to Macedonia to collect troops' (Arr. *Anab.* 3.11.9). On other occasions, however, Arrian appears to identify a unit by the name of the current commander without commenting on whether this was a temporary command. As a result, in the campaigns of 327 for example we seem to have 10 or 11 different *taxis* commanders. This is combined with the occasional use of *taxis* in a non-technical sense, to mean a body of infantry – for example, Arr. *Anab.* 4.24.10, the *taxeis* of Attalos and Balacros, where the latter may be the same as the javelinmen Balacros commanded at Gaugamela, 3.12.3. This means that we cannot be certain of the numbers of phalanx *taxeis* in the later campaigns. At the Hydaspes, there appear to be seven *taxeis* at least, but only four are actually listed as such. Alexander divided his forces for the crossing of the river into three. One part under Crateros remained in camp with 'from the Macedonian phalanx the *taxeis* of Alcetas and Polyperchon' (Arr. *Anab.* 5.11.3). Alexander himself took 'from the phalanx, the Hypaspists and the *taxeis* of Cleitos and Coinos' (5.12.2). Between these two forces, 'Meleagros and Attalos and Gorgias were posted with the mercenary cavalry and infantry' (5.12.1). As these three are known taxiarchs (*taxiarchoi*, taxis-commanders), the usual assumption is that these three each had their own *taxis*, as well as the mercenaries, though characteristically, Arrian does not say so. Nor does he describe them crossing the river or joining Alexander's force, though presumably they did so at some point. The extra *taxis* since Gaugamela is that of Cleitos, which first appears in 327 (4.22.7), without further comment from Arrian. Perhaps, following the influx of reinforcements in 331, the number of *taxeis* was increased from six to seven.[15]

The taxiarchs, commanders of the six *taxeis*, at the three major battles (Granicus, Issus and Gaugamela) were, according to Arrian, and in order right to left:

Granicus	**Issus**	**Gaugamela**
(Arr. *Anab.* 1.14.2–3)	(Arr. *Anab.* 2.8.3–4)	(Arr. *Anab.* 3.11.9)
Perdiccas	Coinos	Coinos
Coinos	Perdiccas	Perdiccas
Amyntas	Amyntas	Meleagros
Philippos	Ptolemaios	Polyperchon
Meleagros	Meleagros	Amyntas (Simmias acting)
Crateros	Amyntas	Crateros

Equipment and Dress

The equipment of the Macedonian phalanx is arguably both the best and least understood aspect of Alexander's army – it is certainly that around which most myths have accumulated. The basic picture is clear enough, though a steady trickle of books and articles still appear proposing alternative interpretations of the scanty evidence. What I will present here is my own take on the question, with conclusions that have been reached after due consideration of the evidence, although there will not be space in the

---

15 Milns (2003), English (2009) pp.10–16.

present volume to present the full argument or to discuss all the alternatives. Interested readers wishing to dig deeper are advised to consult the works referenced in the bibliography.[16]

As we saw above in the section on the Hypaspists, the equipment of the Macedonian phalanx was devised by Philip. It will have been assigned first to the regular infantry, the original Pezhetairoi, and then to the mass of the phalanx. However, we cannot assume that it remained unchanged, either across the 20 years of Philip's reign or the campaigns of Alexander. Experiment, adaptation and evolution are surely to be expected. The original equipment was that identified by Polyaenus (4.2.10): sarissa, helmet, rimless shield (*pelta*), and greaves. These items will be considered individually below. Note that no armour is mentioned. Body armour had generally fallen out of fashion in Greece in the fourth century, and the combination of lack of armour and the lighter type of shield (*pelta*) will have made these early phalangites more lightly equipped than many hoplites and certainly lighter than earlier Classical hoplites. The sarissa, in its largest size, would, to some extent, have cancelled out this lightness. However, the early sarissa was probably shorter than that used under Alexander and certainly shorter than the full-size sarissa used under the Successors and the early Hellenistic kingdoms. This equipment is that of peltasts, in the Hellenistic sense of the word (Iphicratean peltasts, not the javelin-armed skirmishers of the Classical era). Philip's first phalanx was a phalanx of peltasts and was formed around his infantry guard. The guard (renamed Hypaspists under Alexander) was to retain this equipment throughout Alexander's reign. It gave them the ability to fight in the line of battle alongside the phalanx but also (perhaps swapping their sarissas for javelins) allowed them to be used for rapid marches and assaults.

When the bulk of the Macedonian infantry were trained to fight in the new phalanx, however, they were not equipped as peltasts but as hoplites (again, in the Hellenistic, not the Classical, sense). As the Tacticians tell us, the hoplites of the phalanx used the largest size of shield and carried the longest type of sarissa (the actual length of which varied across the Hellenistic period). The shield was usually called an *aspis*, though in some forms, particularly the traditional Macedonian style of shield, it might still be called a *pelta* since it did not have the offset rim of the Argive *aspis* of the Classical hoplite. This Macedonian shield appears to be of a lighter design overall than the Classical *aspis*, presumably made of thinner wood, or perhaps lacking the bronze facing. It was carried using handles that left the left hand free for the two-handed grip required by the sarissa. But not every phalangite necessarily carried a Macedonian shield – the Argive *aspis* could also be carried with a sarissa, providing the same modified holding arrangement was used.[17]

Given the lack of literary references to the equipment of Alexander's phalanx, the scarcity of artistic depictions, and the lack of archaeological evidence, it is impossible to be certain what type or types of shields were

---

16 For a fuller exposition of the arguments, Taylor (2020) pp.26–81.
17 Sekunda (1985) and (2010) also accepts the use of the Argive shield by the men of the phalanx. Karunanithy (2013) pp.100–115 on infantry equipment generally.

used. However, I argued above that the Hypaspists, as peltasts, will have used the smaller and lighter type of shield; the main phalanx will have had larger, heavier shields. The evidence of the Alexander Sarcophagus is that at least some Macedonians used Argive *aspides* at this period – these must, therefore, have been men of the main phalanx. However, the prevalence of the Macedonian shield in art, particularly in depictions on coinage (identifiable by its distinctive decoration and the lack of rim), suggests that this shield too was widely used, and indeed under the Successors and later was to become something of a badge of identity for Macedonians in Asia. Therefore, we should expect to find two types of shields in use in Alexander's phalanx: an Argive *aspis* carried with the new handles and a Macedonian shield. Whether these shields were used concurrently by different units, or one was adopted first and then replaced by the other, is an open question (on which I will speculate below).[18]

One of the myths surrounding the Macedonian army is that the phalanx always carried shields of 'eight palms width', as described by the Tacticians. Some shields may well have been of this size, but the Macedonian phalanx existed for nearly three centuries across an area of land stretching from Italy to India, and we cannot conclude that all used the type of shield described by a late drill manual, especially when that manual is itself internally inconsistent. Another myth is that the phalangite carried his shield on a strap around his neck, or even in some extreme forms of the myth, on his back. There is no evidence for this, though it is likely that a strap was used on the march – such straps account for the depiction of straps in some coin images. The strap idea seems to originate from a misreading of Plutarch's description of the reform of the late third-century Spartan army to fight in the Macedonian fashion, that 'they used an *ochane* (handle) instead of a *porpax* (armband)' on their Argive shields (Plut. *Cleom.* 11.2) but an *ochane* is a handle (of unknown configuration), not a strap. The description of the Macedonian phalanx at Pydna in 168 bringing their shields round to their front is also sometimes adduced as evidence of a strap – bizarrely, since it suggests nothing of the sort. The purpose of the supposed neck strap has never, to my knowledge, been clearly elucidated. A shield cannot be controlled, still less held rigid against blows, by a strap around the neck, nor can such a strap help take the weight of the shield unless it is too short to be useful when the shield is not raised for action. It is an accessory for which there is no evidence and which has no function.[19]

So, we should expect to find two types of shields in use in Alexander's phalanx, both carried on the arm, and both of larger size than those of the Hypaspists and differing from each other in their shape and construction rather than their size. The Argive shields on the sarcophagus appear more or less of normal hoplite shield size or a little smaller, and the Macedonian shields were likely of similar size, based on the depictions of such shields in use in the later Antigonid army.

---

18   Macedonian shields – Liampi (1998).
19   The shield and strap theory is advanced by Markle (1982) and especially (1999) and is followed without question by innumerable subsequent modern authors, for example, Connolly (1998).

THE MACEDONIAN INFANTRY

Fourth or third century Macedonian equipment from the 'Tomb of Lyson and Kallikles', Lefkadia, Greece. The helmets are red and yellow, and the shield has a blue central rondel with a red surround. (PD)

Fourth or third century Macedonian shield and armour from the 'Tomb of Lyson and Kallikles', Lefkadia, Greece. All are shown in yellow, probably indicating plain bronze for the shield. (PD)

As to decoration, Macedonian shields always carried the traditional pattern, which appears across the southern Balkan region, of a series of hoops around the outside surrounding a central rondel, which might contain a portrait or the initials of the king, or some other national or unit symbol. The painted decoration of the shields on the sarcophagus has largely faded, though it is possible to discern, with a certain application of the imagination, painted portraits depicting Alexander, perhaps, and various gods or mythological figures. Portrait shields of this sort are unusual in Greek history; hoplite shield devices had traditionally been drawn from a varied stock of symbols, many mythological, and by the fourth century, it was becoming common to have an insignia of the home city – an initial letter, or a symbol such as the club of Thebes. It may be that some Macedonian shields carried such a symbol, an obvious candidate being the 'starburst' or 'star of Vergina', which was widely used as a symbol of the Hellenistic kingdom, is depicted on the shield carried

Fragments of an ancient Macedonian shield found in Bonče, North Macedonia. (Beat of the tapan, CC BY-SA 4.0)

on the Kinch tomb painting (though it appears not to be carried by a Macedonian) and formed the central device on a number of Macedonian shields. Other shields depicted in Macedonian tomb paintings, particularly those on the exterior of the Agios Athanasios tomb, do have painted decoration similar to that on the sarcophagus, so perhaps this was an indicator either of an elite unit or of officer status.

Given that there were two components of the phalanx – Pezhetairoi and Asthetairoi – and two types of shield, one of which, the Macedonian, might be considered of a lighter design than the Argive, we should note there are several references to Alexander selecting the 'lighter' or 'nimbler' part of the phalanx to take on special missions. For example, in 334–333 against the city of Selge, Alexander took 'the archers, the *taxeis* of the javelinmen, and the nimblest of the hoplites' (Arr. 1.27.8); in the pursuit of Darius, Alexander 'took the Hypaspists and the nimblest of the Macedonian phalanx and some of the archers' (3.23.3); pursuing the rebel satrap Spitamenes, he took 'half the Companion cavalry, all the Hypaspists, the archers and Agrianians, and the nimblest of the phalanx' (4.6.3). It is not clear exactly what is meant by 'nimblest', and the word *kouphotatous* is sometimes translated as 'lightest armed'; but, for example, at 6.18.5 Alexander selected 'the lightest-armed (*kouphotatous*) of his light-armed (*psilon*)', which seems meaningless. In Classical Greek armies, it was often the youngest age classes that were selected for missions requiring special speed, such as chasing down skirmishers, so it is possible that this is what is meant here – the youngest, and therefore fastest and nimblest, age classes were chosen from the phalanx. However, I also suggest that the 'nimblest' of the phalanx could, after all, be those with lighter equipment, perhaps those with Macedonian rather than Argive shields, and perhaps corresponding to the Asthetairoi, mountain men from Upper Macedonia, as opposed to the less agile Pezhetairoi from the lowlands (an equivalent would be Highlanders, or later Ghurkas, in the British Army). So it may be that the Pezhetairoi, lowlanders, carried Argive shields and the Asthetairoi, highlanders, carried Macedonian shields of similar size. In the course of the various updates of equipment in Alexander's campaigns, particularly at the outset of the Indian campaign when huge amounts of new equipment were issued, including new silver shields for the Hypaspists (see Chapter 6), the phalanx shield may have been standardised across the phalanx to the Macedonian type, bearing the traditional Macedonian decoration, along with the new helmets that were also issued at this time (see below). Admittedly, the Alexander Sarcophagus, which was probably produced in Sidon after Alexander's death, depicts equipment that would by then have been superseded, but it is not surprising if the sculptor chose to represent Alexander's army as it looked when it passed by Sidon, rather than on its return from the east.

Aside from the shield, the distinguishing feature of the Macedonian phalangite was his pike, or sarissa (*sarisa* is the more common Greek spelling, but in English, it is usually written as sarissa). Again, there is a common view of this weapon that is likely at variance with the facts. What is not disputed is that it was a long weapon, significantly longer than the spear of the Greek hoplite, and long enough to need to be wielded in both hands. Even this is not certain, however, as a number of scholars have proposed that in Alexander's day, the sarissa was shorter than it became in the Hellenistic period or even that Alexander's phalanx did not use sarissas at all. I am not convinced by these arguments and find it more likely that the Hellenistic phalanx, as we see it in action in the third century and as it is described by the Tacticians, was broadly similar to that of Philip and Alexander, certainly in terms of its offensive weaponry. Arguments that Alexander's phalanx was not a Macedonian phalanx (in the Hellenistic sense) are usually based on the apparent flexibility and mobility of Alexander's men, but this is more likely because the inflexibility of the later phalanx has been overstated than because Alexander's was armed differently. The exact length of the sarissa is open to more doubt. It is not sound to lift (as so many do) a stated length from 100 or 200 years after Alexander and apply that uncritically to Alexander's time. On the other hand, the attested lengths of the Hellenistic sarissa, 10 to 16 cubits (roughly 5–8 metres) probably do define a range within which Alexander's sarissas will have fallen, and the closest source to Alexander in time (Theophrastus, *Plants* 3.12.1–2) gives a length of 12 cubits (6 metres); it seems reasonable to suppose that the sarissas of Alexander's army were usually of about this length. But whatever the typical length, in practice, there must have been considerable variation, so absolute precision is pointless.[20]

There are a number of other doubtful modern beliefs about the sarissa. It is supposed that it had a large spearhead, and some large spearheads discovered in or associated with Macedonian tombs have been identified as sarissa heads accordingly. It is also thought that the sarissa had a large butt spike (*sauroter*), and a single very large, flanged spike found in one of the royal tombs at Vergina has accordingly been confidently identified as a sarissa spike (resulting in countless reconstructions with such a butt spike). The sarissa is said to have been made from cornel wood (like the spears of the Companions), based on Theophrastus' comment that the sarissa was the same height as the Cornelian cherry tree. And (most bizarrely of all), it is said to have been made in two parts, slotted together in the middle with a metal 'connecting tube', an example of which was again discovered in a Macedonian tomb. None of these assertions can be disproved completely, of course, but they all seem extremely unlikely, at best.[21]

20　On the sarissa – Andronikos (1970), Markle (1977), Markle (1988), Hammond (1980a), Connolly (2000), Sekunda (2001a), Anson (2010a), Matthew (2015) pp.47–91, Juhel (2017b), Taylor (2020) pp.29–42; shorter spears, Taylor (2020) pp.42–6; peltasts, Griffith (1981).
21　Andronikos (1970); *contra*, Sekunda (2001a).

The archaeological identification of large spear heads as sarissa heads appears to be based on the assumption that a sarissa, as a large weapon, must have had a large spearhead. But any pike, being long, might be expected to have a smaller than usual spearhead, otherwise it creates problems with balancing the weapon. The only direct literary reference we have to the sarissa, admittedly from a late source, is that it had 'small teeth'(Grattius, *Cynegeticon* 117–20), as we would expect. Weapons fittings discovered in or near tombs are always lacking their essential wooden parts, making identification of the weapon they belong to largely speculative, while royal or high-status tombs are not the places we would expect to look for weapons of the rank-and-file infantry. It seems likely that the tomb spearheads either come from cavalry spears or do not belong to regular weapons – they may be from ceremonial or hunting spears. Similar arguments apply to the butt spike. Such a large lump of metal would be an awkward addition to an already long and unwieldy shaft, and this particular item (of which only two have ever been discovered) could have had a number of uses: the butt of a standard, or of a boar spear, or of a ceremonial spear for a guard or attendant. There is no compelling reason, at any rate, to associate it with a sarissa. More compelling are the spearheads found in the Polyandrion, the mass tomb (taken to be of Macedonians) on the battlefield of Chaironeia, but these are in generally poor or incomplete condition and while at least one spearhead is of large size (around 38 cm long) it is fairly narrow, and could also be from a cavalry spear.[22]

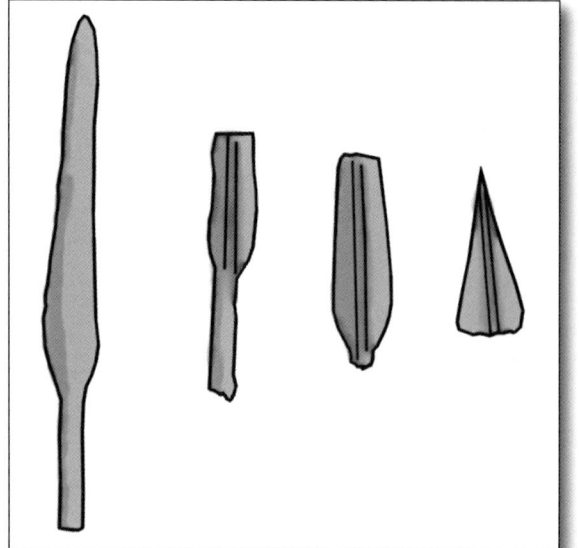

Macedonian spear parts now in the Archaeological Museum, Chaeronea.

As to the wood, cornel wood is notable for its weight, so while its hardness is useful for shortish weapons (up to the length of the cavalry *xyston*, evidently), for longer weapons, especially those which, unlike the cavalry lance, could not be held near their centre point, a lighter wood would be far more practical. Ash is the usual wood for such spear shafts, and it also has the benefit of growing to a suitable height. Theophrastus notes that the Cornelian cherry was as tall as the tallest sarissa, but this is the total height of the tree, not that of its thickest, straightest stems, as it is a branching tree. Finally, the 'connecting tube' is another unique and unexplained object found in a high-status tomb, and there is no reason to suppose it has anything to do with a sarissa. No other pikes throughout history were made in two parts, and the practical difficulties inherent in creating a weapon that could literally be pulled apart by the enemy would be enormous. This strange idea should be dismissed, for all that it has, unhappily, been so widely accepted. It is also worth noting in the context of sarissa myths that the identification of the spears in the background of the Alexander Mosaic as sarissas is extremely uncertain. Although the artist has apparently taken

---

22 Chaeronea spearheads – Markle (1977) pp.325–6.

some liberties with the length of these spears, especially the foremost one, it seems obvious, from the composition if nothing else, that they are Persian cavalry spears, not Macedonian.

Other items of phalanx equipment can be dealt with more briefly. Evidently the phalangites wore a helmet (listed among the items of equipment detailed by Polyaenus in Philip's training programme). Later Hellenistic phalangites wore helmets of two main types, Thracian or Phrygian, and the *konos*, a developed form of the *pilos*. It may be that Alexander's men also wore these types of helmet – the Thracian/Phrygian is the type worn by the infantry on the Alexander Sarcophagus. This helmet continues to appear in art from Macedon after Alexander's reign, such as the Agios Athanasios tomb frieze. But coin depictions of a *pilos* type helmet, a simple conical hat with cheek pieces, became common immediately after the reign of Alexander. It is likely that these formed part of the equipment manufactured and distributed to the phalanx as one of Alexander's reforms before or during the Indian campaign, becoming so ubiquitous that they could be used as a sort of logo on the coinage. The helmet was also the place to display rank insignia, which for the infantry may have been a transverse (side to side, rather than front to back) crest or two vertical feathers in tubes above the temples. Although we tend to think of helmets as plain bronze, they are often depicted in art as brightly coloured – several of those on the sarcophagus are blue, while the tomb of Lyson and Kallikles shows red and yellow helmets. A coloured helmet might have been another mark of rank. As well as metal helmets, the phalangites will have worn the *kausia*, in a variety of colours from purple through grey-brown to white, especially when off duty or marching.[23]

Polyaenus' list does not mention body armour, but as we have seen, he is describing the light equipment of peltasts, not that of the hoplites of the phalanx. The Alexander Sarcophagus represents infantry as either naked or wearing armour of an organic type – the *linothorax* or *stolas*, of linen or leather, and this was probably the standard armour of the phalanx. Diodorus (17.95.4) reports that Alexander in India received from Greece 25,000 sets of armour, which he distributed to the army, and Curtius (9.3.22) notes that the old armour was burned, which suggests that linen or leather armour was widely worn. However, not all men in the phalanx need have been equipped identically, and there could have been distinctions between front and rear-rank men (who were on higher pay and at greater risk) and those in the centre ranks, so it may be that some wore armour while others did not; this might also be relevant to the identity of the 'nimbler' men considered above. Greaves are also mentioned by Polyaenus, so presumably, they were sometimes worn. Of the figures on the sarcophagus, some do, and some do not, wear greaves, so again, there could have been variation between units or between ranks (in both senses) within a unit.

Finally, the infantry depicted on the sarcophagus carry swords, so this was no doubt the standard secondary weapon, and usually the straight pattern *xiphos* rather than the curved *kopis* of the cavalry. As with the

---

23 On the pilos helmet, Juhel (2009); Karunanithy (2013) pp.100–5. Juhel (2017a) for the transverse crest.

THE ARMY OF ALEXANDER THE GREAT

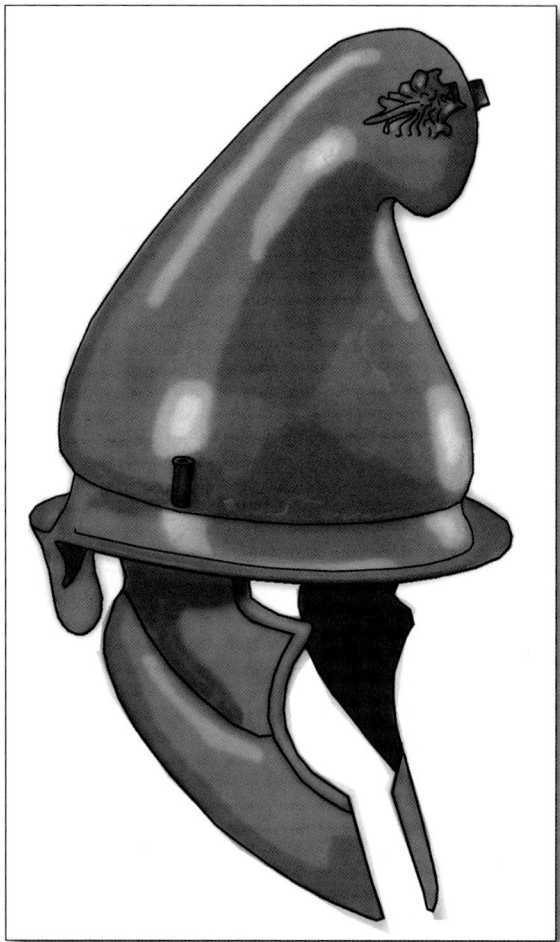

A Phrygian or Thracian helmet. Note the tubes to hold plumes on sides and crest.

Greek simple *pilos* helmet, fifth century or later, Metropolitan Museum, New York. (Metropolitan Museum)

The reverse of an 'elephant medallion', depicting Alexander in a crested and plumed helmet (Numismatica Ars Classica NAC AG, Auction 124, 2021, lot 84)

A Macedonian shield and *pilos* or *konos* helmet on a Macedonian coin, fourth-third century. (With permission of wildwinds.com, ex CNG auction Sept. 2013)

Hypaspists, it is probable that men of the phalanx could carry short spears or javelins when they were undertaking special duties outside the main line of battle. Certainly, there can be no question that sarissas were carried by men climbing siege ladders or towers in assaults on cities, and handier weapons would be needed for such occasions, the javelin being the weapon with which all Macedonians would be familiar. This is illustrated by the siege of Halicarnassus (334), where 'two Macedonian hoplites of Perdiccas' *taxis*' drunkenly launched an impromptu attack on the walls; the defenders sallied out against them, and 'they killed those who came up close and discharged missiles at the more distant enemies' (Arr. *Anab.* 1.21.1–2). The type of missile is not specified, but javelins are far more likely than arrows or sling stones.[24]

The same comments apply to the colours worn by the infantry as to the cavalry and Hypasists. Surviving depictions suggest little uniformity, which could be because artists chose to depict men from multiple different units or (more likely to my mind) because there was indeed little uniformity. Figures on the sarcophagus wear brightly coloured armour and tunics, with purple and red featuring strongly, and later tomb paintings confirm the use of bright colours and purple. Such colour choices can inform reconstructions of the appearance of Alexander's phalanx, provided it is remembered that high-status tombs might not have depicted men who were typical of the rank and file, and that there was likely considerable variation in quality as well as hue. It is, at any rate, impossible to assign any particular uniform colour to any individual unit, with the exception of the Hypaspists, where later Antigonid practice suggests there may have been a uniform red tunic.

Bronze greaves from the tomb of Philip II, Vergina, Greece (Mary Harrsch, CC BY-SA 4.0)

Drill and Tactics

For the drill of the later Hellenistic phalanx, we have almost an overabundance of information in the testimony of the Tacticians. As usual, there is some doubt about how well this can be applied backwards to the army of Alexander. Still, it was clearly the belief of the Tacticians themselves that what they were describing applied to Alexander's time, and it seems inherently likely

---

24   Swords – Karunanithy (2013) pp.137–44. Dual armament – Taylor (2020) pp.42–6.

that the phalanx, as developed by Philip, already used specific drills and formations needed to make the phalanx effective. However, there will have been some evolution and perhaps some increase in sophistication over time. That Alexander's phalanx was very well drilled was demonstrated early in his reign when, in 335, he was cornered by a force of Taulantians (an Illyrian people) and mesmerised them with a display of drill:

> In the circumstances Alexander draw up his phalanx with a depth of 120 ranks … the hoplites were ordered first to raise their spears upright, and then on the word to lower them for a charge, swinging their serried points first to the right, then to the left; he moved the phalanx itself smartly forward and brought it forward on each wing. Thus he deployed and manoeuvred it in many difficult formations in a brief time, and then making a column from the phalanx on the left, he led it to the attack. The enemy, long bewildered both at the smartness and the discipline of the drill, did not await the approach of Alexander's troops, but abandoned the first hills. (Arr. *Anab.* 1.6.2–4).

This level of drill was the product of Philip's 20 years of training, which created a professional, drilled force capable of battlefield control and manoeuvre that must indeed have been daunting to the tribal forces and undrilled or poorly drilled militias that the Macedonians usually faced.[25]

The normal formation for the phalanx was (needless to say) the phalanx, which in this technical sense means a linear formation of much greater width than depth and, generally, quite shallow compared with other formations of the time. The normal depth of Alexander's phalanx is uncertain – the 120 ranks quoted above was a special formation, not a normal battle deployment. By the time of the Tacticians, 16 ranks had been settled on as the best depth, combining the best combination of defensive solidity and attacking impetus without overly narrowing the frontage of the formation. A deeper formation was generally stronger but had a narrower front, so it could be in danger of being outflanked. In Polybius' criticism of Callisthenes' account of the Battle of Issus (Pol. 12.19), it is evident that the phalanx was deployed eight ranks deep. But when Alexander was planning to incorporate Persians into the phalanx, each file had 16 men, and because only the first three and last rank were Macedonians, there would be little opportunity to alter this depth. We can perhaps conclude that the phalanx was deployed according to circumstances with eight or 16 ranks; in pitched battles against numerically superior forces (as at Issus or Gaugamela), eight ranks would be preferred, but later in the campaign, against smaller numbers of more irregular opponents, depth may have become standardised on 16.[26]

The Tacticians (and Polybius) also detail the file and rank intervals, and the number of sarissa points that would project from the front of the formation. These details can probably be applied to Alexander's phalanx also, with due allowance made for the slightly shorter sarissa in use. In the Tacticians, the 'normal' interval between files is four cubits (two metres), and this is the

---

25 Lloyd (1996); Anson (2008).
26 For details of phalanx drill see Taylor (2020) pp.82–124.

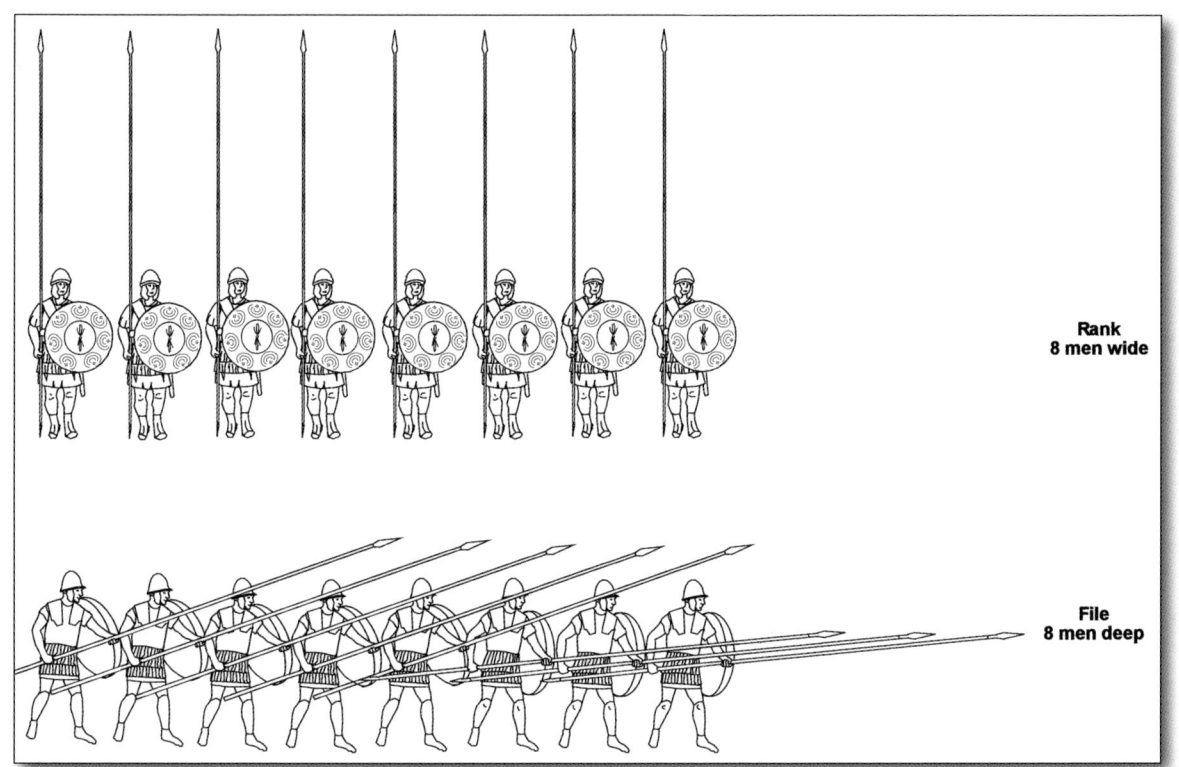

Files and ranks of the phalanx, with two-cubit (one metre) intervals.

interval Polybius assumes for Alexander's phalanx at Issus (Pol. 12.19.7). The close-order battle formation of the Tacticians is two cubits (one metre) per man, and Polybius too assumes this was a possible formation at Issus. The Tacticians add a third, closest order of one cubit (half a metre) per man, although Polybius does not mention this formation, either in his account of Issus or in his discussion of the contemporary Macedonian phalanx (Pol. 18.28–32). It is likely that this closest order was not used in Alexander's time. In the Hellenistic phalanx, the sarissas of the first five ranks projected beyond the front of the formation; in Alexander's phalanx, perhaps only the first three or four ranks' sarissas would have projected. The mixed phalanx with incorporated Persians had three ranks of Macedonians at the front, which suggests three ranks of projecting sarissas may have been the norm.[27]

In the Tacticians, the basic manoeuvre unit of the phalanx is the *syntagma*, also called *syntaxiarchia* or *semeia*, a formation of 256 men in 16 ranks of 16 files. Asclepiodotus (2.9) suggests that an earlier 8-by-8-man formation was called a *taxis* – this might have been the manoeuvre unit of Alexander's reign, not, of course, to be confused with the 1,500- or 2,000-man *taxis*. There is no trace of such units, however, in the literary accounts of Alexander's campaign, which always deal with manoeuvres at a much higher level and never at a level below that of the (large) *taxis*. The high level of drill and the ability to perform complex manoeuvres, like those

---

27   Taylor (2020) pp.85–97.

used to dazzle the Taulantians, meant that the Macedonian phalanx was a relatively highly manoeuvrable formation. Much is made by modern authors of the inflexibility and monolithic character of the phalanx, but this is clearly not entirely accurate, or only in comparison with later formations like the Roman legion with its small, independent units which did not need to maintain a continuous front. Similarly, the phalanx was obviously not ideally suited to operating over difficult terrain, but it was not incapable of doing so, making river assaults at Granicus and Issus, while the ability to switch to lighter equipment and weapons meant that the men of the phalanx could fight effectively in assaults and special operations, out of phalanx formation.

Archers, Javelinmen and Slingers

Identity

Diodorus' listing of the forces in Alexander's army at the start of the campaign includes 12,000 Macedonians, taken to be the phalanx (with or without the Hypaspists), then allies, mercenaries, various Balkan peoples, 'and of archers and the so-called Agrianians one thousand' (Diod. 17.17.4). The Agrianians will be considered in the next chapter, but the archers, lacking an ethnic designation, may be Macedonians. This is made explicit at Gaugamela, where these two units are still together; on Alexander's right, 'half the Agrianians under Attalos were posted next to the Royal Squadron, along with the Macedonian archers under Brison' (Arr. *Anab*. 3.12.2). The other half of these units were nearby. The rest of the Companions 'had half the Agrianians and archers stationed in their front, with the javelinmen of Balacros' (3.12.3). These javelinmen are another unidentified unit but are perhaps also Macedonians, given their lack of ethnic identifier.

Archers had appeared in Alexander's army from the start of his reign. In 335, fighting the Triballians (on the occasion where they rolled wagons downhill against Alexander's phalanx), we find the archers deploying in front of the phalanx and holding back the Thracian attackers with their volleys (Arr. *Anab* 1.1.11–12), and in these campaigns we already find Alexander grouping 'the Hypaspists, the archers and Agrianians' (Arr. *Anab*. 1.5.10) to form a special task force, with the archers providing support for the assault units. The combination of archers and Agrianians recurs frequently throughout Alexander's later campaigns. Against the Illyrians in 335, 'Alexander sent for the Agrianians and the archers, up to the number of two thousand' (1.6.6), which gives an idea of their strength. Companions, Agrianians and archers formed the assault force at the Granicus (1.14.1), while the commander of the archers (*toxarches*), Clearchos, was killed in the assault on Halicarnassus in 334 (1.22.7), and his successor, Cleandros, was killed battling the Pisidians in 334–3 (1.28.8), indicating again the use of this force as the spearhead of the attack. At Issus, the archers again fronted the phalanx under their new commander, Antiochos (2.9.2). We have seen the deployment at Gaugamela (under another new commander), and archers and Agrianians frequently appear in the subsequent campaigns, forming the assault force at the Jaxartes in 329 – 'the archers, the Agrianians and the other light troops under Balacros' (4.4.6 – Balacros' men being presumably the same javelinmen as those at Gaugamela). Balacros' men appear again in one of the three columns into which the army was divided in the Indian campaign; Arrian confusingly refers to 'the *taxeis* of Attalos and Balacros' (Arr. *Anab*. 4.24.10), but in this case, he must be using *taxis* in a general sense to mean a body of infantry, rather than a *taxis* of the phalanx.

The archers stayed in the army throughout the Indian campaign, continuing to be paired with the Agrianians, alongside select forces of Companions, Hypaspists and Asthetairoi. They played an important role at the Hydaspes, under another *toxarches*, Tauron (5.14.1). Their last appearance was at Pasargadai on Alexander's return from the east (6.29.1). Not all of these archers need have been Macedonians, where it is not clearly stated that they were, since the army also included Cretan allies or mercenaries fighting as archers. It may be that the total force of archers was made up of a combination of Cretan and Macedonian units. For example, at the siege of Thebes in 335, an attack by archers was repulsed, and 'Eurybotas the Cretan, *toxarches*, fell with seventy of his men' (1.8.4). How the Macedonian element was recruited can only be guessed – they may have been from an age or, more likely, a property class that was not eligible for phalanx service or from an ethnic group specialising in archery from within the kingdom. At any rate, they were evidently something of an elite force, being chosen repeatedly for special missions.

The slingers are an even more enigmatic unit. They first appear in the campaign against the Triballians, where along with the archers, they skirmished ahead of the phalanx (Arr. *Anab*. 1.2.4). There is no further mention of them until 329, where slingers, archers and javelinmen combine to clear the walls of Sogdian Gaza of their defenders (Arr. *Anab*. 4.2.3). Then at the Jaxartes crossing, archers and slingers led the attack and helped keep the Scythians away from the landing point (Arr. *Anab*. 4.4.5). Their final appearance is at the assault on the Aornos Rock in 326, where they were also used to keep Indian defenders away from the attacking infantry (Arr. *Anab*. 4.30.1). Curiously, however, there is no mention of a unit of slingers at any of the major battles. It is possible that these slingers, rather than forming their own unit, were subsumed into the archers to form a mixed unit of missile-using light infantry, which the sources usually refer to, for convenience, simply as 'archers'.[28]

Organisation

The organisation of the archers, javelinmen and slingers (as with almost all the non-Macedonian units in the army) is largely a matter of guesswork. It may be that the various commanders listed above, sometimes identified as *strategos* (general), sometimes as *toxarches* (archer-commander), sometimes simply as 'leader' or 'commander', indicate different levels of a chain of command, with a *strategos* in command of all the archers, and a *toxarches* in command of sub-units, which, following usual Greek practice, may have been called *lochoi*. By

---

28 Use of the sling was likely widespread in Macedon – see the many sling bullets discovered in Olynthus, Lee (2001).

this reckoning the *toxarches* named above (Clearchos, Eurybotas) will have commanded *lochoi* (perhaps of 500 men), with the *strategos* in command of the whole force, which will have numbered (depending on reinforcements received and losses suffered), some 1–2,000 men. I am not confident that our sources use these ranks with enough accuracy and consistency to make such conclusions possible, but at any rate, some similar organisation into *lochoi* must certainly have been in place, not least because it was easy to divide the archers up into halves for deployment at different points in the battle line, which suggests on these occasions that there were two sub-units each of 500 men. The javelinmen and slingers probably followed similar principles.

Equipment and Dress

Archers will, of course, have been equipped with bows, arrows and quivers. The usual Greek bow was a relatively short recurve bow, rather than the longbow used by Indians, or the composite bow of the steppe peoples (meaning, in Greek experience, chiefly Scythians). Depictions of archers in Greek art are almost invariably of Scythians or Persians, there being very few depictions of any sort of light infantry. Such light infantry as are shown, tend to wear a simple tunic and perhaps a cloak. On their heads they may have a hat (*petasos* sun hat, or *kausia* for Macedonians), though it is possible that a metal helmet was worn or (more likely) a felt *pilos*. Archers and light infantry generally are usually unshielded, though it is possible that Cretan archers carried a small shield on the left arm. The better off or luckier (in terms of plunder) among them may also have carried a sword, but it was generally the intention of archers to remain out of hand-to-hand combat with any enemy and rely entirely on distant shooting. Javelinmen and slingers will also have used the dress and equipment typical of Greek light infantry. Javelinmen are more likely to have carried a shield (making them in effect peltasts, in the Classical sense).

A Thessalian javelinman, reverse of a fourth century coin of Pelinna, Thessaly. This figure, with *petasos* hat, round shield, bunch of javelins, and sword, is probably typical of the light infantry of northern Greece. (Classical Numismatic Group, CC BY-SA 3.0)

Drill and Tactics

We also have almost no information on formations or drill for such units. The Tacticians imply that the light infantry would use the same system of intervals and the same basic formations as the heavy infantry. Certainly, we might expect the 'normal' four cubit, two metre, spacing of the heavy infantry to be used by light infantry also. Whether they would ever adopt the closer formations of the hoplites is more uncertain, since it is usually supposed that skirmishing and shooting would require a looser order, which would also benefit such units when moving rapidly over rough terrain, as was their usual practice. Similarly, although there may have been formal ranks and files in these formations on the parade ground, in battle, they may have operated more as a loose 'cloud' of individuals. Deep formations, up to eight ranks deep, as suggested by the Tacticians, would not be practical for archers or missile users generally unless there was a process of filtering men to and from the rear ranks.[29]

When deployed in the line of battle, such light infantry were often deployed ahead of the phalanx to provide protection against enemy missile users and to use their own missiles to disrupt an enemy before the main attack. This meant that, when the heavy forces of the main line were ready to go into action, the light infantry must have been able to withdraw back through the main line, a process that is often hinted at in the sources but never clearly described. Whether the main line left gaps between sub-units through which the light infantry could pass or whether the light infantry passed between the files of heavy forces while they were still in open formation is not clear – perhaps both methods were used, depending on circumstances. All forms of light infantry could also, like the Royal Hypaspists, be used as *hamippoi*, mingling among the cavalry, though this role would be better suited to javelinmen than to archers.

---

29 Lee (2001) p.16 – an underarm swing could allow slingers to operate in tight formations.

5

Subjects, Allies and Mercenaries

So far, we have been looking at the core units of the army, the native Macedonians, or at least those who lived within the official borders of the Macedonian kingdom. These, however, made up less than half of the army with which Alexander began his campaign and less than a third (and probably very much less than a third) of the army he led into India. The rest of the army was made up of the forces of subject and allied states (including, later in the campaign, subjects of Alexander's new Asian Empire – covered in the next chapter) and of mercenaries. Many of these allied forces were dismissed from the army when Alexander reached Ecbatana in 330 after the defeat of Darius at Gaugamela since the official purpose of the campaign – the Hellenic League's retribution on Persia for the invasion of Greece by Xerxes a century and a half earlier – was fulfilled. Some rejoined as mercenaries. The mercenaries who were already with the army continued in service, and indeed, their numbers increased dramatically as Alexander sought to expand his own forces to provide garrisons and occupation armies, and as his new Empire became the sole employer of mercenaries in the eastern Mediterranean and Near East. The ultimate fate of many of these Greeks was to be settled by Alexander in one of his new city foundations, while mercenaries continued to find their services in high demand in the wars of the Successors. These men and their descendants, alongside the Macedonians of the army, were to form the core of the Greco-Macedonian populations of the newly founded Hellenistic kingdoms.

Thessalians

Identity
Thessaly is the mostly lowland region – an area of good horse-rearing country – lying to the south of Macedon, between Macedon and the city states of central and southern Greece. It was usually divided politically between numerous regions or cities. It had a similar social and political structure to Macedon, with a large, horse-rearing aristocracy being

politically and militarily dominant and a lack of city-based heavy infantry, such as was to be found in most of southern Greece. Thessalian infantry, like Macedonian infantry before Philip, seem to have fought mostly as javelin-armed skirmishers, while the cavalry, like Macedon's Companions, formed the main component of Thessalian armies. In the fourth century, the region became more politically united than had formerly been the case, with leaders such as Jason (Iasōn) of Pherai establishing control over the whole of Thessaly and the formation of a Thessalian League (*koinon*). Philip II had himself elected *archon* of Thessaly, head of the League, and was succeeded in this role by Alexander. As a result, Alexander was able to call on the cavalry levy of Thessaly as their ruler, though Thessaly remained a separate region independent of the Macedonian kingdom itself. The Thessalian nobility does not appear to have undergone any expansion equivalent to the extension of the Macedonian Companionate to newly settled Greeks, but even so, they could produce impressive numbers of horsemen. Alexander crossed to Asia with 1,800 Thessalians (Diod. 17.17.4). The Hellenic League stipulated that each member was to provide 500 infantry and 200 cavalry for each vote it had on the Council of the League, and Thessaly had 10 votes (Dem. 6 22), so was due to provide 2,000 cavalry to the League army, which leaves them, with 1,800, slightly short. When Alexander was at Gordion in 333, he was joined by reinforcements including 200 Thessalian cavalry (Arr. *Anab*. 1.29.4), which sounds as if it was the missing unit, perhaps delayed in Greece for some reason.[1]

While many of the allied Greek forces on the campaign were less than enthusiastic and deliberately sidelined (see below), the Thessalian cavalry were clearly far more committed to the campaign and played an important role in all of Alexander's battles (where they were present); indeed, the Vulgate tradition would have it that the Thessalians were the best cavalry in Alexander's army.

Organisation

We have no certain indications of how the Thessalian cavalry was organised, but there are some hints. At Gaugamela, Arrian states that 'on the left were the Thessalian cavalry under Philip son of Menelaos. The commander of the entire left was Parmenion son of Philotas, and round him rode the Pharsalian cavalry, the finest and most numerous of the Thessalian horsemen.' (Arr. *Anab*. 3.11.10). Pharsalus was one of the larger and more important cities of Thessaly, so it seems that Thessalian cavalry, like Macedonian, were recruited by region, and therefore, that other Thessalian cities and regions will have had their own units of cavalry. The presence of a large and high-quality cavalry unit forming a personal escort to the commander of the Macedonian left has been compared with the Royal Squadron of the Companions around Alexander on the right. So we might tentatively suggest that the Thessalians had a similar organisation to the Companions, perhaps being formed into eight *ilai* (they were certainly formed in *ilai*, as noted by Diodorus, 17.21.4;

---

1   Strootman (2011) for Thessalian numbers; Thessalians generally, English (2009) pp.60–66.

17.60.8). If this is so, then perhaps a normal *ilē* contained just over 200 men, and the Pharsalian *ilē* was stronger, with 400 (matching the strength of the Royal Squadron). However, as Thessaly likely provided 10 units of 200 (see the comment above on the reinforcement at Gordion), this could mean that we should not read too much into the 'most numerous' comment on the Pharsalians. Note that, like the Companions (commanded by Philotas, but with Alexander riding with the Royal Squadron), the Thessalians had their own commander (here, Philip), although Parmenion, overall commander on the left, rode with them.

Equipment and Dress

In the fifth century, Thessalian cavalry were probably armed similarly to most Greek cavalry of the period, that is, as light cavalry, generally without armour and armed with javelins. There seems, however, to have been an increase in the quality and quantity of defensive equipment in the fourth century (perhaps because of increased wealth among the Thessalian nobility). Although definite depictions of Thessalian cavalry in Alexander's time are lacking, it is certain that they were equipped as, and fought as, heavy cavalry, probably very similar in equipment and function to the Companions. Most of what we know about Thessalian dress comes from coin images, which, though informative, are obviously highly restricted in the amount of detail they can depict. That said, fourth-century Thessalian coins are consistent in depicting cavalry in armour – sometimes a 'muscled cuirass', metal armour shaped as an idealised human anatomy, with *pteruges* beneath. Helmets are frequently of the Boeotian type, sometimes with the addition of cheekpieces, or sometimes a Thracian/Phrygian helmet. The nature of the spear carried is often difficult to determine, but one coin depiction shows a butt-end spearhead like that used by Macedonian cavalry, so it seems safe to conclude that the Thessalians used a *xyston* similar to that of the Companions (unless, as it is sometimes interpreted, the spear is being carried backwards). Two figures on the Alexander Sarcophagus identified as Thessalians based on the style of their cloaks have a Boeotian helmet and linen (or leather) cuirass, with a long-sleeved tunic. The identification is admittedly speculative since cloaks of this style appear in other Macedonian contexts (such as the Agios Athanasios tomb), so it is not a given that such cloaks indicate Thessalians. Still, these figures provide the only possible evidence for colours; they are shown with red tunics and dark purple-blue cloaks with white borders.[2]

Thessalian cavalry, obverse of coin of Pelinna, Thessaly, early fourth century. Note the blade on the reverse end of the spear. (Classical Numismatic Group, CC BY-SA 3.0)

---

2   Sekunda (1984) pp.18–19; English (2009) p.62.

SUBJECTS, ALLIES AND MERCENARIES

Thessalian cavalry, reverse of a stater of Pherai, Thessaly, mid-fourth century. (Numismatica Ars Classica NAC AG, Auction 116, 2019, lot 119)

Thessalian cavalry on a funerary stele from Pelinna, Thessaly, mid-fourth century, now in the Louvre, Paris.

Drill and Tactics

According to the tactician Asclepiodotus, 'the Thessalians were the first to use the rhomboid formation for their *ilai* in cavalry fighting, and this with great success both in retreat and in attack, that they might not be thrown into disorder, since they were able to turn in any direction' (Asclep. 7.2). According to Aelian (*Tact.* 18), this was first done by a Jason (presumably Jason of Pherai), which if true would mean that we should expect Alexander's Thessalians to still be using the rhombus. This is a diamond-shaped formation, in effect a double-wedge with points at front and back, and like the wedge, gave the cavalry greater manoeuvrability as they could turn to follow the officers at the points or sides. Asclepiodotus' comments about the value of the rhombus 'in retreat and in attack' – literally, 'in *apostrophe* (or *anastrophe*) and *epistrophe*' – reminds us that the precise way ancient cavalry functioned is not well understood today. Ancient authors frequently draw attention to the way that cavalry, unlike infantry, would alternate attacking and retiring, presumably riding up to an enemy and showering them with javelins, or perhaps into contact with lances, then turning back and riding away again, something that was generic enough to be called simply 'fighting like cavalry'. Polybius (Pol. 12.18.3) records that cavalry formations needed gaps between each subunit with the same frontage as the subunits themselves to allow these alternating attacks and retreats. In a similar way, we hear of attacks being made 'by squadron' or 'squadron after squadron' (for example, Arr. *Anab.* 3.13.4), which is a description of the same phenomenon, with squadrons attacking in sequence rather than all at once, and one squadron breaking off and withdrawing as the next attacks. Fighting of this sort must have been tentative and more time-consuming than the usual modern image of cavalry

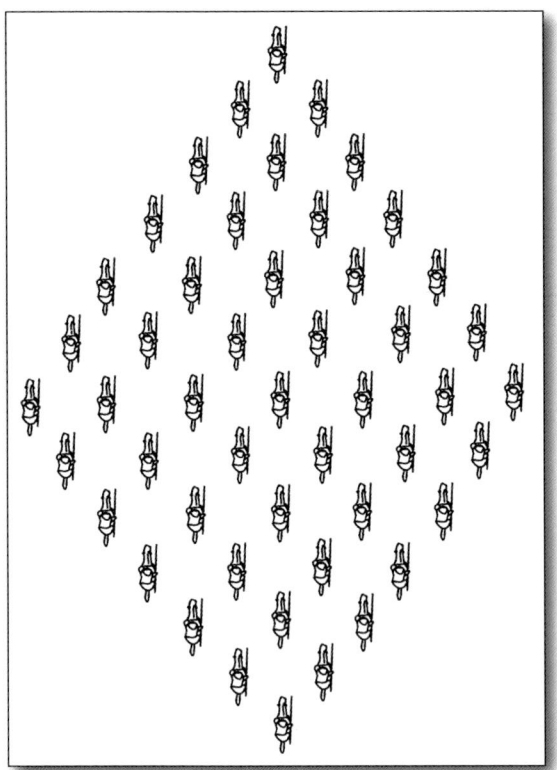
Cavalry in rhombus formation.

all flinging themselves on an enemy and engaging in a swirling hand-to-hand melee. It is fighting of this sort that the Thessalians will have engaged in (and probably the Companions also), something that may seem more akin to skirmishing even though Thessalians were heavy cavalry and probably armed with lances. The option would still be available (as for the Companions) to press home a charge more forcefully against a shaken, disordered or fleeing enemy, where the cavalry could ride in amongst the enemy and strike them down from behind.

Thracian and Balkan Cavalry

Identity

We have already encountered Thracian cavalry in the list Diodorus provided of the invasion army, where there were 900 'Thracian *prodromoi* and Paionians' (Diod. 17.17.4), and the difficulties caused by this passage since the Prodromoi proper are apparently Macedonians. Various theories have been advanced to resolve this issue, as we saw, with some proposing that Diodorus meant 'Thracians and *prodromoi*', or that the Prodromoi are included in the Macedonian total (reducing the size of the Companions – I am unconvinced by this theory), and others that *prodromoi*, in this case, might be in a generic sense – Thracian light cavalry. Whatever the case, there certainly were Thracian cavalry with the army later. The Paionians, who made up one of the original 13 *ilai* at the Granicus, were a Thracian (or Thraco-Illyrian) people. Also at the Granicus, and stationed on the left beside the Thessalians, were a force of 'Thracians under Agathon' (Arr. *Anab*. 1.14.3), and at Gaugamela we find 'the Odrysian horse under Agathon son of Tyrimmas' (3.12.4) – presumably the same men, Odrysians being another Thracian people. Arrian also records 500 Thracian cavalry joining the army in Egypt (Arr. *Anab*. 3.5.1).

Thrace was the region to the north and east of Macedon, and its people were considered by the Greeks somewhat backward, little better than 'barbarians' (the general word for non-Greek foreigners). Economically and politically underdeveloped, the Thracians lived in smaller or larger tribal groupings under local chieftains or kings (depending on the size of the group). These groupings usually acted independently, though a strong ruler of one group might be able to forge an alliance with others, which would, however, quickly dissolve on the ruler's death. Thracian peoples included Agrianians, Paionians and Odrysians, all of which appear under their own names in Alexander's army, as well as numerous smaller tribes, which tend to be grouped together as generic 'Thracians'.[3]

---

3   Thracian warfare: Best (1969), Papazoglu (1978), Webber (2011), Valeva (2015), Nankov (2021).

Thracians had a formidable military reputation, not for any disciplined or well-equipped armies, but because of their numbers (Herodotus noted in the fifth century that 'were they under one ruler, or united, they would … be invincible and the strongest nation on earth', Hdt. 5.3), their predilection for a lifestyle of raiding and pillaging, and as probable originators of a type of arming and fighting that was highly influential in Greece, that of the peltast. Peltasts were (originally) skirmishing infantry armed with javelins and light shields (*peltai*), who might also have carried a thrusting spear, giving them something of a dual role as missile users and in hand-to-hand combat. Thracian peltast mercenaries were in high demand in Greece during the fifth century, though Greeks eventually learned to equip their own poorer classes with peltast equipment. But alongside these peltast infantry, Thracian peoples maintained their own noble cavalry, drawn from the wealthier horse-owners, as in Macedon and Thessaly (both regions also noted for their large, if variably effective, forces of javelinmen). These would often be analogous to the Macedonian Companions, the personal retainers and close associates of the king. These cavalry were available in Thrace in very large numbers (though with the usual dangers that these numbers may be exaggerated); in the wars of the Successors, Diodorus (18.14.2) records an Odrysian army of 8,000 cavalry and 20,000 infantry. However, the forces attached to Alexander's army were more like token forces (of cavalry at least), in part hostages for the good behaviour of the tribes at home, in part providing specialist troops (light cavalry, skirmishing infantry) to supplement the heavy Macedonian forces.

Organisation

The internal organisation of Thracian cavalry is largely unknown. The Paionians, forming an *ilē* alongside the Prodromoi, could reasonably be assumed to have used a similar organisation – an *ilē* of around 200 men. Thracian cavalry operating in their own units – like the Odrysians – might have adopted similar organisation, but there is no reason to suppose that there was any great consistency in unit size or composition, nor that any Macedonian system of organisation would have been imposed on these allied units. Nevertheless, the likelihood is that squadrons (*ilai*, or *lochoi*) of 200 to 300 men were normal for all cavalry in this period. Some of these units were commanded by their own leaders (such as Ariston, commander of the Paionians, or Sitalces, who commanded Thracian infantry at Gaugamela, Arr. *Anab*. 3.12.4, who were members of the Paionian and Odrysian royal families). Others had Macedonian officers placed over them (such was Agathon, commander of the Odrysians). We cannot know what the reason was for these different arrangements – perhaps some forces were recruited as official contingents of their home state or tribe, while others were volunteers or mercenaries recruited individually from a region.

Equipment and Dress

The equipment and appearance of Thracian units are greatly complicated by the fact that we are dealing with a large number of more or less independent Thracian tribes or kingdoms, each with their own traditions, fashions, and styles of fighting. Even within a given ethnic grouping, there will have been social differences and, as each man doubtless provided his own equipment, there must have been a mix of better or worse-equipped men, which would have affected the presence or absence of body armour, metal helmets, swords and so on. We cannot assume any uniformity of equipment in such tribal forces, nor even that all men in a unit would have had similar types of equipment.

We are also, as usual, hampered by the nature of the evidence. There are some coin depictions of Thracians of this period, particularly Paionians, and there was also a tradition of Thracian tomb-building, similar to the Macedonian, meaning that a number of Thracian tomb paintings straddling the period of Alexander have been discovered. These can allow us to view samples of Thracian equipment and dress, but do not tell us how representative they might have been. We also have a few hints from the literary sources, with all their usual contradictions and problems. For example, Thucydides notes that during a fifth-century Thracian invasion of Macedon, the Macedonian cavalry were able to make harrying attacks on the invaders: 'Whenever they did so, being excellent horsemen and armed with breastplates, no one could stand up to them' (Thuc. 2.100). Xenophon, however, records meeting the Thracian king Seuthes, at the end of the fifth century: 'When it was about midnight, Seuthes was at hand with his horsemen armed with breastplates and his peltasts equipped with their arms' (Xen. *Anab.* 7.3.40). It is impossible from references such as this to conclude that 'Thracians' (all of them) either did or did not wear armour. Circumstances varied, as we must expect, and when it comes to those Thracians who happened to find themselves serving alongside Alexander, we can only guess into which group or groups they might have fallen. What follows, therefore, can only be general remarks on the nature of Thracian equipment.

The traditional Thracian costume consisted of a tunic, a long cloak (*zeira* – longer and warmer than the usual Greek *chlamys*), leather boots and a leather (traditionally, fox skin) cap with neck and ear flaps. Xenophon describes Seuthes' men in this gear as having good protection against the cold (Xen. *Anab.* 7.4.4). The cloak is often depicted in Greek art as decorated with zig-zag or castellated lines, and it appears to have been of thicker, stiffer material than the typical cloak, more like a blanket. The Thracian boot was calf length and enclosed, unlike southern Greek examples, and traditionally had a number of flaps hanging down from the upper edge.

Tomb paintings of the late fourth and third centuries suggest that this traditional costume was being supplanted by clothing more like contemporary Greek examples (at least, among those likely to be depicted on high-status tombs), so Alexander's Thracians may have dressed in a manner similar to that of the other Greek cavalry. Colours of tunics and cloaks include a wide range of hues – whites, reds, blues and greens – and there is no suggestion of uniformity. Although most tunics are short-sleeved or sleeveless, there are some long-sleeved tunics, perhaps inspired by Macedonian (or Persian) influence. Striped tunics were also worn, and there is a chance that these were an indication of low status.[4]

---

4 Thracian dress and equipment: Webber (2003), Webber (2011), Webber and McBride (2001), Valeva (2015). Thracian tactics: Webber (2003) pp.551–2.

SUBJECTS, ALLIES AND MERCENARIES

Cavalry from the Thracian tomb of Kazanlak, Bulgaria, fourth or third century. The tunics are white, and the saddle cloths are red and yellow. (Mincov, CC BY-SA 3.0)

Thracian horseman hunting, from the Thracian tomb of Alexandrovo, Bulgaria, fourth or third century. He wears a cream tunic over a dark grey long-sleeved tunic and red leggings. (Bulgarian Heritage Foundation & NAIM-BAS. Photo: A. Cosentino)

Thracians were traditionally javelin users, and this would have also applied to their light cavalry, although wealthier men (who could afford armour) might have carried a spear similar to their Macedonian neighbours, with a spearhead at both ends. Shields were not usually carried by cavalry until after Alexander's reign. However, earlier depictions of Thracian cavalry sometimes show a light shield, *pelte*, being carried on the back, probably for use when dismounted. Helmets appear to be of a wide mix of types, including but by no means limited to the Thracian, which also became very popular in the rest of Greece. The 'Chalcidian' type was also common throughout Thrace. A sword was also invariably worn over the shoulder. Armour, in the form of the usual linothorax or *spolas*, was worn by some, as we saw above, but probably only ever by a minority and only by the wealthiest, who would serve either as the bodyguard of a chieftain or as officers of a larger group.[5]

Thracian horses appear to have worn rich harness decorations, many examples of which have been discovered in tombs, such as those at Vratsa. Horses also had coloured saddle blankets and, in some cases, were starting to make use of an early saddle (most Greek cavalry of this period did not use a saddle, sitting directly on the blanket) – tomb paintings show what appears to be a stuffed pad that would have provided some of the benefits of a saddle.

Drill and Tactics

We can say little in detail about Thracian cavalry tactics. According to the Tacticians (for example, Asclep.7.3), it was the Scythians and Thracians who invented the cavalry wedge, so Thracian cavalry in Alexander's army probably deployed in a similar manner to the Macedonian units – in small wedges with gaps, each the same width as the wedge, between them. Their combat techniques, however, might have been rather different; Companion cavalry and lance-armed Sarissophoroi definitely intended to close with an enemy after first softening up their formation with threatened attacks. Arrian describes Macedonians fighting Triballians (a Thracian-Illyrian people) at the start of Alexander's reign: 'While the battle was still at long range, the Triballians did not have the worst of it, but when [the infantry and] the cavalry, no longer shooting, but actually thrusting them with their horses, fell on them here, there and everywhere, they turned in flight' (Arr. *Anab*. 1.2.6). Thracians, like their Triballian neighbours, probably hoped mostly to fight 'at long range', charging forward in wedge, throwing javelins, then wheeling away in the gaps between units (like an early version of the caracole). For the lighter-armed units at least, charging into contact with any enemy was mostly to be avoided, unless the enemy was already broken or in flight. As such, these are true light cavalry, unlike the Macedonian Prodromoi lancers.

---

5   Stoyanov (2015).

SUBJECTS, ALLIES AND MERCENARIES

Thracian and Balkan Infantry

Identity

The Thracian cavalry formed a relatively modest component of Alexander's army. In contrast, there was a large contingent of Thracian and other Balkan infantry. Diodorus' list of the invasion army includes 7,000 Odrysians, Triballians and Illyrians among the infantry forces – as large as the allied Greek contingent supplied by the Hellenic League – as well as half of the 1,000 Agrianians and archers. The Agrianians were one of the key units of the army, later expanded to 1,000 men on their own.

The Agrianians are to be found in Alexander's army from the earliest of his campaigns, being present alongside the archers in the Balkan campaign of 335. Arrian tells us that the Agrianian King, Langarus, was already a personal friend of Alexander and that he joined the campaign with 'the finest and best armed hypaspists he had' (Arr. *Anab*. 1.5.2). 'Hypaspists' here indicates guard or household troops, the sense in which Alexander applied the name to his own infantry guard. It is not clear how this elite force was armed, but the bulk of the Agrianian force in this campaign, and the 1,000 men who joined the Asian expedition, were certainly javelinmen; they were most likely peltasts in the Classical Greek sense, skirmishing light infantry armed with light shields (*peltai*) and javelins. Agrianians are to be found throughout Alexander's campaigns and are often selected (alongside archers, Hypaspists, and 'the nimblest' of the infantry) for special missions and forced marches. Clearly, they were a highly regarded unit. They remained with the army right through the Indian campaign and were part of the strike force selected by Alexander for the initial assault across the river Hydaspes (Arr. *Anab*. 5.12.2).

The other Balkan units do not figure so prominently in the campaigns, and as they included peoples who had only recently been brought under Macedonian control, or who had recently been in revolt, it is tempting to see them as much as hostages for good behaviour, and as a way to remove numbers of military-age men from the borders of Macedon, as being present for the own military capabilities. Nevertheless, they fulfilled a military need, since the transformation under Philip of the bulk of the Macedonian military population into heavy infantry had (ironically) left the native Macedonian army short of good light infantry. This need was met partly through mercenaries but also through the addition of Balkan javelinmen. Thracian infantry under Sitalces, an Odrysian ruler, performed a similar role to the Agrianians at the battle against the Pisidians in 334–3 (Arr. *Anab*. 1.27.4), but on the left, while the Agrianians were on the right, and they are to be found in the same post at Issus (2.9.3) and Gaugamela (3.12.4), still under Sitalces. A force of Thracians – perhaps a much larger one – also formed the guard for the baggage train at Gaugamela (3.12.5), which suggests that Alexander did not wish to entrust them with a front-rank role. It is likely that 'Thracians' here is used as a catch-all term for all the 'Odrysians, Triballians and Illyrians' of Diodorus' list.

Organisation

Nothing is known about the internal organisation of the Balkan forces. The fact that the Agrianians formed (alongside the archers) part of a force of 1,000 men, and later numbered 1,000 on their own, suggests there may have been subunits (*lochoi*) of 500. As the example of Sitalces shows, these units could be under their own native leaders rather than having Macedonian officers imposed on them.

Equipment and Dress

Where Thracian infantry are described in any more detail than simply by their ethnic origin, it is invariably as 'javelinmen' (*akontistai*). This is explicit for the Agrianians and Sitalces' men and is a safe assumption for the others. Thrace was the birthplace of the peltast, a type of light infantry that became highly important in Greece during the fifth century. Traditionally, Greek light infantry fought as *psiloi* or *gymnetes* (literally, 'naked men'), armed with javelins or whatever other weapon was available (sometimes just large stones) and lacking any defensive equipment, even a shield. However, in Thrace and neighbouring regions (including, in all probability, Macedon), the local peoples were slightly more heavily equipped, and most importantly, they carried shields. These were not the heavier *aspis* used by Greeks, but a lighter *pelta*, a shield that was usually smaller, of lighter construction (wicker or leather rather than solid wood), and without the heavy dished shape and offset rim of the Greek *aspis*. Fifth-century depictions of these shields often show them crescent-shaped (or circular with a 'bite' taken out of the top edge), although *peltai* could also be circular, and the name itself does not specify any particular shape. From the name of the shield, infantry of this type were called 'peltasts', and their value in irregular warfare and settings outside of the formal pitched battle was amply demonstrated during the Peloponnesian War, often at the expense of traditionally-equipped Greek hoplite armies. Illyrians are sometimes depicted carrying oval shields, the construction details of which are unknown but which were presumably also light shields and could fall under the general name of *peltai*. Shields of this oval shape, though larger, became very popular in Greece and the Hellenistic world from the early third century, when they were known as *thureoi*, but, in Alexander's time, they were not in use in Greece. It is possible, however, that some of the western Thracians or Thraco-Illyrians may have had shields of this type.[6]

Offensive weaponry generally consisted of a bundle of javelins, though there are also suggestions that Thracians sometimes carried a long spear as well as javelins. The purely javelin-using forces of Alexander's army are identified as such, so other Thracian infantry and those similar to the earlier peltasts were likely more of a dual-role type of infantry, able to skirmish with javelins but also able, when required, to fight hand-to-hand in the battle line. This would make them similar to the 'Iphicratean peltast'. Thracians themselves seem to have had a tradition of carrying hand-to-hand weapons, in the form of swords with a forward-curving blade, or the enigmatic counterpart of

---

[6] On Thracian peltasts, Best (1969).

Thracian (and perhaps Macedonian – note the kausia of the figure on the left) infantry, with javelins, curved swords and shields, from Kazanlak, Bulgaria, fourth or third century. The tunics are red, and the left hand figure has a blue cloak. (PD)

this weapon, the *rhomphaia*, which appears in the Hellenistic era but may have had earlier antecedents. The *rhomphaia* appears to have been a sort of short polearm, consisting of a wooden handle around a metre long, with a forward curved metal blade attached to one end, a little like a scythe. There is no direct evidence for the use of such a weapon in Alexander's army, but we may reasonably suppose that some Thracian infantry will have carried bladed weapons suitable for close-quarters combat.[7]

Thracians hunting, from the Thracian tomb of Aleksandrovo, Bulgaria, fourth or third century (reconstruction). Tunics are white with red stripes, and red with white stripes. (Kmrakmra, CC BY-SA 3.0)

---

7   Rhomphaia, Sekunda (1981).

In terms of dress, Thracian infantry will have been similar to Thracian cavalry, though being drawn from the less wealthy classes, there will have been less expensive metallic equipment. The traditional Thracian costume was probably still worn by some, though many would have worn clothing like that of southern Greek peltasts – a simple tunic and a cloak. Helmets were probably rare among the infantry, and the traditional Thracian cap may have been more prevalent. Boots were probably also widely retained.

Drill and Tactics

As noted above, Thracian forces can be divided into two types. There were the pure skirmishing javelinmen or *akontistai*, such as the Agrianians, who would have fought in open order and loose formations, showering an enemy with javelins and running away from any counter-charges, avoiding hand-to-hand combat if possible. Then there were peltast-style infantry with some close combat capability, from either long spears or bladed weapons, who had javelins with which they could harass a slower enemy, but who could also close to fight with lightly equipped opponents or (importantly) form into close order to resist enemy cavalry (against whom open order javelin skirmishers would have been largely defenceless).

Men equipped to fight with javelins were particularly useful against the special troop types encountered on the campaign: chariots and elephants. At Gaugamela, the Persian scythed chariots charged unsuccessfully into the Macedonian line: 'For first, as they approached, the Agrianians and javelinmen under Balacrus, who had been stationed in front of the Companion cavalry, met them with volleys; and then they snatched hold of the reins, pulled down the drivers, and crowding round the horses, cut them down' (Arr. *Anab*. 3.13.5). Elephants at the Hydaspes were met in a similar way by those deployed in front of the phalanx: 'Then Alexander sent the Agrianians and the Thracian light-armed against the elephants, for they were better at skirmishing than at fighting at close quarters. These released a thick barrage of missiles on both elephants and drivers' (QC 8.14.24–5). Curtius adds that 'the Macedonians' also used axes and 'gently curving, sickle-like swords called *copides*' (8.14.28–9) – most likely this is a garbled reference to the weapons of the Thracians since the Macedonians themselves were better off with their sarissas, and the *kopis* was a common type of Greek sword.

Greek Allied and Mercenary Cavalry

Identity

I have grouped together the Greek forces, allies and mercenaries here, as they would have been similar in terms of equipment and tactical use, though they were different in the way they were raised and recruited. The following account will apply equally to both infantry and cavalry, although infantry were far more numerous. There were two sources of Greeks (non-Macedonian Greeks) in Alexander's army – official contingents supplied by the members of the Hellenic League and mercenaries hired on an individual basis. In the Hellenistic period, we see a third hybrid group, mercenaries hired by official recruitment agreements with their home cities, but it is likely that this sort of recruitment was less of a feature in Alexander's day. Hellenic League forces, generally classed as 'allies' (*symmachoi*), were city contingents of hoplite infantry or heavy cavalry recruited by and provided by their home cities. Greek military service usually followed the pattern of citizen militias called up for short and defined campaigns and who returned home at the end of the campaign. During the fourth century, there was an increase in the use of professional forces, *epilektoi* (picked men), specially chosen from the general levy and kept on the books permanently (or at least, long term), and therefore able to undergo some formal training. Most city forces, however, were still citizen militias. Precisely which group the League allies in Alexander's army fall into is unclear. Given the length of the campaign and the requirement to be away from home for several years, we might expect professional *epilektoi* to have been sent, but cities might have been unwilling to commit their best troops to foreign service abroad. Alternatively, volunteers might have been sought among the general levy.

Mercenaries, in contrast, were most likely always recruited as individual volunteers, without the direct involvement of their home cities. Mercenary service had been a feature of Greek warfare for centuries, with Greek adventurers seeking a period of foreign service in one of the armies of the Mediterranean great powers (such as Persia or Egypt). These earlier mercenaries might often be relatively wealthy men and their retinues, but the upheavals of the fifth century and the Peloponnesian War caused the rise of a new type of mercenary, a poorer man or often a political exile expelled from his home city in the course of the endless cycle of rise and fall of factions known as *stasis*. Such men sought mercenary service as a way to make a living rather than as a route to wealth, and long service overseas would have been highly attractive to them. In the fourth century, the large numbers of such landless men offering mercenary service to the highest bidder was a cause of social and political problems, and Greek politicians and rhetoricians saw the conquest of the Persian Empire as a possible solution to this problem, hoping it would open up new territory into which landless men could be settled. This was indeed to happen under Alexander and the Successors, though the landless men themselves were sometimes less than enthusiastic. Mercenaries in Alexander's army would have been a mixture of such men and some better-off volunteers, similar to the volunteer League forces but not serving in city contingents.[8]

Identifying and categorising these allied and mercenary forces in Alexander's army is often fraught with difficulties, the main one being the near-invisibility of these forces in many of our sources' accounts of the campaign. In the major battles, while mercenary units are identified individually, the Greek allied infantry remain largely anonymous. For example, at Gaugamela, Arrian describes in detail the deployment of the Macedonian phalanx then adds 'This was the order in which Alexander had marshalled his front, but he also posted a second line, so that his phalanx

---

8   Parke (1933), Griffith (1935), English (2009) pp.67–8.

was double-fronted' (Arr. *Anab.* 3.12.1). The identity of this second line is never stated, and we are left to infer that these were the allied Greeks from the fact that they are not mentioned elsewhere. At Issus, Arrian describes the formation of the Macedonian phalanx and the order of its *taxeis* but does not mention the allied Greeks at all – we might guess that here too they formed a second line. This is rather surprising, so much so that it led Polybius into difficulties (Pol. 12.19) since he assumed that Alexander's entire infantry force would be deployed in a single line and, calculating the frontage such a line required, concluded they could not have fitted into the plain of Issus in the formation they are described as adopting. Yet Alexander seems, in fact, to have been happy to leave almost half of his heavy infantry out of the line of battle, at all his major battles, despite the fact that he was regularly outnumbered by the Persian forces. There were no doubt both political and military reasons for this. The reliability of the allied forces might have been in doubt – not so much that they might have defected to the enemy during a fight (which would likely have been fatal to themselves in the confusion of battle), as that it meant Alexander considered them something of a weak link in his overall battle line. The fact that Alexander deployed the Greeks behind his phalanx, where they could do most harm if they did defect, suggests he did not consider defection a real danger. In terms of training and equipment as well, amateur Greek militias with weaponry that had, as recently as Chaironeia (338), proven inferior to Macedonian weapons would not have been appealing to use as front-line troops. There was also an element of rivalry and hostility between Greeks and Macedonians (exemplified by the fighting between the Macedonian phalanx and Darius' Greeks at Issus, Arr. *Anab.* 2.10.7), with the Greeks being recent and not necessarily enthusiastic converts to the Macedonian cause. All this, no doubt, made Alexander more inclined to give the Greeks secondary roles. The main use of Greek (particularly mercenary) forces appears to have been as garrisons in captured cities and, later, as settlers in newly founded cities.

Looking specifically at the cavalry, mounted forces in Greek cities were usually drawn from the wealthier elements of society, those who could afford to raise horses. They formed a relatively small component of most Greek city armies. Men such as these – aristocrats from each city – may have formed a part of the allied Greek force under Alexander, but there was also a tendency in the fourth century for wealthy men to 'contract out' their military service, providing a horse and paying for a man to ride it – indeed it was sometimes thought militarily preferable to employ a professional cavalryman rather than an unwilling aristocrat.[9]

The allied forces, along with the Thessalians, were dismissed from the army when Alexander reached Ecbatana (in 330), Alexander 'giving the agreed pay in full, and adding as a personal gift two thousand talents' (Arr. *Anab.* 3.19.5), a reminder that allied forces too were paid so that the difference between them and mercenaries was just the method of recruitment. In addition, 'any individual who wanted to continue serving in his army as a mercenary was

---

[9] Spence (1993).

to enrol, and a great many did so' (3.19.6) – thus converting paid members of a city contingent into paid individual volunteers. It is worth noting that this means that later references to mercenary cavalry will, in practice, often have been to units with at least a large proportion of Thessalians. The number of mercenaries in Alexander's army also increased dramatically over the course of the campaign – just as the allied forces were sent back to Greece – but these later mercenaries will be considered in the following chapter on the Imperial army.

Organisation

In Diodorus' list of the army at the start of the campaign, we find a force of 'six hundred from the rest of Greece [other than Macedon and Thessaly] under the command of Erigyios' (Diod. 17.17.4). At Gaugamela, 'the allied cavalry under Erigyios son of Larichos' was posted on the Macedonian right (Arr. *Anab*. 3.11.10), while on the Macedonian left was 'the allied cavalry under Coiranos' (3.12.4). Diodorus provides more details about these units; he describes 'the combined Peloponnesian and Achaean horse, then cavalry from Phthiotis and Malis, then Locrians and Phocians, all under the command of Erigyios of Mitylene', although he appears to place them alongside the Thessalians on the left (Diod. 17.57.3). Curtius also has allied cavalry on the left – 'Crateros was in charge of the Peloponnesian cavalry, to which were attached squadrons of Achaeans, Locrians and Malians' (QC. 4.13.28, Crateros was of course in command of infantry, not cavalry, at this battle). At the Granicus, the allied cavalry (under Philip son of Menelaos) were posted on the left (Arr. *Anab*. 1.14.3), and at Issus similarly, 'the Peloponnessians and other allies were sent to Parmenion on the left' (Arr. *Anab*. 2.8.10). We also know that a force of 150 Eleians, probably cavalry, had joined Alexander at Gordion in 333 (Arr. *Anab*. 1.29.4), and there may have been other reinforcements that we have not been told about.

Not much can be extracted from these brief and, in the case of Diodorus and Curtius, clearly confused references. If the allied cavalry suffered no losses to sickness, battle or detached duty, and if the Eleians were indeed cavalry and were attached to this unit, then the overall strength would be 750 at Gaugamela, though there may have been other reinforcements received. The number of 600 at the outset of the campaign might suggest three squadrons (*ilai*) of 200 men each, and if Diodorus' details are correct (though he misplaces the unit), these may have been mixed squadrons of, respectively, 'Peloponnesians and Achaeans', 'Phthiotians and Malians', and 'Locrians and Phocians'. The Eleians may have formed a new squadron or been combined with the other Peloponnesians (Achaea and Elis are both in the Peloponnese, while the other regions named are in central Greece, bordering on Boeotia).

Mercenary cavalry are not included in Diodorus' initial campaign list, but a number of reinforcements reached the army (as well as the volunteers enrolled from the allies noted above, which will be considered in more detail in the next chapter). At Memphis in 331, 400 Greek mercenaries joined the army under Menoitas or Menidas (readings of the manuscripts differ) son of Hegesandros (Arr. *Anab*. 3.5.1). More reinforcements reached Alexander in Persia after the overthrow of Darius, but at Gaugamela mercenary cavalry formed part of both flank guards, with 'the mercenary cavalry under Menidas' on the right (Arr. *Anab.* 3.12.3), and 'the foreign mercenary cavalry under Andromachos son of Hieron' on the left (3.12.5). It is unclear what distinction, if any, there is between these units, the addition of 'foreign' (*xenoi*) to Andromachos' men probably meaning no more than that they were non-Macedonian. These might be two units each of 400, or Menidas' original force of 400 might have been split into two; in either case, multiples of 200 again suggests standard-sized squadrons, 200 strong.

Equipment and Dress

Nothing specific is known about the equipment of the allied and mercenary cavalry or whether they differed. The likelihood is that they were equipped like most cavalry from central and southern Greece in the fifth and fourth centuries (so, unlike Thessalians and Macedonians), as a sort of medium cavalry, armed with javelins or short spears, shieldless, helmeted (probably with Boeotian helmets, which were regarded as especially suitable for cavalry use, Xen. *Hipp.* 12.3), with short boots, tunics and cloaks. Armour will have been worn or not as a matter of personal preference and affordability, and will have included bronze cuirasses (probably rare) and the usual linen or leather armour, as worn by the infantry. Whether there were any city or contingent uniforms we can only guess – it seems likely that individual volunteers (in the mercenary units) would have brought their own clothes and equipment, while city contingents might have standardised clothing, but if so, we do not know what it was.

A reconstruction of grave stele of an Athenian cavalryman, early fourth century, in the National Archaeological Museum of Athens.

Drill and Tactics

According to the Tacticians, Greek cavalry usually fought in square formations consisting of 16 files of eight ranks, with the rank spacing being double that of the file spacing, so that the formation had the shape of a square, although the number of men in rank and file was not equal (Asclep. 7.4; Aelian 18.9). 'Some', the Tacticians go on to say, instead increased the number of files to three times the ranks and used triple rank spacing (which seems more likely from a practical point of view, given the length of the horse). Adapting a formation of around 128 men (as suggested by the 16 by eight formation) this might suggest something like 18 files and six ranks (108 men total), but no doubt absolute mathematical precision was rarely achieved in practice. Two such formations would have made an approximately 200-man formation, such as we encountered above. The Tacticians call the smallest formation the *ilē*, and a formation of two an *epilarchia*. The file spacing used is never clearly stated, though calculations suggest it was the same two cubits, one metre, as the infantry. Even at triple rank spacing, this would give an improbable rank

SUBJECTS, ALLIES AND MERCENARIES

interval of three metres, barely enough to contain a horse, so it is likely that wider spacings were used, and a two metre file spacing, with six metres between ranks, may be more typical. There would also have been gaps between the squadrons equal in width to the squadrons themselves, as Polybius informs us.

While Thessalian and Macedonian cavalry, and the Prodromoi in their role as *sarissophoroi*, lancers, were armed with long spears and intended to charge into contact with enemy forces, most Greek cavalry probably fought using the tactics of the previous two centuries – a sequence of charges, throwing javelins, then retreating, whether as a body or by individual squadrons. Speed and manoeuvrability were the keys to this sort of fighting, and whether we class such cavalry as 'light', 'medium' or 'heavy' is a moot point. This was probably the commonest form of fighting used by most cavalry forces in antiquity, including by the javelin-armed Persians, even though the Persians were often more heavily armoured.

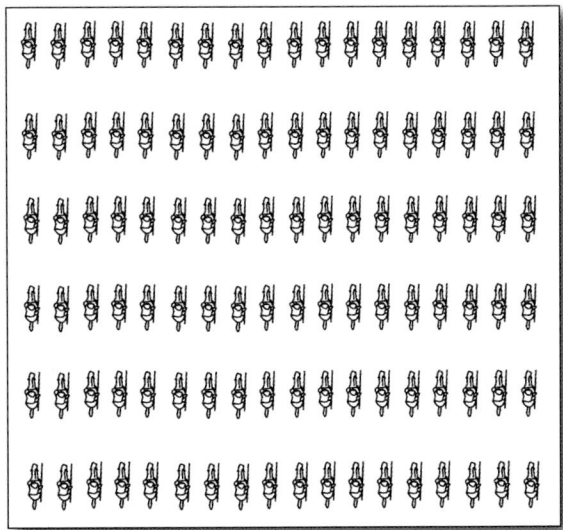

Square or rectangular formation of cavalry in six ranks of eighteen files.

Greek Allied and Mercenary Infantry

Identity

The comments above about allies and mercenaries apply to the infantry as well as to the cavalry. The infantry were far more numerous, right from the outset. Diodorus lists 7,000 allied infantry in the invasion army, along with 5,000 mercenaries (Diod. 17.17.4). To these must be added some proportion of the advance force of 10,000 which probably contained a high proportion of mercenaries. It may well have contained Macedonians as well, but would be unlikely to have included allied League forces. Arrian reports 300 Greek mercenaries in Persian pay being enrolled in the Macedonian army at Miletus (Arr. *Anab* 1.19.6) and an additional 4,000 Peloponnesian mercenaries joining the army at Sidon (Arr. *Anab*. 2.20.5), while Curtius records 3,000 more mercenaries in Persian service from Chios being captured and enrolled (QC. 4.5.18). Large draughts of mercenaries were recruited after Gaugamela, as we will see in the next chapter. Up to Gaugamela, then, we have definite records of 7,000 allied infantry and 12,300 mercenaries, plus whatever proportion of the advance force was retained – we might estimate a total of around 20,000 mercenaries.[10]

The allied infantry, as we saw above, were probably hoplites provided as official contingents (whether *epilektoi*, conscripts or volunteers) by their respective cities. The mercenaries are rather harder to pin down. Many

---

10 English (2009) pp.74–8 (especially for list of mercenary reinforcements).

mercenaries in Persian service certainly fought as hoplites, and the political turmoil and incessant warfare of the fifth to fourth centuries meant there was a plentiful supply of hoplite-class men (though probably from the lower end of the economic spectrum) seeking this sort of employment. However, the great growth of mercenary service in the fourth century had been not in hoplites but peltasts. As Alexander had no shortage of good quality heavy infantry (in the shape of his Macedonians), we may well expect that he would have preferred to recruit peltast generalists rather than inferior hoplites. Such peltasts may have been of the sort familiar from the Classical era, javelin-throwing skirmishers, but would also have included at least a proportion, perhaps a preponderance, of the heavier-equipped 'Iphicratean' peltasts, armed with spears and shields and able to fight in the line of battle.

Both forces – allies and mercenaries – are strangely absent from many of the battle accounts. We have seen how the allied infantry played a secondary role, at most, in the major battles. Both allies and mercenaries are absent from the accounts of the Granicus. At Issus, Arrian merely comments cryptically, that 'The foreign mercenaries were drawn up in support of the whole line' (Arr. *Anab.* 2.9.3). This suggests that they formed a second line, similar to the second line formed by the allies at Gaugamela (3.12.1). It is most likely that mercenaries and allies were both posted as a second line at both battles, a fact obscured by our sources. At Gaugamela, however, some mercenaries received a front-line posting (of sorts), 'the so-called old mercenaries under Cleandros' forming part of the right flank guard (Arr. *Anab.* 3.12.2). Characteristically, Arrian does not tell us the strength of this unit, nor anything about its equipment, nor does he explain why they were called 'old' (*archaioi*) mercenaries. The usual assumption is that these were some of the original mercenaries who crossed with the invasion force, or even the advance guard, rather than the reinforcements who had joined the army since and that they were armed as peltasts or Iphicratean peltasts. Diodorus places a unit of Achaean mercenaries on Alexander's left, but his account of the battle is so confused as to be almost useless, and as Arrian does not mention this unit, they are probably an error.

The main use of mercenaries, however, was not as front-line troops in battle but to bulk out detached forces and to form garrisons. Garrisons and settlers were to become particularly important after Gaugamela, as were detached forces given the counter-insurgency nature of the fighting. Large garrison forces had to be left in conquered territories. Arrian (3.23.6) describes 'three thousand mercenary foot and two hundred horse' being left as a garrison for Caria, while Curtius (4.8.4) records 4,000 men being left as a garrison or occupation army in Egypt (Arrian 3.5 lists the command arrangements, which are confused). Such large garrisons could not have been formed from Macedonians without critically depleting the phalanx, so mercenaries provided long-service soldiers who could be expended this way, freeing up the Macedonians themselves for the field army. This pattern was to be followed throughout Alexander's campaigns and the following Hellenistic period. As for detached forces, these were to become a particular feature of the post-Gaugamela phase of the campaign, but we see allies and mercenaries performing detached duties earlier, such as the force with which

Parmenion seized the Cilician Gates in 333, consisting of 'the allied infantry, the Greek mercenaries, the Thracians under Sitalces and the Thessalian horse' (Arr. *Anab*. 2.5.1).

Of particular note also are the Cretan archers, referred to in Chapter 4 as fighting alongside the Macedonian archers (according to some modern views, there were, in fact, no Macedonian archers and all the archers were Cretans, but this seems to be going too far). Like their Macedonian counterparts, these were treated as an elite unit and often included, alongside the Agrianians, in special missions. Crete was noted for its archery skills, and Cretan mercenaries were sought after as specialist archers throughout the Hellenistic period. It is possible that the total archery force in the army was (when it reached full strength at Gaugamela) 1,000 men, split evenly between Macedonians and Cretans.

Organisation

No specific information is preserved in our sources for the organisation of any of the allied or mercenary infantry, and we are left to fall back on general statements. Greek infantry of the time were usually formed into a fairly rudimentary hierarchy of units, except in the Spartan army, which had a more complete four-level hierarchy, as did armies based on the Spartan model, such as the mercenary Ten Thousand with which Xenophon campaigned in Persia. Greek forces generally were formed into companies (*lochoi*) of a few hundred men (200, 300 and 400 are typical figures), which might then be grouped into larger units under a variety of names (sometimes *taxeis*, like the battalions of the Macedonian phalanx). As the allied forces consisted of individual city contingents, they were probably formed into separate units by city or region, which would, therefore, have been of variable sizes. The mercenaries would have been formed into more regular units since there was no need to divide them according to city of origin. Allied forces doubtless served under their own commanders, while mercenaries might have Macedonians placed over them. There were probably Macedonian commanders for contingents as a whole; Arrian tells us that Balacros, commander of the allied infantry (presumably all of them), was left in Egypt in 331 and that he was replaced by Calanos (Arr. *Anab*. 3.5.6).[11]

Equipment and Dress

As noted above, there will have been two types of mercenaries, peltasts and hoplites, while allied infantry most likely were all equipped as hoplites. Hoplite equipment during the fourth century followed a general trend of becoming lighter, with body armour and, in many cases, greaves being discarded. The mercenary hoplites will have used this lighter equipment, with the Argive aspis (itself the heaviest piece of equipment), a spear of around two to three metres in length, a helmet, often the conical *pilos* type popular in Sparta, and the usual tunic and (on campaign) cloak. Footwear would have consisted of boots, sandals or in combat, bare feet.

---

11   Taylor (2021) pp.98–155.

Grave monument of Aristonautes of Athens, late fourth century, in the National Archaeological Museum of Athens. (Marsyas, CC BY 2.5)

Allied hoplites would often have worn similar equipment, but there is evidence that many Greek states were trying to increase the protection of their hoplites by adopting (or re-adopting, since it had been popular in the fifth century) metal body armour in the form of a 'muscle cuirass' (decorated with a stylised musculature of the torso). This type of cuirass had a curved lower edge to protect the lower abdomen and was often worn with leather *pteruges* protruding below it over the groin. Helmets would have been of a variety of types, including *pilos* and Thracian or Phrygian styles, as well as Chalcidian or Attic, and there was probably little uniformity within or between units.

Peltast equipment would have been of two types; there would still have been some traditional peltasts, forming a type of infantry akin to the Agrianian javelinmen, with a bundle of javelins and a light shield that would

SUBJECTS, ALLIES AND MERCENARIES

Funerary stele of Panchares of Athens, killed at Chaironeia, in the Piraeus Archaeological Museum. (Furius, CC BY-SA 4.0)

A reconstruction drawing of relief of peltasts in action on the Tomb of Payava, Lycia, Turkey, mid-fourth century. (G. Scharf, in A. Smith, *A Catalogue of Sculpture in the Department of Greek and Roman Antiquities* (Harvard))

have been crescent-shaped or, more often, round. Then there would have been 'Iphicratean' peltasts, armed with a long spear that would have allowed them to fight in the line of battle. The equipment of such men would have been very similar to that of the lighter type of hoplite, but instead of the heavy Argive shield they would have carried lighter rimless shields, round and superficially similar to hoplite shields.[12]

---

12   Sekunda and Burliga (2014), Taylor (2021) pp.467–9.

Cretan archers were equipped similarly to the other light infantry and the Macedonian archers, with a tunic, hat or light helmet, and bow. However, there is some evidence that Cretan archers, unusually for archers, carried a small shield. This would have given them a degree of extra protection if they came to hand-to-hand fighting, which they would do all they could to avoid.[13]

Drill and Tactics

Again, we can only draw some general conclusions based on what we know about Greek armies of the fourth century. Although we have detailed accounts of the drill and formations of the hoplites of the Macedonian phalanx, the extent to which this can be extrapolated backwards onto Greek hoplites is controversial, and it is certain that many Greek militias would have had a standard of training and drill far below that of the Macedonians, or the more professional Greek units such as Spartans and the cities with *epilektoi*. Most likely, hoplites usually formed up in bodies eight deep (a 200 man *lochos* would then have had 25 files), and with a file spacing of two cubits (one metre), the intermediate spacing of the later Macedonian phalanx. Such units had limited manoeuvre ability, though they could countermarch to face a threat from their rear, as the second line did at Gaugamela (Arr. *Anab.* 3.14.6). They would charge to contact at the run over the last hundred metres or so, and then fight hand-to-hand using their spears or, if those broke, their swords. Despite their equipment having become lighter over the years, hoplites were still considered highly effective in hand-to-hand combat, which is why they were always employed in such large numbers by Persian commanders, as Persia (and its various subject peoples) lacked a native tradition of heavy infantry specialising in close combat.

The combat techniques of peltasts are more obscure. They were probably drawn up in a looser formation, though Iphicrateans would have formed in a close order identical to that of the hoplites when required to fight at close quarters. Old-style peltasts fought by rushing forward, as a group or a crowd of individuals, throwing javelins at their opponents, then running away when their victims attempted to countercharge them – a tactic that could be very effective against slower infantry but was obviously dangerous against quicker, or mounted, enemies. Iphicratean peltasts could have fought the same way or maintained a closer formation, perhaps using a javelin or two to 'soften up' an enemy before an attack. This would represent a type of fighting – in massed formation and close order, but with more tentative contact with the enemy and relatively low-intensity combat – that was probably the default form of combat throughout antiquity (and beyond), with forces such as Greek hoplites, who for equipment and cultural reasons were willing to close to full close combat, being the exception not the norm.

---

13 Sekunda (2001b).

SUBJECTS, ALLIES AND MERCENARIES

A hoplite phalanx from the Mausoleum of Pericles, Limyra, Turkey, now in the Antalya Archaeological Museum. Note the variety of helmet styles in use. (Jona Lendering, CC0)

An Achaemenid (Phrygian) heavy cavalryman with Greek (right) and Anatolian (left) light infantry, Altıkulaç Sarcophagus, Troy Museum, Turkey. The rider has red armour (compare him with the Persian figures on the Alexander Mosaic).

Engineers

Identity

It is convenient to consider the engineers and the siege train in this chapter, although many of the men involved in these roles will have been Macedonians. As we have seen, Philip II's ability to capture defended cities was one of the key factors in the success of his campaign to dominate Greece; although he did not always need to call on his engineers, bribery and betrayal often did the job for him. Alexander inherited the siege train and the body of engineers (*mechanopoioi*, literally 'machine-makers') and made extensive use of them in his campaigns. However, in Alexander's case, too, cities could often be captured using non-violent means, or in the case of the smaller towns of the Eastern provinces, simply stormed by infantry with ladders.[14]

The siege train consisted of two main types of siege engine, both generally referred to by Arrian as 'machines', which can make it difficult to identify which type is meant on any given occasion. First, there were the various types of missile-engines or artillery, which in turn can be divided into light and heavy types. Light artillery shot bolts or arrows (larger arrows than those shot by bows) and were termed *katapeltai* (sometimes qualified as *oxybeles*, 'sharp-missiled' for example, Diod. 20.48.1). These were anti-personnel weapons (the name *katapelta* means 'anti-shield'), and their primary use was to clear walls of defenders, though they were portable enough that they could also be used in the field. Their first large-scale use was at the siege of Olynthus in 348, and bolt heads have been discovered there with Philip II's name inscribed on them. Heavy artillery shot stones, hence *lithoboloi* or *petroboloi* (stone-throwers), and their primary use was to directly batter the walls of a defending town, either to strip away battlements and shooting apertures or to breach the wall completely to permit an infantry assault. These large machines were too heavy for use in the field and would have been constructed where they were required for a formal siege and dismantled afterwards.[15]

The second main type of machine were the various types of siege engines, which did not shoot missiles, consisting chiefly of siege towers and rams. Siege towers were primarily a means of getting assault troops up to wall height – they were mobile towers on wheels, with internal stairs or ladders and a drawbridge. They would be pushed up against a city wall, and the drawbridge lowered, allowing infantry to climb the tower and assault the walls. Rams (and their cousins, borers) were intended to batter down (or bore through) gates or walls from ground level. Early rams were simply a beam suspended from a sling, but by Alexander's day, there were mobile covered rams with roofs and walls covered in hides to protect against fire and missile weapons, with rams mounted on rollers. Later, under the Successors and in the Hellenistic period, we hear of various more complex and sophisticated siege engines, but there is no clear evidence that such machines were used in Alexander's day, towers and rams being sufficient for most purposes, although it was possible, for example, to place stone-throwing artillery inside siege towers, as at the siege of Halicarnassus (Arr. *Anab.* 1.22.2). Alexander's engineers also showed great ingenuity in getting these machines into action, building ramps and mounds to cross moats or natural defences, or mounting engines on ships for amphibious assaults (see Chapter 9).

Towers and rams had developed gradually throughout the Greek world (and beyond), but the missile-engines were a relatively new invention. They were probably first used in Syracuse under Dionysius in the early fourth century when the principle of torsion catapults – those that gained their power from twisted rope or sinew rather than from bent wood, like

---

14 Marsden (1977); Campbell (2003); English (2009) pp.100–109; English (2010) pp.1–21.
15 Olynthus, Lee (2001) (note it can be difficult to distinguish arrow heads from catapult bolts).

normal hand bows – was probably first developed. However, it is not certain that Dionysius had torsion engines, and it is possible that they were only invented later under Philip II. It was the discovery of torsion power that first made such missile-throwing engines really practicable. There may have been earlier giant bows using the bent wood principle of the hand bow, but such engines were less efficient and harder to dismantle and transport. Small versions, termed the *gastrephetes* or 'belly shooter' (so named because the stock was pressed against the belly to bend the bow), are said to have been used in the fourth century, but there is no reason to link them particularly with Alexander's army. Greeks also seem never to have developed gravity-powered engines like the Medieval trebuchet. Philip and Alexander by no means had a monopoly on the use of torsion engines. They were, by the later fourth century, used extensively throughout the Greek world and the Persian Empire, and in all Alexander's major sieges, we see the defenders also making use of such artillery. For example, Alexander was wounded by a shot from a catapult at the siege of Gaza (Arr. *Anab*. 2.27.2, in 332) which penetrated his shield and armour, and Diodorus (17.24.6) reports the defenders of Halicarnassus using bolt-shooters. Catapults were also used as field artillery by armies other than the Macedonian – Philip II himself is said to have suffered defeat at the hands of the Phocians early in his reign when they used catapult field artillery against his phalanx (Polyaen. 2.38).

Essential to the construction of these machines were the engineers themselves, the 'machine-makers'. These were the technical experts who designed, built, fitted together, and perhaps operated the machines. The actual spade work of building mounds and ramps and other such hard labour was done by the rank-and-file Macedonians, the men of the phalanx. At the siege of Tyre, Alexander was building a mole to reach the island defences and 'ordered his men to make the mole broader, and the engineers to construct new engines' (Arr. *Anab* 2.19.6). But just as Alexander depended on local forces to supplement his navy, he also collected local engineers; as the siege progressed, 'many engineers had been collected from Cyprus and the whole of Phoenicia' (Arr. *Anab*. 2.21.1). So, the engineers were a multinational group, and the Macedonian army was open to all talents, in this field at least. The Tyrian defenders also depended on the 'engineers and artisans of all sorts who were in the city' (Diod. 17.41.3). Even so it was not always easy, in a competitive market, for an engineer or other skilled expert to attract attention. The Roman engineer Vitruvius tells of the efforts of the architect Dinocrates to gain employment in Alexander's army. Letters of recommendation from friends and family to senior officers and courtiers produced no immediate result, so, relying on his imposing physique, he stripped naked, put on a Heracles costume (lion skin and club), and appeared in front of Alexander as he was hearing legal cases in public – this did the trick, and Alexander employed him (Vit. 2.Pref.1–2).

Organisation
Engineers were talented individuals offering their skills rather in the fashion of mercenaries, so it is unlikely that they had any formal organisation within the Macedonian army. No mention is made of any system of ranks, although

there were senior men whose skills and knowledge were particularly valued; these include Aristoboulos, the writer of the biography of Alexander used as a source by Arrian, who was an architect and military engineer, and most importantly Polyeidos, a Thessalian who served with Philip, and Charias and Diades, his pupils. Diades was the inventor of many different types of siege engine and the writer of a treatise on siege engines, which was quoted by the Roman engineer Vitruvius.

Equipment

Details of the construction of the siege engines themselves come mostly from later authors, chiefly Heron and Vitruvius, working under the Roman Empire, so it is uncertain precisely how closely their descriptions match the machines Alexander will have used. The catapults and stone-throwers of the artillery will have been similar in appearance to equivalent machines, the ballistae and scorpions, of the Roman army, the stone-throwers being simply scaled-up versions. Vitruvius records Diades' detailed descriptions of his towers and rams; the towers, he specifies, should be 30 metres tall (for the small towers) to 60 metres (for the large type) and eight to 12 metres wide at the base, diminishing to one fifth less at the top. They should be 10 or 20 stories high, with windows all around (presumably, arrow slits), and the whole covered in rawhide (Vitr. 10.13.4–5). The mobile ram had a base of 15 metres and was six metres high (excluding the pitched roof), with a small tower on top to house catapults. The ram itself was mounted on a roller and operated by ropes, and the whole again covered in rawhide (with stores of water kept inside the ram housing to put out fires) (Vitr. 10.13.6). Although Diades does not say so, we must assume that both types of machines were mounted on wheels – Curtius (QC 4.6.9) describes the wheels of the towers sticking in soft sand at the siege of Gaza.[16]

Tactics

The use of such machines in practice will be described during the sieges in Chapter 9. The range of the various artillery machines is never stated but it was probably in the region of 200 metres or so. There are some indications of range, for example, in the siege of Aornos Rock (Arr. *Anab.* 4.30.1–2), where the Macedonians had to fill a ravine to get their artillery within range; the first 180 metres of this ravine were filled in on the first day, after which slingers and machines were able to engage Indians making sallies against those building the mound. This suggests that the range of the machines (presumably catapults in this case) was similar to, or not much greater than, that of slingers, though unfortunately, we do not know if the walls could be reached at this stage – another two days' mound-building was needed to get close to the walls, and we do not know at what point the machines could reach them.

In a siege, light artillery, shooting from fixed positions, would be used to suppress the defenders on the walls, while the heavy artillery, probably

---

16   Marsden (1977), Connolly (1998) pp.281–5 for reconstructions.

with similar ranges, would batter the walls themselves, in the ideal case, aiming to breach the walls completely, or at least to damage them and reduce the defenders' ability to hold them. Rams and towers could then be pushed forward to the walls, which would have required level ground, with any obstacles filled in, if necessary, with ramps and mounds, and either the walls breached for a ground-level assault or infantry assaulting over the tops of the walls using the bridges on the towers.

In field operations, the two uses of catapults in Alexander's reign both involved river crossings (Arr. *Anab.* 1.6.8, in 335, and Arr. *Anab.* 4.4.4, in 329) where the machines could be set up in fixed positions on one bank, without fear of interference from enemy forces over the river, and shoot to clear the opposite bank, allowing infantry and cavalry forces to cross the river unopposed.

It is worth also noting that although artillery was invented early in the fourth century, its adoption in the Greek world was slow, primarily for social and cultural reasons, the dominant hoplite class being reluctant to introduce weapons which would (by their range, power and randomness), cancel out their own *arete* (courage). Philip and Alexander did not feel bound by such restrictions and were able to take full advantage of the technological advances. The Hellenistic age, an era of absolute monarchs, was to see continued development in the field of artillery and siegecraft.[17]

---

17 See Keyser (1994) esp. pp.50–3.

6

The Imperial Army

The previous chapters have described the army of Alexander as it was on the invasion of the Persian Empire, up to the period 331–330 when, with the defeat of Darius at Gaugamela and his death at the hands of Bessus and Alexander's entry into the Persian homelands, Alexander became the de facto ruler of the Persian Empire, the new King of Kings. From this point on, Alexander was no longer just King of Macedon (and Hegemon of the Hellenic League), and his army began to change accordingly. Some of the differences were due to a change in available resources; with the seizure of vast Persian treasures, Alexander went from being the relatively impoverished king of a small Greek kingdom to being the wealthiest man by far in the known world. This meant that, when it came to hiring mercenaries and other professional soldiers, money was no object. Alexander also became the ruler of the peoples of the Persian Empire (increasingly so as he campaigned further east) and was able to use traditional Persian recruitment systems (we assume) to mobilise these peoples for his army. In addition, the Hellenic League components of the army, having fulfilled their obligations under the terms of the League, were able to return home (though many stayed on as mercenaries). Other changes arose from a series of reforms to the core Macedonian elements of the army, some of which we have already encountered above. Overall numbers were (perhaps) expanded with the addition of new recruits from home, and there were a number of organisational changes, some of them tactical in nature, to meet the demands of the changed nature of campaigning in the eastern provinces of the Empire, and some political to avoid the concentration of power in the hands of possibly untrustworthy subordinates and to empower a particularly trusted new class of officers. These changes combined to bring about a new, 'Imperial' army, similar in its core elements but different in many details from the Macedonian and allied army with which Alexander began the campaign. Although not all these changes took place at the same time, place or rate, it will be convenient to group them all together as the subject of this chapter.

Reforms to Macedonian Units

The Hipparchies

After Gaugamela, Alexander undertook reforms of the organisation of the Companions, the details of which are unfortunately obscure and which have provoked considerable discussion. Firstly, Arrian tells us (Arr. *Anab* 3.16.11) that, after receiving reinforcements from Macedon (of which 500 were cavalry, according to QC 5.1.41), which he enrolled in the Companions, Alexander 'formed two companies (*lochoi*) in each squadron (*ilē*)', noting that there had previously been no cavalry *lochoi*. The division of units into subunits was normal practice in Greek armies (and in all military forces since), and it is surprising if, up to this point, the smallest unit in the cavalry was really the squadron of around 200 men, which would be a rather large formation. However, Arrian may mean that there had been smaller units (perhaps the *tetrarchia* of Arr. *Anab*. 3.18.5, see Chapter 3), but no intermediate-sized unit. With the addition of 500 extra Companions (assuming these were not just making up losses, which they might have been), it may be that the *ilai* were indeed unwieldy, and greater flexibility was required.[1]

The second stage of the reform is more controversial, and involves organisation above the level of the squadron. Following the implication in 330 of Philotas, commander of the Companions, in a plot and his subsequent execution, Alexander decided that he could no longer trust the command of the Companions to a single man, so he appointed two commanders, Cleitos (formerly commander of the Royal Squadron) and Hephaistion (his own closest confidant and partner). These men were termed *hipparchoi*, literally, 'cavalry commanders', usually anglicised to 'hipparchs'. A hipparch would, we might reasonably imagine, command a *hipparchia*, or hipparchy (literally, 'cavalry command'), and we do indeed start to see hipparchies of cavalry appear in the accounts of Alexander's campaigns after this date. There are also some references to hipparchies before this reform was carried out; as early as 334, Arrian (Arr. *Anab*. 1.24.3) describes Parmenion being sent on a mission with 'a hipparchy of the Companions' and the Thessalian cavalry. It may be that the word was used anachronistically here (by Arrian or by his source), or it may have been an informal usage to indicate a group, perhaps of two or four *ilai*, though on other occasions, such as Arr. *Anab*. 1.18.2, 2.20.4, Arrian just calls these *ilai*. In 329, we find Ptolemy being put in charge of 'three hipparchies of the Companions' (Arr. *Anab* 3.29.7), while in battle against the Scythians in 329, Alexander 'ordered three hipparchies of the Companions and all the mounted javelinmen to charge' (Arr. *Anab*. 4.4.7). This is surprising if there were still only two hipparchs.

Curtius records further reforms to cavalry and infantry organisation. He notes (QC 5.2.6) that cavalry were previously 'enrolled in separate units according to their nationality, but he [Alexander] now abolished tribal distinctions and gave command of the units to men of his own

---

[1] Hipparchies – see Brunt (1963); Griffith (1963); Apergis (1997); English (2009) pp.44–50, Here I follow Sekunda (2010) p.453.

choosing without regard to race'. This is a difficult statement to unpick. The different words used by the translator ('nationality', 'tribal', 'race', translating Curtius' 'gens' and 'natio') used to refer to ethnic origins make it difficult to understand exactly what distinctions are meant (Macedonians, Greeks, Thracians, or regional differences within Macedonia or between Greek cities). However, the placing of commanders over units according to choice rather than ethnic origins was surely not a new development since allied units had often previously had Macedonian commanders. We perhaps see here a trace of the hipparchy reforms, in which cavalry began to be formed into uniform hipparchies rather than being separated into different ethnic or regionally recruited units. So far as we can tell, no equivalent changes were made to the infantry, and the Macedonian units continued to be separate and ethnically distinct.

The greatest changes seem to have occurred after Cleitos was killed by Alexander, in 328. After this date, we find a total of six men named as hipparchs. However, it is not certain that they were all hipparchs at the same time, so there could be some overlap, and although there is no single list (as there is for the *ilai* at Gaugamela), it is possible to make the number of hipparchies recorded add up to eight, including the Agema (the new name for the old Royal Squadron). Campaigning in India in 327, Alexander 'divided his army, and sent Hephaestion and Perdiccas to the territory of Peucelaotis towards the river Indus, with … half of the Companion cavalry and all the mercenary cavalry' (Arr. *Anab* 4.22.7), and a little later 'he himself took … the Agema of cavalry and other Companions up to about four hipparchies'. Presumably, this means the Agema plus three other hipparchies, so 'half the Companions' appears to be four hipparchies. Similarly, in 326–325, while campaigning against the Mallians in India, Alexander 'took with him… all the mounted archers and half the Companion cavalry' (Arr. *Anab*. 6.6.1) and subsequently issued independent orders to three hipparchies, those of Perdiccas and Cleitos (Arr. *Anab* 6.6.4 – this is a different Cleitos, 'White Cleitos', from the one killed in 328, 'Black Cleitos'), and Demetrios (Arr. *Anab*. 6.8.2). At the Battle of the Hydaspes, 'Crateros was left in charge of the camp, with his own hipparchy' and other forces (Arr. *Anab*. 5.11.3), while 'Alexander himself selected the Agema of the Companions, the hipparchies of Hephaistion, Perdiccas and Demetrios' and some infantry (Arr. *Anab* 5.12.2). This would give four hipparchies plus the Agema, but in the course of the battle, we hear that 'Coinos was sent to the right, with the hipparchy of Demetrius and his own' (Arr. *Anab* 5.16.3), which makes at least five hipparchies (six including the Agema) – and not long afterwards we hear again of the hipparchy of Cleitos (Arr. *Anab*. 5.22.6).

All of this might suggest that there were indeed eight hipparchies (including the Agema), but this poses two problems. Firstly, in the mutiny at Opis (324), one of the mutineers' grievances was that Alexander had enrolled Asians ('barbarians') in the Companions, and that he had created, in addition 'a fifth hipparchy, though it was not entirely barbarian, but when the whole cavalry force had been augmented, barbarians had been enrolled for the purpose' (Arr. *Anab*. 7.6.4). This would mean that before the creation of this fifth hipparchy there were just four hipparchies. The second problem is that if eight squadrons (*ilai*) were converted into eight hipparchies it is hard to see what the purpose or effect of the reform was. The end result would seem to be a very similar organisation and unit size and just a change of name.

Neither of these problems is insoluble. It could be, for example, that the losses suffered on the march through the Gedrosian desert so reduced the Companions that they were consolidated into four hipparchies, which could then be expanded again to five with the addition of Asians. As for the difference between eight *ilai* and eight hipparchies, it may be that hipparchies were larger (in terms of numbers of men) than *ilai* due to the addition of reinforcements. We have a very imperfect record of the reinforcements that reached Alexander during the campaign, and most were either infantry or mercenaries, but we have already seen above that Alexander received 500 Macedonian cavalry (QC 5.1.41). In addition, the Prodromoi/Sarissophoroi (on which see below) disappear from the accounts after the 329 battle against the Scythians, where Alexander 'launched at the Scythians first a hipparchy of the mercenaries and four *ilai* of the sarissophoroi' (Arr. *Anab* 4.4.6 – note here that mercenary cavalry too are formed in a hipparchy). It may be that these units, perhaps 800 strong, were incorporated into the hipparchies, so that the overall numbers of cavalry (now not strictly Companion cavalry) increased, allowing larger hipparchies to be formed, still eight in number. In addition, the difference between *ilē* and hipparchy was as much to do with the status of their commanders (on which see Chapter 7) and the tactical uses to which the unit was put – performing more detached, independent actions – as it was a simple organisational change.

These explanations are reasonable though not, to my mind, wholly satisfactory. That the Companions lost half their strength in Gedrosia seems unlikely, and it is not clear what would have happened to the hipparchs of the disbanded hipparchies. A total of eight hipparchies, even if containing around 3,000 men, does also seem too small a change from the eight *ilai* of 1,800 men. The evident confusion in Arrian over the designation of hipparchs and hipparchies and the lack of any clear listing of all the commanders together in one place leaves me with a low estimate of the likelihood that all the details of names and numbers of the hipparchies to be found in our sources are accurate and tell the whole story. To take an example, the confusing identity of the hipparchies at the Hydaspes has been mentioned above, but as Arrian himself relates (Arr. *Anab* 5.14.3–6), his two major sources, Aristoboulos and Ptolemy, gave different, incompatible, accounts of an important skirmish before the battle at which they were both probably present, and the details are different again in the accounts of Diodorus and Curtius. It seems likely that details of the designation of the hipparchies in the battle could also have become confused, and we do not know from which source Arrian drew each piece of information. The usual scholars' practice of extracting references to individual hipparchs from Arrian or other sources to reach a total of eight, on the assumption that they all record accurate, complete, and compatible information, may, therefore, be unsound.

As such, a more speculative account of the formation of the hipparchies may have as much chance of being correct as one derived directly from the confused and conflicting evidence in the sources. My own guess is that the name *hipparchia* was already in general use for a body of cavalry of indeterminate strength (like the *taxeis* of the infantry we encountered above) and *hipparchos* for a commander of cavalry, well before any of these reforms took place. When Alexander first appointed two commanders to the Companions (Hephaistion and Cleitos) and titled them *hipparchoi*, hipparchs, this would not have been directly related to the formation of hipparchies. The hipparchies themselves were formed subsequently by grouping together two squadrons (*ilai*). We might note, for example, that at Hydaspes the cavalry 'attacked not in line but by *ilai*' (Arr. *Anab.* 5.15.2), while the 'three hipparchies of Companions' charging the Scythians had attacked with '*ilai* in column' (Arr. *Anab.* 4.4.7), and in 325 Alexander split his army in two, taking among others half the archers, the Asthetairoi, and one *ilē* from each hipparchy (Arr. *Anab.* 6.21.3). This, combined with the creation of *lochoi* mentioned above, would give the Companions an organisation analogous to that of later Hellenistic cavalry we encounter in the Tacticians (though the precise unit names have changed), with two *lochoi* making an *ilē*, and two *ilai* a *hipparchia*. Reinforcements, the addition of the Prodromoi, and the inclusion of allied and mercenary Greeks (including volunteer Thessalians), and, later, Asians, would have increased the total number of hipparchies available, but there may only ever have been four hipparchies specifically of Companions, including the Agema, until the addition of an Asian hipparchy that so upset the men at Opis. The excess numbers of named hipparchs can be explained as hipparchies other than those of the Companions. We saw above that there was a hipparchy of mercenary cavalry, while Curtius' (5.2.6) story that after 331 Alexander ceased to divide the cavalry by tribal or national affiliations may reflect the creation of generic hipparchies formed from all the non-Companion cavalry available (mercenaries, ex-Prodromoi, Thessalians and other Greek volunteers). So, all cavalry of any origin (including perhaps the Asians, although they were not yet added to the hipparchies of the Companions) were formed into hipparchies, and Arrian's failure to distinguish clearly between Companion and non-Companion hipparchies is characteristic of his somewhat haphazard approach to unit identities. There may have been eight hipparchies in total (or even more, including all the Asian cavalry), but only four of these hipparchies were Companions. This interpretation has the benefit of fitting more easily with Hellenistic practice and with the importance attached by the Opis mutineers to the formation of a fifth hipparchy, specifically of Companions. Each hipparchy could have contained around 500 men, divided into two *ilai* of around 250, each in turn made up of two *lochoi* of 125. Certainty is, however, impossible, and no doubt debate on the question will continue.

One final point to note is that while the *ilai* of the Companions often had regional designations from the area where they were recruited, the hipparchies were named after their commander. Arrian records that on the death of Hephaistion, 'Alexander never appointed anyone in place of Hephaistion as chiliarch over the Companion cavalry, so that the name of Hephaistion might never be lost to the unit; the chiliarchy was still called Hephaistion's, and the standard went before it which had been made by his

THE IMPERIAL ARMY

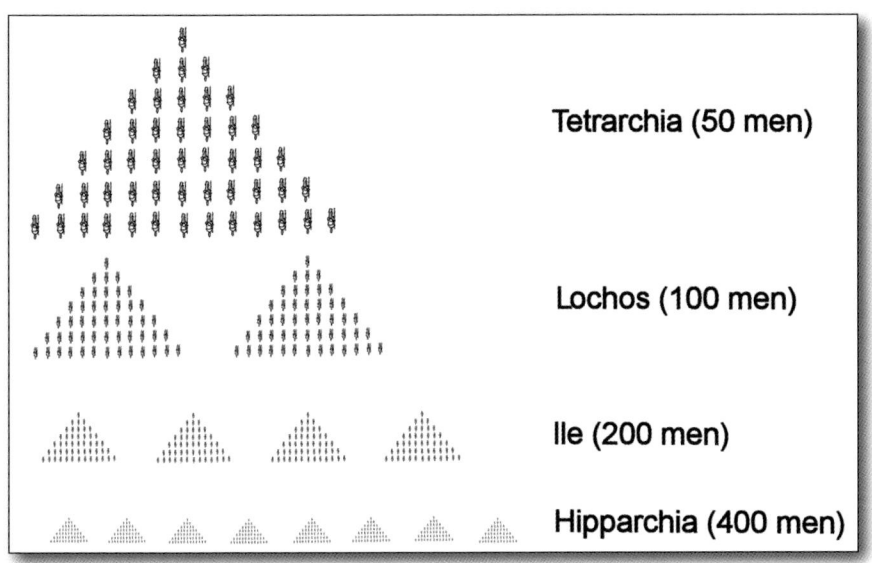

A possible organisation of cavalry into *hipparchiai* (hipparchies).

order' (Arr. *Anab*, 7.14.10). The use of 'chiliarchy' in place of 'hipparchy' is surprising and is probably an error of Arrian's.[2]

Note also the reference to the standard (*semeia*). There is only scattered evidence elsewhere for the use of such unit standards in Alexander's army, standards being better known among the Romans, but it is likely that each Macedonian unit carried a standard (probably a square flag mounted on a pole), evidently designed by its commander.[3]

The Infantry

Reforms to the infantry were of a more modest nature. The phalanx of Pezhetairoi and Asthetairoi seems to have continued largely unchanged into the eastern and Indian campaigns, although as we saw, it is possible that a seventh *taxis* was formed, commanded by Cleitos at the Hydaspes.[4]

During 331, when Alexander was at or in the vicinity of Susa (the old Persian capital), substantial reinforcements were received from Macedon, which might have gone toward forming the seventh *taxis*. According to Arrian (3.16.10-11), Amyntas, son of Andromenes, arrived at Susa with an unspecified number of reinforcements: 'Of these Alexander assigned the horsemen to the Companion cavalry, and attached the foot to the other *taxeis*, assigning them in accordance with their national origins (*kate ethne*).' According to Diodorus (who places their arrival before Susa), the reinforcements consisted of '500 Macedonian cavalry and 6,000 infantry, 600 Thracian cavalry and 3,500 Trallians, and from the Peloponnese 4,000 infantry and little less than a thousand cavalry' (Diod. 17.65.1). Curtius

---

2   Sekunda (2010) pp.453–4; Collins (2001).
3   Karunanithy (2013) pp.134–6; 199–201.
4   Milns (2003).

(5.1.40-41) agrees on most of the numbers but places their arrival at Babylon. Presumably, the reference to assigning these '*kata ethne*', 'by nationality', means Macedonians to Macedonian units (Pezhetairoi, Asthetairoi and Hypaspists), Trallians to Thracian units and so on, though it might also mean the Macedonians were assigned to their regional battalions. This was the largest reinforcement of Macedonians received, though further Greek forces arrived during the subsequent campaign, as will be considered below.

Curtius also records the reform we encountered in Chapter 4, where he relates that Alexander set up a panel of judges to award eight senior commands as prizes and divided the army for the first time into chiliarchies, units of 1,000 (QC 5.2.3). The men appointed do not appear again in the campaign, except Antigenes, who won the second prize and later appears as commander of the Argyraspides (Hypaspists). I do not believe it is possible to make much sense of Curtius' account, and he must have garbled some other reforms (perhaps separate rewards for valour and possible reorganisation into chiliarchies), and without further information, we cannot tell which units were so reformed. At any rate, in the later campaigns the *taxeis* of the phalanx appear to be referred to in the same way as they had been earlier, as Pezhetairoi and Asthetairoi, and named after their commanders.

However, the Hypaspists were at some point renamed as the Argyraspides, 'Silver Shields'. In Diodorus' account of Gaugamela, the Hypaspists are already referred to by this name (Diod. 17.57.1), but it is clear from Arrian's account that this is an anachronism and that 'Hypaspists' was still the correct name at this date. However, by the end of Alexander's reign, the unit had clearly become the Argyraspides, and this change is generally dated to the adoption of expensive new equipment noted by Curtius: in 327, preparing to enter India, Alexander 'added silver-plating to his soldiers' shields' (QC 8.5.4), and Justin (12.7.5) states that it was at this time that he 'called a body of his men, from having silver shields, Argyraspides.' Whether the design, style, or shape of the shield also changed at this point is not recorded; if not, then the Hypaspists would simply have had their smaller (and probably Macedonian-style) shields replaced with silver-plated equivalents. We need not read too much into the 'aspides' part of the name since as we saw in Chapter 4, Macedonians always called their shields 'aspides', and it is a generic word for shield, not a specific technical term.[5]

It may be that there were also equipment changes for the rest of the infantry. At the very least, there must have been a need for replacements for lost and damaged equipment after such long campaigns. Curtius (9.3.21–2) records issues of new equipment during the Indian campaign – arms sufficient for 25,000 men, with the old equipment being burned. It may be that this included changes to the shape or design of the shields of the phalanx, and if it is valid to see a switch between Argive shields, as depicted on the Alexander Sarcophagus, and Macedonian shields, of similar dimensions but different shape, as depicted on coins of the Successors, then it might have been at this time that the change was made. It is also likely that a new standard helmet

---

5   On the Argyraspides, Anson (1981), Lock (1977), Roisman (2012).

THE IMPERIAL ARMY

A Roman copy of Hellenistic painting depicting a Macedonian with kausia, purple clothing and Macedonian shield, from the Villa of P. Fannius Synistor, Boscoreale, now in the National Museum, Naples. (ArchaiOptix, CC BY-SA 4.0)

design – the pilos helmet with cheekpieces – was first distributed around this time. This helmet was commonly depicted on coins dating from around and after the end of the reign of Alexander, and the Roman writer Julius Africanus tells us that Alexander introduced 'Lacedaemonian' helmets (that is, the pilos) to his army (Jul. Afr., *Kestoi* 1.1.40-46).[6]

Greeks and Mercenaries

As we saw in the previous chapter, the Hellenic League contingents, and the allied forces such as the Thessalians, were dismissed when Alexander reached Ecbatana in 330, but were given the option to re-enrol as mercenaries, an option which many took up. In addition, there continued to be large drafts of reinforcements received from Greece and from the already-conquered territories, and as

---

6   Helmets – Juhel (2009).

Alexander and his commanders were now the only employers of mercenaries in this part of the world, large numbers would have been available. Although we clearly do not have accounts of all the reinforcements received, there are still some impressive numbers recorded. Curtius recounts that at Zariaspa in the winter of 329–328, Alexander was joined by 4,000 infantry and 1,000 cavalry, all mercenaries, as well as 8,000 Greeks sent by Antipatros, and other smaller forces (QC 7.10.11–12 – Arrian *Anab*. 4.7.2 mentions the arrival of these forces but not their numbers). Curtius records an even larger reinforcement reaching Alexander in 326, after he had turned back at the Hyphasis: 5,000 Thracian cavalry and 7,000 infantry (QC 9.3.21 – Diodorus 17.95.4 somewhat less plausibly estimates there were 30,000 infantry). As a result of such flows of reinforcements (and local recruitment, as we will see below), the total size of the army expanded dramatically. From the 47,000 men at Gaugamela, the army had grown at the start of the Indian campaign to 120,000 men, according to Curtius (QC 8.5.4), although this figure must be extremely doubtful. Arrian (Indica 19.5) repeats the 120,000 figure, but this is later in the Indian campaign and may include other units, sailors, and many Asian and Indian units. The total number of Europeans in Alexander's army at the outset of this campaign has been estimated at around 35,000 (including the Macedonians), though this figure may, in turn, be too low.[7]

Exactly what sort of soldiers these were – their equipment, their organisation, their ethnicity – is, however, largely unrecorded, nor is it clear how they were incorporated into the army. As we have seen, mercenary cavalry were probably enrolled in hipparchies equivalent to (but still separate from) the Companions. Infantry were evidently not added to the Macedonian contingents (except in the cases where they were ethnic Macedonians), so must have been added to, or formed, their own independent units, but as with the mercenaries in the earlier army, we have no clues as to what these units were. There is also no definite statement as to the equipment of such units – presumably both hoplites and peltasts were represented (the latter both Classical peltasts and Iphicrateans).

As with the earlier mercenaries and Greeks, these units are also largely invisible in the various battles, sieges and assaults of Alexander's later campaigns, and many must have been brought along largely in order to be left behind as garrisons or settlers in conquered territories. An example is Alexandria in the 'Caucasus' (in fact, the Hindu Kush mountains on the borders of India), where according to Curtius 7,000 older Macedonians and other retired soldiers were settled (though Diodorus reports in neighbouring towns 7,000 native settlers, 3,000 camp followers, and an unspecified number of volunteers from among the mercenaries, and Arrian 4.22.5 does not give numbers). If these muddled figures are anything like accurate, and given that it is unlikely that a large proportion of the settlers were Macedonians, these must mostly be Greek mercenaries. When Alexander advanced from Bactria towards India in 327, he left behind a garrison of 3,500 cavalry and 10,000 infantry (Arr. *Anab*. 4.21.3), presumably also mercenaries.

---

7   See the tables of unit strengths, losses and reinforcements in Engles (1978) pp.146–52.

1 – Alexander the Great
(Illustration by Renato Dalmaso © Helion & Company) *See Notes to Colour Plates for further information*

2 – Companion Cavalry
(Illustration by Renato Dalmaso © Helion & Company) *See Notes to Colour Plates for further information*

3 – Prodromoi Cavalry
(Illustration by Renato Dalmaso © Helion & Company) *See Notes to Colour Plates for further information*

4 – Hypaspist
(Illustration by Renato Dalmaso © Helion & Company) *See Notes to Colour Plates for further information*

5 – Pezhetairos
(Illustration by Renato Dalmaso © Helion & Company) *See Notes to Colour Plates for further information*

6 – Asthetairos

(Illustration by Renato Dalmaso © Helion & Company) *See Notes to Colour Plates for further information*

7 – later Pezhetairos or Asthetairos
(Illustration by Renato Dalmaso © Helion & Company) *See Notes to Colour Plates for further information*

8 – Javelinman
(Illustration by Renato Dalmaso © Helion & Company) *See Notes to Colour Plates for further information*

9 – Archer
(Illustration by Renato Dalmaso © Helion & Company) *See Notes to Colour Plates for further information*

10 – 'Iphicratean' peltast
(Illustration by Renato Dalmaso © Helion & Company) *See Notes to Colour Plates for further information*

11- Thessalian Cavalry
(Illustration by Renato Dalmaso © Helion & Company) *See Notes to Colour Plates for further information*

12 – Greek cavalry
(Illustration by Renato Dalmaso © Helion & Company) *See Notes to Colour Plates for further information*

13 – Thracian cavalry

(Illustration by Renato Dalmaso © Helion & Company) *See Notes to Colour Plates for further information*

14 – Thracian infantry
(Illustration by Renato Dalmaso © Helion & Company) *See Notes to Colour Plates for further information*

15 – Greek infantry (Hoplite)
(Illustration by Renato Dalmaso © Helion & Company) *See Notes to Colour Plates for further information*

16 – Hippotoxotai (horse archers)
(Illustration by Renato Dalmaso © Helion & Company) *See Notes to Colour Plates for further information*

17 – Hippokontistai (Arachotians)
(Illustration by Renato Dalmaso © Helion & Company) *See Notes to Colour Plates for further information*

18 – Persian Companion
(Illustration by Renato Dalmaso © Helion & Company) *See Notes to Colour Plates for further information*

19 – Indian infantry
(Illustration by Renato Dalmaso © Helion & Company) *See Notes to Colour Plates for further information*

20 – Epigonos/Persian 'phalangite'
(Illustration by Renato Dalmaso © Helion & Company) *See Notes to Colour Plates for further information*

When Alexander reached Opis on his return from the Indian campaign, he sent back 10,000 of the oldest Macedonian veterans (Diod. 17.109.1) and selected a force of 13,000 infantry and 2,000 cavalry – presumably mostly or all Macedonians – to retain as his field army (QC. 10.2.8). It was possible to have such a small army, Curtius notes, because Alexander 'had deployed garrisons in a number of places and populated the recently established cities with colonists who wanted only to make a fresh start'. However, as events after Alexander's death were to show, many of these settlers were less than keen, and there was a large-scale revolt and attempt to return to Greece. This does illustrate, however, that even though the army had grown during the campaign to a prodigious size, the core of the army that did most of the fighting was still relatively small and consisted of the original Macedonian units of Companions, Hypaspists-Argyraspides and Pezhetairoi-Asthetairoi. It was Alexander's attempt to supplement or replace these core units with non-Macedonians that triggered the Opis mutiny.[8]

Asian Contingents

Native Recruits

Once Darius was defeated and killed and Alexander became officially the ruler of the Persian Empire, he began to recruit from among his new subjects, the native inhabitants of the Empire, who, so far as we know, would have owed military service to Alexander on the same terms as they had done to Darius. Alexander may have begun recruiting from the conquered territories at least by 330 when he was joined by Lydian forces consisting of 2,600 'foreign' infantry and 300 cavalry 'of the same race' – Lydians, presumably (QC. 6.6.35). In 329, Alexander received reinforcements of 4,000 infantry and 500 cavalry from Lycia and the same number from Syria (QC. 7.10.11–12); these could conceivably have been Greek mercenaries previously stationed in those districts, or they may be native troops.

Perhaps the first Asian unit to be created was the *hippakontistai*, 'mounted javelinmen', recorded by Arrian as forming part of a select force for the campaign against the Mardians in 330. Alongside the expected Hypaspists, archers, Agrianians, two battalions of (probably) Asthetairoi, and Companions, are the *hippakontistai*, 'for by this time they formed a battalion [*taxis*]' (Arr. *Anab.* 3.24.1). Unfortunately, Arrian says nothing of their ethnic origin, and it is possible that these were Greek or Thracian cavalry, using their own native equipment. Arrian's use of the word *taxis* is also presumably non-technical in this sense, meaning just a 'unit' (cavalry would usually be formed in *ilai* or *hipparchiai*). These *hippakontistai* feature in a number of Alexander's selected forces over the next few years; for example, in 329, Ptolemy was sent in pursuit of Bessus with three hipparchies of the Companion cavalry, all the *hippakontistai*, a *taxis* of infantry, a *chiliarchia* of Hypaspists, all the Agrianians and half the archers (Arr. *Anab.* 3.29.7). At the

---

8   English (2009) pp.82–4 for garrisons.

crossing of the Jaxartes against the Scythians, Alexander sent ahead 'three hipparchies of the Companions and all the *hippakontistai*' (Arr. *Anab*. 4.4.7). They were evidently, given their selection for these special forces, considered to be among the elite units. The only time they are associated with Asian units is when in 328–327, they were sent to overwinter in Sogdiana with Coinos' and Meleagros' *taxeis*, 400 Companions and 'the Bactrians and Sogdianians attached to Amyntas' (Arr. *Anab*. 4.17.3). So, it is impossible to be certain as to the ethnic origins of this unit, but it remains a possibility they were locally recruited.[9]

We can be more certain, however, about a similar unit, the *hippotoxotai*, 'mounted archers'. These first appear – without comment from Arrian, or hint as to their origins – in 327–326 in India, when Alexander took 'the Hypaspists, archers and Agrianians, with Coinos' and Attalos' *taxeis*, the Agema of cavalry and other Companions up to about four hipparchies and half the *hippotoxotai*' (Arr. *Anab*. 4.24.1). They were to play a prominent role at the Hydaspes (326), where Arrian finally divulges their strength and identity; for his assault across the river, Alexander selected a force of cavalry and infantry including 'the cavalry from Bactria and Sogdiana and the Scythians, with the Dahai, *hippotoxotai*' (Arr. *Anab*. 5.12.2). A little later, in the battle itself, 'Alexander launched the *hippotoxotai*, about 1,000 strong, at the Indians' left wing' (5.16.4). These *hippotoxotai* had played an important advance role throughout the build-up to the battle, screening Alexander's force and engaging the Indian advance party (5.13.4; 5.14.3; 5.15.1), and their casualties (10 men) were singled out for special mention (5.18.3). Like the *hippakontistai*, they could be selected for special missions such as the force Alexander led against the Mallians, consisting of the Hypaspists, the archers, the Agrianians, Pithon's *taxis* of Asthetairoi, all the *hippotoxotai* and half the Companions (Arr. *Anab*. 6.6.1 – although at 6.5.5 the *hippotoxotai* were also left behind with Krateros, so in that case or this, *hippakontistai* might be meant).

So, these *hippotoxotai* – mounted archers, or horse archers – were Dahai, an Iranian nomadic people from east of the Caspian Sea, associated with the Sacai (Eastern Scythians) from the same region. They had fought in Darius' army at Gaugamela on the left flank, along with the Bactrians (Arr. *Anab*. 3.11.3). However, in the course of the battle only Bactrians and Scythians are mentioned (3.13.2–3) – perhaps they were considered interchangeable, as the Sacai too were *hippotoxotai*, who fought in Darius' army on the strength of an alliance, not as subjects (3.8.3). Evidently, Alexander was sufficiently impressed by their performance to recruit them at some point before the Indian campaign into his own army. They were probably armed and equipped similarly to the Sacai, that is, with trousers tucked into boots, a long-sleeved tunic with a coat worn over the top, all often decorated in bright colours and patterns, and wearing a pointed hat (the Persians distinguished between various groups of Scythian peoples by the pointiness of their hats). They were armed with bows, for which a combined quiver and bowcase was

---

9   Badian (1965), English (2009) p.51.

THE IMPERIAL ARMY

Saca tribute bearers depicted on the Apadana Palace, Persepolis, Iran, sixth or fifth century. (Amin Berenjkar, CC BY-SA 4.0)

The reverse of a coin of Idrieus of Caria, Turkey, depicting cavalryman, mid-fourth century. (Classical Numismatic Group, CC BY-SA 3.0)

The 'Solokha Comb', depicting a Scythian armoured cavalryman, early fourth century, now in the Hermitage Museum, St Petersburg. (PD)

carried, and perhaps with the traditional *sagaris*, a short pick and hammer. Nothing can be deduced about their organisation except that units of 1,000 were common in Persian and Asian armies generally, probably subdivided into smaller subunits of a few hundred.

As well as these frequently occurring units, we have a number of Asian units mentioned by name, particularly in the Hydaspes campaign, though without any further details. When Alexander prepared his crossing of the Hydaspes, Crateros was left in camp with 'his own hipparchy, the cavalry of the Arachotians and Parapamisadae', some Macedonian infantry, and 'the nomarchs [governors] of the Indians of these districts and their five thousand men' (Arr. *Anab.* 5.11.3), while Alexander's own assault force included, as we saw above, cavalry from Bactria, Sogdiana and Scythia as well as the Dahai (3.12.2). The 5,000 Indians are best dealt with first. As Alexander marched through Indian territory, he frequently required cities that surrendered to him to provide men (and animals) for his army. An example is the city of Nysa, from which Alexander 'requested' a force of 300 cavalry and 100 of the 'best' (wealthiest) men – the city persuaded him instead to accept 200 poorer men, but he still required the governor's son and grandson (Arr. *Anab.* 5.2.1–4). Clearly these forces are present as hostages rather than as real additions to the field army, and they were sent back to Nysa not long afterwards (6.2.3). Auxiliary forces or hostages of this sort will have been picked up frequently – shortly after Nysa, the city of Taxila provided another 700 Indian cavalry (5.3.6) – and served with the army probably for short periods. The Oxydracae provided 1,000 men for Alexander 'to keep as hostages if he desired or, if not, to have them serving with his army, till he had finished his wars against the rest of the Indians' (Arr. *Anab.* 6.14.3). Such forces would have provided local security where Macedonian or friendly local leaders like Taxilas or Poros were left in charge, supplemented by Greek or Macedonian garrisons. Poros, defeated at the Hydaspes but reinstated by Alexander, provided 5,000 Indians and a force of elephants (5.24.4), which Alexander employed in the siege of Sangala, another Indian city. Poros and his force were then sent to place garrisons in the cities that had surrendered to Alexander (5.24.8). In this way, Alexander was able both to secure the loyalty of cities that had come over to him and place garrisons without depleting his core forces of Greco-Macedonians. The downside, of course, was that Macedonian control over these regions proved short-lived. The Indian forces provided would have been a mixture of infantry and cavalry, along with some elephants. For example, Taxilas had provided Alexander with 25 elephants as early as 327 (Arr. *Anab.* 4.22.6). Alexander appears to have been unimpressed by Indian chariots, which were used to little effect by Poros at the Hydaspes, and, although he is said to have taken 500 offered to him by the Oxydracae and surviving Mallians in 326–325, we never see them used in action (Arr. *Anab.* 6.14.3) – perhaps they were pressed into service as transports.

Indian dress and equipment was described by Alexander's admiral Nearchos, and his account is preserved in Arrian's *Indica*. Indians, Nearchos tells us, wore linen (cotton) calf-length tunics, probably white ('bright in colour'), a cloak or stole around the shoulders, and a turban (Arr. *Ind.* 16.1–2). Some Indian infantry used long bows 'as tall as the archer', which Nearchos controversially reports they placed on the ground and braced with their left foot while shooting (Arr. *Ind.* 16.6). This has been doubted by modern scholars, with good reason, since it would make for an extremely awkward stance and the bow was probably shot in the normal way from a standing position. Other infantry instead used javelins. All, including the archers (Nearchos implies), used light shields (*peltai*) of rawhide, 'narrower than their bodies, but not much shorter' (Arr. *Ind.* 16.8–9). All, archers and javelinmen, also had a sword 'not less than three cubits long' (nearly one and a half metres, an astonishing size if true), wielded with both hands (16.9), but Indians preferred to avoid hand-to-hand combat. Cavalry carried two javelins and a smaller shield (*pelte*) than the infantry. Elephants were ridden bareback, without howdahs, with a driver and one or perhaps two fighting men on their backs, armed with javelins (as Poros was, Arr. *Anab.* 5.18.7).

The other Asian units mentioned – Arachotians, Paropamisadae, Bactrians, Sogdians and Scythians – were all cavalry recruited from the Upper Satrapies, the eastern regions of the Empire in which Alexander campaigned prior to his advance into India. They will have served in part as subjects of Alexander as the new ruler of the Empire and in part as auxiliary 'hostage' forces similar to the Indians. Many of these peoples fought on the Persian side at Gaugamela – Bactrians, Scythians and Arachotians forming the left flank cavalry (Arr. *Anab.* 3.11.3–6). We have few clues as to their equipment or organisation, except that the Scythian cavalry at Gaugamela are said to have been more heavily armoured than the Greeks (Arr. *Anab.* 3.13.4). They were probably organised in units of 1,000 men, though up to what total numbers we do not know.[10]

An Indian archer, on the obverse of an 'Elephant Medallion'. Note the long bow reaching to the feet of the archer. (Numismatica Ars Classica NAC AG, Auction 114, 2019, lot 123)

Asian Replacements

So far, we have been considering separate ethnic units of Asians added to the army as auxiliary forces or as local security and garrison troops. But Alexander, in the later years of his life, was also undertaking a more ambitious programme of incorporating Asians into the core units of the army, alongside or even (as they believed) replacing the Macedonians. Alexander evidently began planning this process quite early, since a large force of infantry had been in training during the Indian campaign. These joined the army at Opis in 324, when Alexander returned from the east, where Alexander 'was joined by the satraps from the new cities he had founded, and the other land he had conquered, bringing about 30,000 boys now growing up, all of the same age, whom Alexander called *Epigonoi* [Successors], dressed in Macedonian dress and trained to warfare in the Macedonian style' (Arr.

An Indian elephant of Poros in combat with Alexander, on the obverse of an 'Elephant Medallion'. (Numismatica Ars Classica NAC AG, Auction 124, 2021, lot 84)

---

10   Persian army units – Head (1992).

THE ARMY OF ALEXANDER THE GREAT

A third century depiction of an Asiatic horseman from Cyprus, typical of many of the cavalry of the Empire, in the Metropolitan Museum, New York. (Metropolitan Museum)

Anab. 7.6.1). Curtius notes Alexander's order for the recruitment of this force before the start of the Indian campaign, 'to serve simultaneously as hostages and as soldiers' (QC 8.5.1). This, combined with Alexander's move to pension off large numbers of Macedonian veterans (Arr. *Anab.* 7.8.1), and changes to the cavalry to be considered below, led to the so-called Opis Mutiny of the Macedonians in the army. When the Macedonians demanded they all be sent home, Alexander's response was to summon 'the picked men among the Persians' and give them command of 'the *taxeis*' (Arr. *Anab.* 7.11.1) and to create a complete replacement army: 'the barbarian force being drafted into the units [*lochoi*], and the Macedonian names – an Agema called Persian, and Persian Pezhetairoi and Asthetairoi too, and a Persian battalion of Argyraspides'. In the event, the Macedonian infantry backed down and were reconciled with Alexander, and it is not clear precisely what became of the *Epigonoi*. Alexander did, at any rate, pension off 10,000 Macedonians, undertaking to bring up their sons by Asian women as a further generation of recruits (Arr. *Anab.* 7.12.1–2). There is no indication that Alexander reversed his decision to enrol Persians in the phalanx, although in the wars of the Successors which followed Alexander's death soon after, we see only modest forces of 'mixed' infantry armed in the Macedonian manner, who may be the remnants of this force. The size of the *Epigonoi* – 30,000 strong, allegedly of a single age class, and largely disappearing after Alexander's death – suggests that their numbers may have been exaggerated. Alexander had no obvious need at this point to employ a phalanx more than twice the size of that with which he had conquered his Empire.

This was not Alexander's only move to augment or replace the Macedonian phalanx. At Babylon the following year, 'Alexander found that

Peucestas had arrived from Persia with an army of about 20,000 Persians' (Arr. *Anab.* 7.23.1), apparently recruited by Peucestas himself in his role as Satrap of Persia. In a passage we have already seen for the light it sheds on Macedonian organisation, Alexander 'enrolled them in the Macedonian *taxeis*' with three senior Macedonian soldiers leading each file, then 12 Persians, and finally another Macedonian. 'Thus the decad comprised four Macedonians, three on extra pay and one in charge, and 12 Persians; the Macedonians were equipped with their traditional weapons and the Persians were either archers or were provided with thonged javelins [*mesangkulai*]' (Arr. *Anab.* 7.23.3–4). This curious hybrid phalanx disappears completely after Alexander's death, and we cannot be certain if it was ever more than a plan or was actually created – Arrian's words certainly imply that the force did exist, at least for a short while. It is also not clear if this phalanx was to serve as well as or instead of the *Epigonoi*, nor is the relationship, if any, between Peucestas' Persian recruits and the *Epigonoi* clear. The terminology used by our sources often does not give clear indications of ethnic origin, with 'barbarian' and 'Persian' both being used as general terms for Asians who may or may not be actual Persians.

In such a mixed unit of Macedonians and Persians, we might speculate about the languages spoken and how orders were communicated. Alexander's army had always been multilingual, since the Macedonians spoke a language (or perhaps more accurately a dialect) that was not readily comprehensible to the southern Greeks. While all the higher-ranking Macedonians would certainly have spoken Greek (and many of the Companions were Greek) this was not necessarily true of the rank and file of the phalanx. The Thracian units would also have spoken their own dialects. With the addition of Asians to the army and the removal of some of the ethnic distinctions between units, this situation would have become even more complicated. The Epigonoi would have been taught Greek (or Macedonian) as part of their training, and we can assume that other recruits, like those of the mixed phalanx, would be expected at least to learn Greco-Macedonian drill commands. Asian units like the Bactrians and Sogdians would have retained their own officers, so that only the overall commander would need to speak Greek to communicate with higher command. The fact that on one occasion Alexander appointed an interpreter to command a mixed Macedonian and Asian force ('Pharnuches … who was expert in the language of the barbarians of these parts', Arr. *Anab* 4.3.7) shows that the language barrier could be a significant factor. It is unlikely that Macedonian officers would learn Asian languages, Arrian noting that Peucestes 'was the only Macedonian to change over to the Median dress and learn the Persian language' (Arr. *Anab.* 6.30.3).

From at least 330, after the death of Darius, Alexander began to recruit selected Persians into his inner circle, including the Royal Bodyguards (the infantry unit, not to be confused with the *somataphylakes*, the seven top-ranking attendants of the king). According to Diodorus (17.77.4), Alexander formed a unit of Persian *doryphoroi*, 'spear bearers' or bodyguards, including Darius' brother Oxathres (who was also made a Companion, Plut. *Alex.* 43.3). These appear to have been largely a ceremonial unit (they are named alongside Persian 'rod bearers' or ushers, who controlled access to the king, see also Plut. *Alex.* 51.1), although they were at least 500 strong, assuming these are the same men as the *Melophoroi*, 'apple bearers' (the name of the traditional bodyguard of the Persian king), mentioned as forming a ceremonial guard around Alexander's pavilion and 'dressed in purple and white uniforms' (Polyaenus 4.3.24). When Alexander fell out with his Macedonians at the Opis Mutiny (324), these Persian bodyguards briefly formed his sole attendants (Plut. *Alex.* 71.3).

As well as these additional infantry recruits, Alexander also began recruiting Asian cavalry, not just to their own separate ethnic units as we saw in the previous section, but to the previously all Greco-Macedonian Hipparchies. The timing of this change is controversial – it is only directly referred to in the context of the Opis Mutiny but in language that suggests that the process may have been ongoing for some years. When the *Epigonoi* joined the army, the Macedonians were aggrieved by this, by Alexander and Peucestas' adoption of Persian dress, and:

> ...at the incorporation of the Bactrian, Sogdianian, Arachotian, Zarangian, Areian and Parthyaean cavalrymen and of the Persian cavalry called Euacae in the Companion cavalry, in so far as they seemed to be specially distinguished by rank, physical beauty or any other good quality; at the addition to these of a fifth hipparchy, though it was not entirely barbarian, but when the whole cavalry force had been augmented, barbarians had been enrolled for the purpose. (Arr. *Anab.* 7.6.3–4)

In addition, a few named individuals had been enrolled in the Agema (of the Companions), and the Macedonians also objected 'at the issue to them of Macedonian spears [*dorata*] in place of barbarian thonged javelins [*mesangkulai*]' (7.6.5).[11]

The difficulties this passage poses for understanding the organisation of the hipparchies have already been considered earlier. We have seen that the Bactrian, Sogdianian and Arachotian cavalry were with the army throughout the Indian campaign. The Zarangian, Areian and Parthyaean cavalry joined in Carmania in 325, brought by their respective satraps (Arr. *Anab.* 6.2.5) – 1,000 strong according to Curtius (QC. 10.1.1) – and the Persian *Euakai* (the significance of the name is unknown, but presumably they were an elite unit) joined in 324. Given that the Asian cavalry in the Indian campaign must have been several thousand strong, and that a hipparchy, while its exact strength is unknown, was unlikely to have been more than a few hundred, we do not see here the wholesale inclusion of Asian units in the regular Greco-Macedonian cavalry organisation, but rather the enrolment of selected individuals, nobles (like the individuals named by Arrian), or those selected for their appearance or 'any other good quality', in the four hipparchies of the Companions, following the Macedonian tradition whereby the Companions were open to all talents. The fifth hipparchy created would have included larger numbers of Asians (though not even the whole of this hipparchy was

---

11 English (2009) pp.51–55.

THE IMPERIAL ARMY

Detail from the Alexander Mosaic depicting the cavalry guard of Darius These are the men who would subsequently have joined the Companions. They wear red armour with white piping, and yellow head coverings. (PD)

Asian, as Arrian notes – it probably retained Macedonian officers). It is also not clear if it was only the individuals enrolled in the existing Companion hipparchies who were re-equipped with Macedonian weapons or if the fifth hipparchy was re-equipped also. Most likely, given the mixed origins and, therefore mixed equipment of the recruits, there was standardisation – to Macedonian patterns – of equipment.

By the end of Alexander's reign, the army was beginning to take on a very different form from that it had at the outset. The numbers of Macedonians were nearly halved with the retirement of the veterans, there was a new Asian phalanx, or a mixed phalanx of Macedonians and Persians, and Asians were being enrolled in the Companion cavalry and the infantry guards. However, all of this ethnic integration was to end abruptly with Alexander's death, as few of his Successors (the possible exception is Peucestas) had any interest in the integration of Europeans and Asians in the army, the policy remained unpopular with the Macedonian infantry themselves, and in the wars of the Successors, and the Hellenistic kingdoms they gave rise to, there was a strict demarcation between Greco-Macedonians who served in the heavy, regular units and Asians who provided only light and auxiliary troops. We can only guess how Alexander's hybrid army might have performed if he had lived to carry out his alleged plans to march west against Africa and Italy.

7

Command and Operations

High-Level Command

We have already seen the low-level command structure of the army in each of the preceding chapters; soldiers of each type were grouped into units under officers, with a probable hierarchy of commands, though we never see more than two levels of officers in practice, aside from the junior officers of the individual phalanx file. These officers were Macedonians, in the case of the native Macedonian units. Mercenary units appear (so far as we can tell) also to have had Macedonian officers placed over them, but allied units may have brought their own commanders with them. In the case of the Greek allies, at least, none of these commanders is ever named and barely even alluded to except in the vaguest terms, as at Gaugamela where 'the commanders of the troops which formed the reserve to the first phalanx quickly learned what had happened [the Persian penetration of the line], turned about face, according to previous orders' and counterattacked the Persians (Arr. *Anab.* 3.14.6). There may however have been an overall commander of the allies: Antigonos, then Balacros, are so named at Arr. *Anab.* 1.29.3.

There was a body of commanders of individual units: the *taxeis* of Pezhetairoi and Asthetairoi, *chiliarchiai* of Hypaspists, *ilai* of Companions and *lochoi* of the allied and mercenary infantry, each had their own named and appointed officer in charge. The selection of these officers was nominally completely at the discretion of the king, Alexander, though in practice, there were limitations on his freedom of action. Allied units might come with their own officer in charge, appointed by their home city, while the Pezhetairoi and Asthetairoi, recruited regionally, were commanded by their own regional nobility, men who were independently powerful within the kingdom and would expect the privilege of leading their own *taxeis*. This meant that command of a given *taxis* could be retained by a single powerful family; for example, the Tymphaean taxis was commanded by Amyntas, son of Andromenes, at the Granicus (Arr. *Anab.* 1.14.2), by his brother Simmias at Gaugamela (3.11.9), and another brother, Attalos, later in India (5.12.1).

Another feature of phalanx command is recorded by Arrian; deploying against Selge (334–333), the Hypaspists were on the right as usual, 'and next to them the Pezhetairoi extended to the left wing, each *taxis* under the commander in the order of precedence for the day' (Arr. *Anab.* 1.28.3). We can compare with the Companions at the Granicus, where Socrates' squadron (under another commander) led the attack, Arrian noting that 'this was on the list as leading the whole cavalry on that day' (Arr. *Anab.* 1.14.6). Apparently, the order of units in the battle line varied from day to day in a rotating order of precedence (the same might have been true of the Hypaspists at the Hydaspes (Arr. *Anab.* 5.13.4), but Arrian's meaning, in this case, is far from certain). This was not a rigid system, as at the major battles, Coinos' *taxis* is on the right and Crateros' on the left, which suggests that on these occasions, at least, the order of precedence was fixed.

In addition, there was a level of command above that of the individual units. However, this appears to have been implemented more haphazardly and was clearly and explicitly driven by political as much as by military considerations. It is a feature of armies of this period that, while there would often be officers in formal positions of command over individual units, there was no formal higher-level command structure, no equivalent to the divisions and corps of more modern armies, and instead, senior commanders were placed over large bodies of men, on campaign and in battle, according to the wishes of the king or general, and political imperatives in force at the time.[1]

In the case of Alexander's army, this means that, for example, while each individual *taxis* of the Pezhetairoi and Asthetairoi had a commander, there was no overall commander of the whole phalanx (in battle, Crateros often effectively had this role). A few higher-level units do have their own commanders – the Hypaspists and the Companion cavalry each had their own commanders, respectively Nicanor and Philotas, both sons of Parmenion, and as noted above, there may have been an overall commander of the Greek allies. For his part, Parmenion was nominally in command of the Thessalian cavalry, although he was also Alexander's second in command and so, in battle, commanded the left wing and, on campaign, received the largest independent commands. Parmenion had been Philip II's right-hand man also, and Alexander 'inherited' him along with the rest of the army. His support was no doubt essential in Alexander's relatively smooth accession to the throne. The first years of Alexander's campaign, up to 330, were characterised by the importance of Parmenion and his family, and senior commands went naturally to them. All this changed after 330 when Philotas was implicated in the 'Pages Conspiracy', and both he and Parmenion were executed (Nicanor had earlier died of natural causes). Alexander, freed from their influence, instituted the reforms to the command of the Companions that we saw earlier, dividing up command between separate hipparchs and having no overall commander. There also does not seem to have been an overall commander of the Hypaspists after Nicanor. Alexander also set his official historian to portraying Parmenion as over-cautious, in contrast to Alexander's own dash and flair, resulting in a series of unlikely stories of Parmenion's advice being overridden. For independent operations, Alexander would often send Parmenion with some subset of the army or would appoint

---

1 High level command in general, Fuller (1960), Griffith (1980), Heckel (1992), Heckel (2003).

some other one of his Companions (that is, of his inner circle, rather than the Companion cavalry) and assign them some units on an ad hoc basis, as required in the circumstances. There was no official ranking among the Companions – selection depended on the favour of Alexander and also on the political power and influence that the individual was able to wield.

After the Philotas affair, Alexander no longer trusted command of the Companion cavalry to any one individual and instead split command between Hephaistion and Black Cleitos. As the organisation of the cavalry was altered to increase the number of hipparchies (whether to four or eight), the commander of each hipparchy, the hipparch, became an important general in his own right, often given command of large sections of the army, as well as or instead of his own hipparchy, and tasked with independent duties. This is in marked contrast to the earlier *ilarchoi*, squadron commanders, of the Companions, who did not receive large independent commands and generally commanded only their own *ilē*. Correspondingly, the *taxiarchoi* of the infantry became less important, and officers like Parmenion or Crateros, who did have battlefield command of their own units but also could command larger subsets of the army independently, were largely, though not completely, replaced by hipparchs.

This change marks an important shift in power relations between Alexander, his officers, and the army. The Companionate of a Macedonian king (in the sense of his circle of adherents) was always open to all talents at the discretion of the ruling monarch, but, in practice, there were also independently powerful aristocrats with regional affiliations who could expect high command by virtue of their own exalted status. Obvious examples of such individuals were Parmenion, whose sons commanded the Companions and the Hypaspists, and Antipatros, who was Regent of Macedon and responsible for maintaining control over Greece in Alexander's absence. As well as being powerful men in the kingdom, these were men who had risen to prominence under Philip. Parmenion's removal marks a partial effort by Alexander to replace Philip's men with his personal friends and followers, men of approximately his age, often his boyhood friends. Such men would have closer personal loyalty to Alexander and little independent influence were they to lose Alexander's approval. This represents a multi-faceted shift: away from established aristocrats towards personal favourites of the king; away from older men who had made their name under Philip and towards men of Alexander's age; and away from infantry commanders and towards cavalry commanders. The growing rift between cavalry (and Alexander's men) and infantry (and Philip's men) was to become more apparent on Alexander's death when the two arms took opposite sides on the question of the succession – Alexander's unborn son or his half-brother by Philip – and was an important element in the early rivalries of the Successors.

The only group with a formal special status was the Bodyguards (*somatophylakes*), sometimes called Royal Bodyguards (*somatophylakes basilikoi*). This was not, however, a level of command but a special group, fixed at seven in number, of personal bodyguards and attendants on Alexander, and the men in these roles were high-ranking officers within the army. They would not hold independent command over any unit while they were serving as bodyguards, though they might hold temporary senior commands. The position was a mark of honour for the holder but was not purely honorific, as bodyguards fought alongside Alexander in battle and presumably were also responsible for his personal security in camp. At the assault on the Mallian city in India, where Alexander set an example by being the first to climb a ladder onto the wall, he was accompanied by Peucestas, not (yet) a Bodyguard, but assigned to carry the sacred shield which Alexander took from the temple at Ilium (Troy), and Leonnatos, who was a Bodyguard, along with (on a different ladder) Abreas, a half file leader (Arr. *Anab*. 6.9.3–104). For his efforts, Peucestas was later promoted to Bodyguard, the number being increased from seven to eight, specially to make room for him (Arr. *Anab*. 6.28.3–4). Arrian quotes Aristoboulos to the effect that Alexander wished to make Peucestas Satrap of Persia, 'but wished him first to enjoy this honour [that is, being made a Bodyguard] and mark of confidence as well'.[2]

Another relevant institution was that of the Royal Pages (*basilikoi paides*). These were formed from the teenage sons of the important men within the kingdom, who were sent to serve the king in various roles, including guarding the king at night (Arr. *Anab*. 4.13.1). Curtius adds additional tasks they performed: to "act as the king's servants at dinner, bring him his horse when he goes into battle, attend him on the hunt, and take their turn to guard before the bedroom door" (QC 5.1.42). This is widely seen as a way of introducing these boys to the life of the army and the court, establishing bonds between them and the king and getting them used to life within the camp, while also acting as hostages for the good behaviour of their fathers. Although sometimes described as an 'officer training school', there is no evidence of any sort of formal military training, though this may have taken place independently, outside the institution of the Pages.[3]

Battlefield Command

On campaign, independent forces were sometimes detached under senior officers and sent on separate missions. But for the major pitched battles, the army would ideally all be concentrated as one force under Alexander's direct overall control. Obviously, one man could not directly command the entire army on the battlefield, however. Hence, Alexander still relied on his officers for command and control, especially given the rudimentary means of communication available on the ancient battlefield. This means that large elements of battlefield command were delegated to a hierarchy of officers, not controlled directly by Alexander.[4]

Each individual unit, or the components (such as *taxeis*) of units, would have their own commander, who would be responsible for the direct command of that unit. In many cases, particularly the core Macedonian units, these commanders are named in our sources (especially in Arrian). Larger

---

2   Heckel (1986) on the *Somataphylakia*.
3   Sawada (2010).
4   Battlefield command – Wrightson (2010), Taylor (2020) pp.211–245.

groups of units could also be grouped together under a senior commander, who usually would also have direct command of a unit. For example, at Gaugamela, Crateros was commander of the leftmost *taxis* of the phalanx and also commanded the whole of the left wing of the infantry; in practice, this presumably meant his own and two other *taxeis*, and perhaps included the second line. We are not told who commanded the right of the phalanx (perhaps Coinos, commander of the rightmost *taxis*). The commander of the entire left wing was (as usual) Parmenion, who was also surrounded by (and perhaps therefore in command of) the Pharsalian squadron of the Thessalians, though the rest of the Thessalians were under Philip, son of Menelaos (Arr. *Anab.* 3.11.9–10). This was the same arrangement as at Issus, where 'Crateros had been put in command of the infantry on the left, and Parmenion of the entire left wing' (Arr. *Anab.* 2.8.4), and the Granicus (1.14.1), though here no senior command for Crateros is mentioned. The Hydaspes was a more complex battle, with several detached forces, but the pattern of delegated command is similar. Here, Crateros was left in command of the camp with his own hipparchy and other infantry and cavalry – characteristically, a hipparch could command both infantry and cavalry – and with orders to make his own crossing (5.11.3–4). Three taxiarchs, Meleagros, Attalos and Gorgias, were left with mercenaries and (presumably) their own *taxeis* to make another crossing (5.12.1), while Alexander himself commanded the main strike force.

Alexander assigned orders to these delegated commands in briefing meetings or councils before the battle, the night before, if there was sufficient notice of the coming engagement. At such meetings, all the senior commanders (which in practice probably means all the named commanders of units and above) were gathered, briefed by Alexander on the overall plan, and issued specific orders that they were to follow in the battle. Our sources often also report motivating speeches supposedly delivered by Alexander at this point; it is doubtful that the actual words of any such speeches have come down to us accurately, but certainly, Alexander would have taken the opportunity to motivate his commanders and remind them of their duties and the risks and opportunities ahead. The types of orders issued can be discerned from the accounts, although we do not have a complete record of any such orders. For example, at Issus, Parmenion was in command of the left 'with orders not to edge away from the sea, for fear the barbarians should surround them' (Arr. *Anab.* 2.8.4). We can assume that he had other more general orders, along the lines of 'engage the enemy right', but specific points to be aware of (staying close to the sea) were emphasised by Alexander. At Gaugamela, we do not hear of specific orders to Parmenion – presumably, the general order was again to engage the enemy right, and avoid being outflanked – but the second line 'had instructions to face about and receive the barbarian attack, if they saw their own forces being surrounded by the Persian army' (3.12.1). Conditional orders of this sort – in the event of A, do B – must have been common, and we see another example at the Hydaspes, where Alexander's orders to Crateros covered multiple eventualities: not to attempt to cross the river until Poros moved away or fled; if Poros split his forces and left elephants, to remain in camp; if Poros split his force but removed the elephants, to cross

(Arr. *Anab.* 5.11.4). Conditional orders like this could cover several options, but of course, Alexander could not predict all eventualities, and often it must have been necessary to inform the subordinate of the overall plan and leave the specific response to their initiative. This was so because Alexander could not see all events on the battlefield, given limitations on visibility imposed by flat terrain, large armies, a low point of view, and dust, nor could he send orders in a timely fashion, given that the fastest means of communication was the mounted courier and events in ancient battles happened quickly. For example, at Gaugamela, Alexander had no idea what events were taking place on the left of his line and depended entirely on Parmenion to manage this part of the battle. The first he knew of the difficulties Parmenion was facing was when Parmenion sent a messenger to report to him (allegedly – the reality of this message is disputed), and even so, by the time Alexander returned with reinforcements, Parmenion had successfully conducted his defence and defeated the Persian forces opposing him.

For units closer to Alexander, however, direct command was possible. Alexander could see the movements of enemy forces in the line directly opposed to him and could send orders directly to the relevant junior commanders of units detailed to respond. Such orders could be transmitted with signal flags or trumpet signals, but it is apparent that the type of orders that could be sent this way was extremely limited (usually, such a signal would be used to trigger the implementation of an already-issued order rather than to send new orders), and mounted messengers must usually have been used. For the unit to which Alexander was directly attached (part or all of the Companion cavalry), direct commands could be sent in the form of instructions that would be translated directly into the necessary drill movements and aided by the use of the wedge formation in which the only command needed might be 'follow me'. Gaugamela provides the best example of these sorts of direct orders. Here, Alexander first led off the whole army toward the right. When the Persian left attempted to head off this movement, Alexander 'ordered his mercenary cavalry under Menidas to charge them' (Arr. *Anab.* 3.12.3). The Persians sent reinforcements, on which 'Alexander ordered the Paionians with Ariston and the mercenaries to charge the Scythians'. The Persians then sent forward their chariots, which were met by the Agrianians and javelinmen who, no doubt following standing orders, met them with volleys of javelins, while the main line 'as they had been ordered, parted where the chariots attacked' (so this too was not a direct order, but a pre-arranged conditional or standing order). When more Persians attacked, Alexander again sent a direct order to Aretas to charge, until finally Alexander turned with the Companions, under his direct control, and the near part of the phalanx (presumably the Hypaspists) and made his decisive charge. This succession of direct orders to nearby subordinates contrasts with events on the Macedonian left, of which Alexander had no knowledge, but where Parmenion would have been issuing a succession of similar orders to the nearby units under his command in response to Persian threats.

This lack of direct knowledge of events on the battlefield outside his immediate vicinity was partly a result of the personal form of leadership adopted by Alexander and is sometimes criticised (in antiquity and by modern writers) as meaning that Alexander 'lost control of the battle'. In contrast, Roman generals, for example, often preferred to station themselves to the rear of the battle line and to retain direct control over a larger part of their army, committing forces as required to shore up breaks in the line or exploit weak points in the enemy line. Persian kings were traditionally stationed in the centre of their armies so that they could retain control over the whole army (Xen. *Anab*. 1.8.21), and at Gaugamela, we see Darius directly ordering each phase of the battle, committing forces to outflank the Macedonian right, sending forward the chariots, then ordering a general advance. However, there were good reasons why personal leadership was preferred in Alexander's army. Partly the reason is cultural – Macedonian military culture, steeped in Homeric values, required the king or general to lead from the front, to set an example, and to directly encourage his men to fight, and the success of this practice speaks for itself. There were also great practical difficulties in direct command, given the limitations of intelligence and communication, so a general with capable and trusted subordinates would be better allowing them to fight their own battles, under some general guidelines, rather than attempting direct personal control (or micromanagement). The nature of battle in this period also favoured personal leadership – Greek armies usually formed up in a single line of battle, and although Alexander often used a double line to guard against outflanking, most of the fighting was still done by the front line. This meant that there was no large body of reserves, as in a Roman army, which the general could use to alter the course of a battle, and battles were generally won or lost in the initial attack. A general stationed at the back in such a case would have had too little influence over the timing and course of the initial attack and no opportunity to use reserves to change the course of the battle. Personal leadership, at every level, therefore, made a great deal of sense in the circumstances of battle of the time, and undoubtedly was a major factor in the consistently high morale of the Macedonian army.

Operations

The marching training instituted by Philip II was intended to increase the strategic speed and mobility of the army, and Philip and Alexander's armies were noted for their ability to make rapid movements, often arriving unexpectedly in the vicinity of the enemy. A good example is the march conducted by Alexander from Illyria to Thebes on receiving news of the revolt of Thebes (Arr. *Anab*. 1.7.4–7). Alexander's army – a sizable force including several *taxeis* of the phalanx, the Hypaspists and Companions, as well as archers and Agrianians – marched from the Illyrian frontier to Thessaly in seven days (a straight-line distance of over 300 kilometres), and in another five entered Boeotia 'so that the Thebans did not learn that he was within the Gates [probably Thermopylae] until he arrived, with all his force, at Onchestos [in Boeotia]' (Arr. *Anab*. 7.1.5). Throughout Alexander's campaigns the ability to perform rapid strategic movements of this sort was an important element of the army's success. This rapid movement was due to a combination of the training instituted by Philip, the ability of the army to travel light without a large baggage train (Philip had restricted the infantry to one servant to every *dekas* or file (Front. 4.1.6), rather than the typical Greek ratio of one per man), a preference for not relying on wheeled transport but rather on pack animals (Plut. Mor. 177a, 790b), and for special operations, the detachment from the army of flying columns made up of selected forces – typically, Companions, Hypaspists, archers, Agrianians, and the 'most nimble' of the phalanx. Daily march rates for the entire army with its baggage, where known, are in the region of 15 to 25 kilometres per day. For smaller, detached forces this could increase significantly with marches of 50 to 60 kilometres being recorded on occasion. Smaller forces could move faster than large ones because they were specially selected for speed, they could leave behind their baggage, and there were fewer delays in starting, halting and traversing constrictions.[5]

In the early years of the campaign in Asia, up to Gaugamela, the bulk of the army tended to move in a single, relatively slow-moving column, with smaller forces detached for special missions, but the army could also be divided to accomplish varied missions simultaneously. An example is the movement of the army in Asia Minor after Granicus, where Alexander needed to take control of several cities and strongholds before Persian reinforcements could arrive from the interior (Arr. *Anab*. 1.18.1–4). After receiving the surrender of Ephesus, Alexander sent Parmenion with 5,000 Macedonian and mercenary infantry and 200 Companions to take the surrender of Magnesia and Tralles, Alcimachos with a similar force to further unspecified Ionian towns, and himself took 'the remainder of the infantry' (probably Macedonian and mercenary infantry), the archers, Agrianians, the Thracian cavalry and four squadrons of Companions to march against Miletus. The remainder of the army, including the Greek allies, remained in Ephesus. Similarly, in the winter of 334–333 (Arr. *Anab*. 1.24.3–4), Alexander sent Parmenion to winter in Sardis with some (a hipparchy according to Arrian) Companions, the Thessalian cavalry, the allies and the wagon train, while he himself with an unspecified force took a string of small towns in Lycia. The pursuit of Darius after Gaugamela involved a particularly gruelling sequence of forced marches, in which the baggage, female camp followers and heavier or slower units were detached, allowing the fastest and most reliable parts of the army – Companions and Prodromoi, mercenary cavalry, and the phalanx – to press the most rapid pursuit (Arr. *Anab*. 3.19–20). 'By reason of the speed of his march many of his troops were left behind worn out, while the horses were dying' (Arr. *Anab*. 3.20.1); clearly, such forced marches could not be sustained for long periods, and Alexander soon had to rest even this force for five days, before pressing on again with just the Companions, Prodromoi and 'the strongest and lightest of the infantry, carefully selected' (3.21.2). Despite marching through two nights this particular pursuit was unsuccessful, with Darius being killed by Bessos before Alexander caught up with him.

---

5   Engels (1976) pp.153–6 for data and discussion; Karunanithy (2013) pp.172–185.

Rapid marches could be especially effective in seizing choke points and passes. The passage of the Cilician Gates in 333 was accomplished by leaving Parmenion to follow with the heavy infantry, while Alexander marched ahead by night with the Hypaspists, archers and Agrianians (Arr. *Anab.* 2.4.3–4), taking the defenders by surprise. Shortly afterwards, Alexander sent Parmenion with the allied infantry (a rare independent mission for them), Greek mercenaries, Thracians and Thessalians to seize another pass, while the rest of the army marched down the coast (2.5.1). A rapid advance against the Uxians, after Gaugamela, was particularly effective (Arr. *Anab.* 3.17.3–5); Alexander advanced with the Hypaspists and 8,000 others in a rapid attack on the Uxian villages, then pressed on to the pass, sending Crateros (with unspecified forces) further ahead, leaving the Uxians 'astounded at Alexander's speed of movement' (Arr. *Anab.* 3.17.5). Immediately afterwards, Alexander detached Parmenion with the baggage, the Thessalians, allies, mercenaries and other heavily armed troops, while he led the phalanx, Companions, Prodromoi, Agrianians and archers to attack the Persian Gates (Arr. *Anab.* 3.18.1–2).

After Gaugamela, while there are many similarities with earlier practice, the strategic problem faced by Alexander was different. Previously, the main threat had been the large centralised Persian army, and the territory traversed contained several large cities, many of which were Greek or with Greek sympathies and could be occupied peacefully. After the death of Darius, with Alexander now in the role of Great King, the campaigns in the Upper Satrapies and India often take on the form of counter-insurgency operations. No single concentrated enemy force could threaten Alexander's combined army, but numerous small forces could conduct guerrilla actions which were difficult to subdue individually, while the few large and possibly friendly cities were replaced by large numbers of smaller towns whose sympathy for Alexander's cause was likely to be doubtful. Alexander's approach continued to be to conduct rapid special operations with flying columns while the main army, with its baggage, marched at a slower pace but with modifications to the command structure. These forces were no longer led by Parmenion or an equivalent but by a pool of trusted hipparchs, all men specially selected by Alexander himself. The campaign in Hyrcania shows the early stages of this process (Arr. *Anab.* 3.23–24). Here, Alexander divided the army (that part of the army that was present, he had already detached a large force) into three; a rapid assault force under his own command, Crateros with two *taxeis* and some cavalry and archers, and Erigyios with the mercenaries, baggage and wagons, to follow on a slower road. Rapid movement was still essential. Hearing of the revolt of the satrap Satibarzanes, who had killed his garrison force, Alexander took the Companions, hippakontistai, archers, Agrianians and two *taxeis* of Asthetairoi and made a swift advance, covering 600 stades (108 kilometres) in two days and frightening Satibarzanes into flight.

Dividing forces and placing them under, in some cases, untried commanders had its dangers. While Alexander was on the Tanais (Jaxartes) river, he despatched against another rebel, Spitamenes, three commanders with 60 Companions, 800 mercenary cavalry, and 1,500 mercenary infantry, under the overall command of Pharnuches, a Lycian diplomat (Arr. *Anab.*

4.3.7). This force fell in with Spitamenes, reinforced by a large force of Scythian horsemen, and met the typical fate of a slower force facing a mobile, missile-equipped enemy, being surrounded and shot down en masse (Arr. *Anab.* 4.5.4–9). In this case, a divided, unclear command hierarchy was a large contributor to the disaster (Arr. *Anab.* 4.6.1–2). Alexander responded by personally leading another selected force – Companions, archers, Agrianians, Asthetairoi – on another forced march, this time of a scarcely believable 1,500 stades (270 kilometres) in three days, from which, however, Spitamenes was able to escape. A long campaign in Sogdiana, employing numerous divided forces to subdue the largest possible tracts of country, was required before Spitamenes was eventually defeated.

The march into India was also conducted with the army divided into different columns. In 327–326, marching toward the Indus (Arr. *Anab.* 4.22–23), Alexander sent an advance force under Hephaistion and Perdiccas with three *taxeis* of infantry, half the Companions and all the mercenary cavalry to prepare a river crossing. Alexander himself took the rest of the Companions, the Asthetairoi, archers, Agrianians and hippakontistai, on a rapid march against the local towns. Numerous small forces sent on independent operations were characteristic of the rest of the Indian campaign. Typical is the campaign following the mutiny on the Hyphasis, where the army was divided into river-borne and land elements (Arr. *Anab.* 6.2.2). The Hypaspists, archers, Agrianians and Agema of the cavalry went by boat under Alexander, Crateros led infantry and cavalry on one bank, and Hephaistion led the bulk of the army, plus 200 elephants, on the other bank. Another force followed three days behind. These forces each had separate missions, although they coordinated camp sites (6.4.1). Shortly afterwards, the army was divided again (6.5.6), Hephaistion being sent on ahead, Ptolemy marching behind (in both cases, to capture fugitives from Alexander's own force), and Alexander leading the Hypaspists, archers, Agrianians, some Asthetairoi, the mounted archers and half the Companions against the Mallians, in a particularly brutal campaign. Before the difficult return march through Gedrosia, a larger division of the army was made, with Crateros being sent with three *taxeis* and the older age classes of the Macedonians, as well as the elephants, to return by an easier route while the main army proceeded across the Gedrosian desert (Arr. *Anab.* 6.17.3).

Although we tend to think of armies of this period marching freely across open countryside, in reality, much of the terrain covered was obstructed by natural vegetation or by farmland with all its walls, fences and ditches, and armies would, wherever possible, have moved by road. Although the centrally built and maintained roads of the Roman Empire still lay some centuries in the future, Greece and the Persian Empire were traversed by a network of roads, mostly built or created by local people going about their business between cities. However, there was also some centralised roadbuilding, notably the Persian Royal Road, which led from the heart of the Empire to its western extremities. Where there were no existing roads for armies to march along, new roads could be built specially for them. In 334–333 in Lycia, Alexander 'sent part of his forces through the mountain passes towards Perge, where the Thracians had made him a road, the approach being otherwise long and difficult' (Arr. *Anab*. 1.26.1). In India in 326, marching toward the Indus, 'his army as it went forward made a road, since the country here was otherwise impracticable' (Arr. *Anab*. 4.30.7). We must assume that these isolated incidents stand in for many similar occasions. Note again that the engineering work was undertaken by the men of the army themselves (or some subset, like the Thracians) and would have been directed by specialist engineers, the equivalent of the *mechanopoioi* siege engineers we saw in Chapter 6. For this purpose, Alexander's army was accompanied by a body of engineers and surveyors (*bematistai*); the special task of the latter was to measure distances along the march – many of their records have survived in the writings of later authors and show a high degree of accuracy.[6]

Among other natural obstacles, Alexander's march featured numerous river crossings. Where existing bridges existed, they could be used, but the army was also capable of building its own bridges. On the approach march to Gaugamela, Alexander first had to cross the Euphrates near Thapsacus, for which an advance force had been sent ahead to build two bridges. A Persian force under Mazaios was holding the opposite bank, which prevented the bridges from being completed, but when Alexander and the main army approached, Mazaios withdrew, allowing the bridges to be extended to the far bank (Arr. *Anab*. 3.7.1–2). On reaching the Tigris, however, which was found not to be held by enemy forces, the army simply waded across at suitable fords. Arrian (Arr. *Anab*. 3.7.5) notes that this 'was difficult because of the swiftness of the current', while Curtius writes a long paragraph about the dangers and difficulties of the crossing (QC 4.9.15–21). Still, the river was safely crossed and it would be nice to think that the Boeotian helmet now on display in the Ashmolean Museum in Oxford and found in the Tigris was lost in the course of this crossing.[7]

Where a river was too deep or swift to ford, and there was no time for building bridges, alternative means had to be found. Most commonly, the method used was to stuff hides with straw to create floats and rafts, on which the army could then swim or float across the river. This was a means of crossing rivers already used by the Assyrians and depicted in ninth-century reliefs, and still in use in parts of Asia to this day, though the usual practice is to inflate the skins with air. This method could be supplemented by boats or even simple dugout canoes. At the crossing of the Ister (Danube) in the campaign of 335, Alexander 'filled the leather tent covers with hay, collected as many as possible of the boats from the countryside made with single tree trunks… and ferried across as much of his force as he could in this way' (Arr. *Anab*. 1.3.6). The River Oxus posed particular difficulties, being wide (over one kilometre, according to Arrian) and swift, with little timber available for bridging, so again the tent covers were filled with straw and formed into rafts, allowing the army to cross in five days (Arr. *Anab*. 3.29.2–4). The crossing of the Jaxartes in Scythia, in 329, was accomplished in a similar way, with Alexander ordering hides to be prepared for the crossing (Arr. *Anab*. 4.4.2); on this occasion the crossing was covered by shooting from catapults set up

---

6 Karunanithy (2013) pp.209–14.
7 River crossings – Karunanithy (2013) pp.218–23.

COMMAND AND OPERATIONS

Skin rafts are still in use in parts of Asia, here to provide tourist trips on the Yellow River, China (PD)

on the near bank (4.4.4). The crossing of the Hydaspes in 326 required both 'rafts made of skins ... filled with chaff and carefully sewn together' (Arr. *Anab*. 5.12.3) and also boats, broken down into sections and carried to the crossing point, including some as large as *triacontoroi* (30-oared ships, quite sizable vessels, 5.12.4).

While rapid marches were an important element of the army's success, just as important was allowing periods of rest and recuperation, particularly before any major engagement. All of Alexander's campaigns contain periods of rapid movement followed by periods of rest in camp to give the army and its mounts a chance to recover, rebuild their strength and also enjoy some leisure activities. Before Gaugamela, for example, Alexander halted the army for a rest after crossing the Tigris (Arr. *Anab*. 3.7.5), then marched on until he received definite intelligence on the Persian army, on which he halted again for four days' rest (3,9,1), and after advancing within sight of the Persians the army halted to rest again (3.10.1). The army also spent the night before the battle sleeping while the Persian army stood to arms (3.11.1).[8]

Supply and Logistics

The logistics of Alexander's army are the subject of an influential (if controversial) specialist modern study and are probably better understood than that of most armies in antiquity, although, as usual, some even of the main points are disputed. The main point at issue is the question of how much food the army could carry along with it. Ancient accounts will sometimes refer to so many days' rations being carried, but calculations suggest that, with food consisting chiefly of grain (milled or unmilled), the weight of more than a few days' rations would be impossible for individual men to carry, while the limitations of wheeled transport at the time mean

---

8   Camping – Karunanithy (2013) pp.186–206.

that supplies could not easily be carried in wagons (and Philip was said to have discouraged the use of wagons by the army). Pack animals, while able to carry larger burdens than men, must also be fed, and would tend to eat more food than they could carry after a few days. Evidently, wagons were still sometimes used despite Philip's strictures – for example, Alexander had the army's wagons burned in 330 in Bactria (QC 6.6.14–16). But while we hear of figures such as 30 days' rations being carried (Front. 4.1.6), it is unlikely that this was possible except in rare circumstances, such as when food could be carried by river or sea, the carrying capacity of ships being vastly greater than that of pack animals of wagons. Instead, men will have carried with them (on their or their servant's persons, on pack animals or in wagons) a few days' supply of food and would have relied on constantly topping up these supplies locally as they marched. It is worth noting in the context of pack animals that the usual mules and donkeys familiar to Greek armies would have been supplemented in Asia by camels (apparently especially valued for carrying treasure, for example Diod. 17.71.2) and elephants, both of which have a much greater carrying capacity than equids.[9]

In Greek armies, resupply was typically accomplished by organising markets for the army, at which the men could buy their own food (often using money provided for them, along with their pay, specifically for this purpose). Alexander's army will have followed this practice also, but it was, of course, possible only in friendly territory and where arrangements could be made in advance, it being necessary to provide advance notice of the army's arrival so that sellers could gather together their produce at the agreed location. The Macedonian army, with its greater degree of professionalism and centralisation, would also more frequently have been provided with supplies rather than this being left to the market. This could take the form of food supplies gathered at central depot locations when in friendly territory, or in disputed territory would more often have involved arranging in advance with captured or surrendered cities for them to provide supplies from their central stores. Cities in antiquity generally laid up large volumes of provisions for their use, particularly to allow them to withstand sieges in times of war, so every city would have been a potential supply depot. In many cases, making such supplies available to the army would have left the citizens themselves short, a point which is rarely mentioned, but as the alternative for a city population to cooperating with the army was usually massacre and slavery, it may have been thought a reasonable deal.

The need for the army to obtain supplies from the local surroundings as it marched, rather than carrying supplies with it for long distances in a supply train, means that the modern concept of 'lines of supply' did not really apply to ancient armies. Although communication with home bases could be important for the receipt of reinforcements, for example, in terms of supply, it would be more accurate to think of a radius of supply extending a few days' march around the army rather than a lengthy line of supply. This means that a scorched earth policy, destroying the local supplies on which an invading

---

9   Engels (1976) (however, for criticisms of Engel's findings see Hammond (1983)); Sekunda (2007) p.330 n.17; Karunanithy (2013) pp.172–4; servants, pp.179–82

army would depend, was a plausible strategy for the Persians and was indeed proposed on several occasions. Before Granicus, Arrian tells us that at a council of war of the local Persian leaders, the Greek mercenary Memnon proposed that they should retreat while 'destroying the fodder by trampling it with their cavalry, and burning the growing crops, not even sparing the very cities' (Arr. *Anab*. 1.12.9). Such a policy was naturally unpopular with the Persian satraps, who would have been destroying their own subjects' livelihoods, and the territories on which their wealth and influence depended, while also admitting their inferiority to the Macedonians. As a result, the Persians continued to offer armed resistance rather than ceding territory. Curtius states that before Gaugamela, Mazaios was tasked with laying waste the area through which Alexander was to march 'for Darius believed that as his enemy possessed nothing but what they gained by looting they could be starved into submission', while Darius' forces could be supplied along the rivers (QC 4.9.7). In the event, a vigorous advance by Alexander drove back Mazaios' force before they could destroy most of the supplies (QC 4.10.12–14). After Gaugamela, and with less to lose, Darius intended to retreat into Bactria 'ravaging all the country and making further progress impossible for Alexander' (Arr. *Anab*. 3.19.1), a policy that was continued by Bessos (Arr. *Anab*. 3.28.8), but in each case, rapid advances by Alexander, combined with a choice of routes, the division of the army into separate columns, and the ability of the Macedonians to endure hardship, meant that the policy was not successful in stopping his advance. Local foraging and the seizure (or voluntary provision) of supplies stockpiled in cities or strongholds were generally sufficient to keep the army supplied through the Bactrian and Sogdian campaigns. After securing the surrender of the Rock of Chorienes, for example, the army was 'distressed by want of provisions', but Chorienes (ruler of the eponymous Rock) 'said he would furnish the army with provisions for two months, gave them grain and wine from the stores in the Rock, and distributed dried meat among the tents', this amounting to less than a tenth of what had been stockpiled for a siege (Arr. *Anab*. 4.21.10). These incidentally should be seen as winter supplies for a static army, and we need not imagine the army marching on with two months' supplies in train.

The march into India was similarly dependent on seizing or being provided with provisions by newly conquered territories, as on the Acesines, where Coinos was left behind to supervise the crossing of the river by the main force and the collection of grain and supplies from the local area (Arr. *Anab*. 5.21.1). The greatest difficulties were presented in moving the army across territory without large and settled local populations, where it became so much harder to find locally grown produce. The disastrous return march across the Gedrosian desert was rendered so difficult because of the sparse local population, and it was complicated by the need for Alexander to find anchorages and, crucially, supplies of fresh water for the fleet to use (Arr. *Anab*. 6.23.1–3). Such supplies as could be obtained were earmarked for the fleet (6.23.5). 'The inhabitants also were commanded to grind and bring down from the upper parts [of the country] all the grain they could spare for supplies for the fleet, with dates from the palm trees, and sheep for the army market' (Arr. *Anab*. 6.23.6). We may well imagine that the judgement

THE ARMY OF ALEXANDER THE GREAT

Modern armies in difficult terrain still use mule transport similar to that of Alexander – here, US marines on exercise. (PD)

as to what they could spare was not made with the welfare of the locals in mind. In the course of a 60-day march to the Gedrosian capital, Pura – where water and supplies were available again – the army suffered very heavy losses, particularly to the horses and baggage animals, which the men would kill and eat for want of other food (Arr. *Anab*. 6.25.1–2).

Intelligence

In the ancient world, strategic intelligence was gathered largely through diplomatic means – ambassadors to other states often had the dual function of performing their diplomatic mission and investigating the war-making capabilities of the visited state. Alexander sent some Companions to the Scythians in 329 'pretending it was an embassy to conclude a friendly agreement', but in fact 'to spy out the nature of the Scythians' land, their numbers, their customs and the arms they use' (Arr. *Anab*. 4.1.2). This could cut both ways, as in the famous story of the young Alexander quizzing visiting Persian dignitaries on military matters within the Persian Empire (Plut. *Alex*. 5). It was also common practice for exiles from a state to find refuge with its enemies, and to supply intelligence on their former home, as in the case of the exiled Spartan king Demaratos, who accompanied Xerxes' invasion of Greece in the fifth century and gave advice on the military capabilities of the Spartans, or the Macedonian deserter Amyntas, son of Antiochos, who advised Darius not to engage Alexander in the narrows at Issus (Arr. *Anab*. 2.6.3).

Operational intelligence, that which immediately concerned the movement of armies, like logistics, should be seen as extending over a fairly limited radius from the army itself, perhaps only a day or two's march (or less). Intelligence at this level was gathered in four main ways: through direct observation by the king or generals riding ahead of the army with a suitable escort (Arr. *Anab.* 4.24.8); by the sending of scouts ahead of the army with orders to report back on what they observed (Arr. *Anab.* 3.7.7); by questioning local inhabitants, particularly on matters of geography, but also for any information on the movements of enemy forces (Arr. *Anab* 4.30.6–7); and by capturing prisoners, or receiving deserters, from the enemy army who could give information with suitable persuasion (Arr. *Anab.* 3.8.1–2).

All these means of intelligence-gathering were utilised by Alexander's army at various times, with the combined information giving him an overall picture of the position and intentions of enemy forces. The approach to the battle of Gaugamela provides good examples. Alexander crossed the river Euphrates at Thapsacus while Darius was encamped, awaiting him. Scouts who had been sent out from Darius' army were captured and reported that Darius was on the River Tigris (Arr. *Anab.* 3.7.4), but when Alexander hurried forward, he found the river unguarded and crossed it. The army was rested, and then Alexander resumed the advance. Scouts (*prodromoi*, but not necessarily the Prodromoi cavalry) 'reported that some enemy cavalry were to be seen over the plain, but they could not guess their numbers' (Arr. *Anab.* 3.7.7); later, further scouts rode in, reporting the enemy numbers at no more than 1,000. Alexander advanced in person with two *ilai* of Companions and the Paionian cavalry and captured some of the Persian cavalry, 'from these they learnt that Darius was not far off with a large force' (3.8.1–2) – he was at this stage a single night's march distant. Alexander advanced through the night and had his first direct view of the Persian army on descending some intervening hills, at a distance of 30 stades (about 5.4 km) (Arr. *Anab.* 3.9.3). Here Alexander halted again and conducted personal reconnaissance of the battlefield, accompanied by unspecified *psiloi* and some Companion cavalry (3.9.5). The battle then took place on the following day.

The Issus campaign amply demonstrates the limitations and short radius of this sort of intelligence. Alexander and the main army were lingering in Tarsus while Alexander recovered from an illness. Parmenion was sent ahead to seize the passes ('Gates') between Cilicia and Assyria (Arr. *Anab.* 2.5.1). Alexander himself advanced to Mallus, subduing any opposition en route. Here, 'a report came that Darius with his full force was encamped at Sochi' in the Assyrian plain (2.6.1), two days' march from the Assyrian Gates (the precise identity of these various Gates is unclear in the sources, and is still disputed). Darius was advised by Amyntas, son of Antiochos, an aristocratic Macedonian deserter, to meet the Macedonians on open ground (2.6.3). Alexander now advanced to confront Darius, stopping at Myriandros (2.6.2). But Darius became impatient at Alexander's delays in Tarsus and beyond, and crossed the Amanian Gates to arrive on the coastal plain at Issus, a day or two's march behind Alexander's army (2.7.1), the two armies having thus passed each other without any knowledge of the other's proximity. Alexander heard (from sources unstated) that Darius was in his rear but, disbelieving the report, sent a shipload of Companions who observed the Persian camp at Issus from offshore (2.7.2). Before starting his march back to confront the Persians, Alexander sent ahead a few cavalry and archers to reconnoitre the road, then marched the army back to the Gates and spent the night there (2.8.1). The following day, he marched down to battle at Issus.[10]

Clearly, the radius of information was remarkably limited, a few days' march at the outside and often less, and the quality of intelligence that could be gathered varied dramatically. Only when an enemy army was directly in sight of the king could reliable information on location and strength be obtained. However, as to strength, Greek observers were notorious in their tendency to overestimate enemy ('barbarian') numbers. We must assume that more accurate estimates as to numbers were made on the field than were subsequently recorded in memoirs or official histories.

---

10 Devine (1985a).

8

Serving in the Army

Recruitment

The various ways in which units of the army were recruited have already been mentioned in previous chapters, varying as they did according to whether the unit involved was Macedonian, subject, allied or mercenary. To recap, Macedonian units were conscripted from the eligible population according to the region in which they lived, and their age. The precise details of how this was administered are lacking, as we have information only for Antigonid Macedonia, a century or more later, but it may be that arrangements were similar. At that time, each household was required to provide one (or more) recruit for the army. The call-up for recruits would probably have been sent around to each region, requiring a certain number of men to be gathered at a central place and time. Local officials would then have used their records to require the households to provide a recruit of the appropriate age, which in most Greek cities meant between the ages of 20 and 60 (the Antigonids, in emergencies, had to lower the minimum age to 16). This incidentally indicates a remarkably high level of efficient bureaucracy, even in a supposedly backward kingdom such as Macedon. The recruits would report to the designated location and be issued with their equipment, which, unlike in the Greek cities where each man provided his own equipment, was manufactured and distributed by the state. They would then be enrolled into the appropriate unit, for example, the local *taxis* of the Pezhetairoi or Asthetairoi or, if they were from a wealthy family, the local *ilē* of the Companions. They would also then begin to receive their basic training, though it is likely that potential recruits were also trained before being called up – more on this below.[1]

For the cavalry forces in particular, the Macedonian king had reserves of royal land within the kingdom that could be distributed to his supporters (in practice, to men in the army) as rewards and also to give them a source of income to allow them to equip themselves (not least with horses), and some financial independence so they could undertake military service.

---

1 Noguera Borel (2006), Hatzopoulos (2001).

Plutarch records that at the outset of the campaign, Alexander 'would not set foot upon his ship until he had enquired into the circumstances of his Companions and allotted to one a farm, to another a village, and to another the revenue from some hamlet or harbour' (Plut. *Alex.* 15.2). The Companions, in particular, would need to maintain a horse and to be absent from home for many years. Horses were evidently acquired by individuals, but army command could redistribute them at need – Curtius (QC. 7.1.15) records Antiphanes, secretary of the cavalry, ordering a Macedonian noble to 'follow the normal practice' and give some of his spare horses to others who had lost theirs.[2]

Much of this system, along with so many other aspects of the Macedonian army, was created by Philip II. In the speech which Arrian says Alexander gave to his mutinous army at Opis, he gives a probably exaggerated account of the social reforms that accompanied Philip's military reform programme:

> Philip took you over when you were helpless vagabonds, mostly clothed in skins, feeding a few animals on the mountains and engaged in their defence in unsuccessful fighting with Illyrians, Triballians and the neighbouring Thracians. He gave you cloaks to wear instead of skins, he brought you down from the mountains to the plains; he made you a match in battle for the barbarians on your borders… He made you city dwellers and established the order that comes from good laws and customs. (Arr. *Anab.* 7.9.2)

It is doubtful whether the circumstances of the entire Macedonian population could have been changed so completely in such a relatively short time, but it is certainly true that Philip and especially Alexander engaged in a massive programme of city foundation and expansion, creating urban population centres to act as the recruitment pool for the phalanx.[3]

Justin provides an image of Philip's reforms in practice:

> [Philip] transferred at his own pleasure populations and cities in accordance with his own idea of what places should be replenished and what places should be abandoned, even as shepherds move their flocks now to winter pastures and now to summer pastures. (Just. 8.5.7).

Justin suggests that the response to these movements was great unhappiness on the part of those transplanted, which may well have been so, but the military effectiveness of the policy cannot be doubted.

Traditionally, Greek armies fought short campaigns in the summer season, returning to their homes and farms in time for the harvest. This is often said to be because the hoplite class were farmers, and so were tied closely to their land, although the entry requirements to hoplite status were sufficiently high that most hoplites were landowners, not farm labourers, and their need to return home was more a need to supervise their estates than to bring in the harvest by their own efforts. Macedonian armies were not

---

2 Karunanithy (2013) pp.64–78.
3 Anson (2008); Hammond (1989a) pp.152–65 for internal reforms.

tied to the campaign season in the same way, with Alexander's army serving overseas for many continuous years. Evidently, recruitment operated in such a way that agriculture could carry on back home while the soldier was absent. The Antigonid recruitment system based on households may be one explanation for this, as, provided the household contained more than one adult male and they were not all recruited at the same time, the farm could be kept running. The urbanisation programme would also serve to break the direct link between soldiers and the land, with slave or poor labour being used to run farms while the soldier classes moved to the new cities.[4]

Subject and allied units would have been formed somewhat differently. We do not know the terms on which Alexander levied soldiers from his newly conquered territory. Presumably, he took over the existing Persian systems, which were broadly similar, being a system of regional conscription, where local administrators were required to provide a stated number of men. Allied units would have been recruited according to the methods of their own state; in this case, Alexander's officials would have required the given city or kingdom to provide a unit of a given strength (specified, for example, by the constitution of the Hellenic League). Men would then have been recruited and supplied according to the providing city's own systems and would come complete as a fully functioning unit, including with its officers, though a Macedonian officer might have been placed in overall command.

Mercenaries were different again. There were two main systems for mercenary recruitment in the Hellenistic period; central recruitment from allies or individual volunteers. In the former case, a treaty would be concluded with another city or state, permitting the signatories to recruit each other's citizens (such treaties usually worked both ways). The resulting units would then have been very similar to allied units but recruited by officials of the other power rather than under local systems. This form of recruitment became common in the Hellenistic period but was rarer in Alexander's time. More common was the recruitment of individual volunteers. Those wishing to serve as mercenaries could come to some central recruiting location and sign up, or recruiting officers could be sent to friendly states to seek volunteers. Either way, individuals would enrol (in practice, it was no doubt very common for groups of men from one location to sign up together) and be assigned, by the officials of the recruiting army, to an appropriate mercenary unit. Rates of pay and length of service would be agreed at this time also, or else men may have signed up for indefinite service. Most such mercenaries, especially if they were to fight as hoplites, would provide their own equipment (shield and spear at a minimum), although wealthier recruiters, like Alexander later in his reign, could provide equipment centrally – this would be particularly necessary if a particular type of soldier was to be recruited, rather than generic hoplites or peltasts.[5]

It is worth noting also that, in Alexander's Empire, the central army under Alexander was not the only recruiter of mercenaries, as individual satraps

---

4   Millett (2010).
5   Karunanithy (2013) pp.40–63 on supply of arms.

could, as they had under the Persian kings, recruit private mercenary armies. Such private armies could pose a threat to central authority, and according to Diodorus, on his return from the Gedrosian desert march, Alexander 'wrote to all his generals and satraps in Asia, ordering them, as soon as they had read his letter, to disband all their mercenaries instantly' (17.106.3). This was said to have been a response to reports of satrapal disloyalty or malpractice, and we may doubt that Alexander really intended to unleash thousands of unemployed mercenaries to wander the kingdom unsupervised, one possibility being that he intended to enrol these men into the central army to make up losses from the desert march.[6]

Training

Traditionally, Greek hoplite armies had eschewed any sort of formal training, believing that the necessary martial skills required of a gentleman hoplite would come naturally, or could be acquired during visits to the gymnasium for exercise. Already by the later fifth century, this picture was beginning to change, with professional trainers in fighting skills (*hoplomachia*) and in organisation and drill (*techne taktike*) being available for hire, though they were usually employed on a private basis by individuals. During the fourth century, we increasingly see small professional bodies of selected hoplites (*epilektoi*), paid and on permanent service, who would also be trained at state expense. One of the most important of Philip II's acts in creating his new Macedonian army was to massively expand this sort of training to cover the entire heavy infantry – the men of the phalanx.

Diodorus describes how, early in his reign, Philip II set about reforming the Macedonian army:

> …bringing together the Macedonians in a series of assemblies and exhorting them with eloquent speeches to be men, he built up their morale, and, having improved the organisation of his forces and equipped the men suitably with weapons of war, he held constant manoeuvres of the men under arms and competitive drills. (Diod 16.3.1)

Here we see all the important components of the reform programme: direct inspiration of the men by speeches at meetings and assemblies (think of the party conventions of modern times); reforming organisation, weapons and formations (that is, creating the Macedonian phalanx); and holding frequent drills to train the men in their new tactics. Note also the use of competitive drills – ancient Greece was a fiercely competitive world, and even military drills could be turned into a competition, with prizes and rewards for those who best learned their lessons. On Alexander's accession, he 'established his authority far more firmly than any did in fact suppose possible, for he was quite young and for this reason not uniformly respected, but first he

---

6   English (2009) pp.90–2.

promptly won over the Macedonians to his support by tactful statements' (Diod. 17.2.2).[7]

Polyaenus provides more details on one aspect of the training:

> Philip accustomed the Macedonians to constant exercise, before they went to war: so that he would frequently make them march three hundred stades [54 km], carrying with them their helmets, shields, greaves, and spears; and, besides those arms, their provisions likewise, and utensils for common use. (Polyaen. 4.2.10).

Building fitness, stamina and endurance were the chief objectives of this sort of training, but given the drill required by the pike phalanx, there would also have been extensive drill training for all recruits. Diodorus reports that on Alexander's accession to the throne, he 'busied his soldiers with constant training in the use of their weapons and with tactical exercises, and established discipline in the army' (Diod. 17.2.3, it would be more accurate to say that he confirmed discipline in the army).

At precisely which point in their careers soldiers received this training is less clear. It is possible that men who were called up were then trained for the first time or that training was provided at a certain age (such as 18 to 20, the typical age for 'ephebic' training – the training of young men, in Greek cities), with possible refresher training whenever these men were subsequently conscripted. This was certainly the case for the 30,000 Epigonoi that Alexander ordered to be trained while he was in India, who received a full programme of training under 'supervisors and teachers of the arts of war' (Diod. 17.108.1; Arr. *Anab.* 7.6.1). As a result of this state-administered training, Philip's army was the first large scale professional army in Greece and was therefore capable of both strategic and tactical manoeuvres which would not have been possible for most Greek city armies of the period, or indeed for the largely conscript Persian armies faced by Alexander (although Persian armies likely had at least a small professional, trained core).[8]

The extent to which such training was extended to other non-Macedonian units in Philip and Alexander's army is unclear. It is likely that mercenaries at least were also trained, since there was a strong precedent in rulers such as Jason of Pherai (in Thessaly), who had also provided training for his mercenary forces (Xen. *Hell.* 6.1.6). Allied units, such as the Greeks and Thracians, were likely not included in Macedonian training programmes. In the case of Thracians, most likely their natural warlike lifestyle and culture were considered sufficient, and fighting in traditional fashion with javelins and more open order they did not have the same training requirements as the men of the phalanx.

Another feature of Macedonian units was the combination of disciplined manoeuvres in silence and a resounding war cry at the moment of attack, both points stressed by Arrian in the speech he claims Alexander gave before

---

7 Training – Karunanithy (2013) pp.19–29, Taylor (2021) pp.182–91 for Greeks. Examples of contests and competitions in English (2009) p.9.
8 Sekunda (2010) p.464; Hatzopoulos (2001); ephebic training under the Antigonids, Gauthier and Hatzopoulos (1993).

Gaugemela (Arr. *Anab*. 3.9.7; cf. 1.6.1). Greek armies had traditionally been subject to a certain amount of chatter in the ranks, even to the extent of men shouting advice to their commanders, but the Macedonians were trained to drill in silence, a matter of practical importance since it made it easier to hear the words of command (cf. Asclep. 12.10-11). When the order was given to attack, however, they would shout their war cry, described by Arrian with the verb 'alalazo' (for example, at the Granicus, Arr. *Anab*. 1.14.7) and often taken to mean literally shouting 'alalala' (though the word can mean to shout in various ways). At the Granicus, the shout was described as 'to Enyalios' (another name for Ares, god of war), so this may be literally what was shouted. The war cry was a Greek tradition, used, for example, by the Ten Thousand as described by Xenophon ('they struck up the paean [battle hymn] and after that raised the battle-cry', Xen. *Anab*. 6.5.27). The effect could be enhanced (though not presumably while charging) by simultaneously clanging the shield against the spear (Arr. *Anab*. 1.6.4).

Pay and Motivation

Once enrolled in the army, the men would have required pay, and also rations, which could take the form either of cash, along with the provision of markets where they could buy their own supplies, or of centrally-provided food stores. There is no reason to suppose that the Macedonians in the army did not receive pay. Just because they were conscripted does not mean they were not paid, probably at a similar rate to mercenaries, and plunder from enemy cities would be in addition to normal pay, not in lieu of it. The actual levels of pay are not known with certainty, the only direct evidence being the reference in Arrian (Arr. *Anab*. 7.23.3–4) to the file leader and half file leaders receiving extra pay. The 'ten stater men' also received enhanced pay, but it is not certain (since the value of the 'stater' varied, and it is not clear over what period this sum was received) what this amounts to in daily terms – likely around eight obols per day. Typical daily pay for a soldier in the Hellenistic period was around six obols (one drachma) a day, an amount which is comparable to the pay for a skilled labourer. Inflation and the changing value of money make comparisons with different periods difficult, but typical pay in Alexander's army was probably in the range of four to six obols per day. A reasonable guess would be that a regular phalangite would earn four obols rising to six for a member of the Hypaspists (a fragmentary contemporary document, a treaty between Athens and Alexander, specifies this amount), or eight for a junior officer.[9]

Particularly at the start of the campaign, this pay was not given out regularly, but in arrears, as and when funds became available. For example, Diodorus records that, following the capture of Babylon, Alexander 'distributed to each of the cavalrymen six minas, to each of the allied cavalrymen five, and to the Macedonians of the phalanx two, and he gave to all

---

[9] Sekunda (2010) p.465; Milns (1987); Hypaspist pay; IG II² 329, with Worthington (2004) for dating.

the mercenaries two months' pay' (Diod. 17.64.6 – Curtius 5.1.45 gives the same figures, with minas translated to denarii for his Roman audience, but specifies three months' pay). A mina is 100 drachmas, so for the infantry, 200 drachmas would represent over 200 days' pay. Rations or payment for food must, of course, have been received more regularly, or else men given the chance to plunder or forage for their own supplies. If pay was not received in a sufficiently timely fashion, it could lead to discontent and even mutiny, as is attested for Philip's army at least, although the men were tolerant of some delay, provided there were reasonable prospects of receiving pay in the not-too-distant future.[10]

The early years of Alexander's campaign, in particular, were marked by a shortage of cash for army pay. Arrian's version of Alexander's speech at Opis claims that Alexander inherited from Philip a treasury of just 60 talents, and debts of 500 talents – which Alexander increased with another 800 talents of borrowing (Arr. *Anab.* 7.9.6). A talent is 6,000 drachmas, so enough to pay (assuming an average of one drachma per man) a day's pay to 6,000 men. An army of 45,000 men, the approximate size of the army at the start of the campaign, at this rate, would consume 60 talents in just eight days. Alexander's borrowing, 800 talents, would last 106 days. Where possible, conquered cities, just as they were made to provide rations for the army, could be required to provide cash for pay; Arrian records that Aspendus, in return for not receiving a Macedonian garrison after its surrender, provided 50 talents for army pay (Arr. *Anab.* 1.26.3). When the Aspendians tried to renege on this agreement, Alexander increased the sum to 100 talents, plus yearly tribute to be paid to Macedon (1.27.4). Later in the campaign, as Alexander captured the main Persian treasuries, such cash flow problems receded significantly.

As the pay received was carried by each individual and there was little or no opportunity in Alexander's long campaign to bank or stash the money in a safe location, it is easy to understand the importance of a fortified camp for the army, of a strong guard for the camp, and the attraction of plundering an enemy camp. Even so, by the end of Alexander's campaign, despite the years of paid service supplemented by potentially vast amounts of Persian loot, many men had run up considerable debts, which Alexander offered to pay off when the men were sent home, said to be a total of 9,870 talents (Plut. *Alex.* 70). It is unclear who the creditors were, presumably the train of merchants that followed the army, who through this transaction alone will have become very rich men.

As well as regular pay, Alexander, once he started to acquire the massed treasures of the Persian Empire, was able to pay out special bonuses to the army. Such bonuses were paid to the allied units when they were dismissed from the army at Ecbatana, Alexander 'giving the agreed pay in full, and adding as a personal gift two thousand talents' (Arr. *Anab.* 3.19.5). We do not know precisely how many allies there were, so the exact amount per man cannot be calculated, but between the 7,000 or so allied infantry, the

---

10   Carney (1996), Roisman (2012) pp.31–60.

(approximately) 2,000 Thessalians and another 1,000 or so allied cavalry, this would average around 1,200 drachmas per man, a generous gift indeed. In addition to monetary bonuses, it is likely that Alexander issued medals, equivalent to modern campaign medals, to those taking part in the Indian campaign. A number of such medals have been discovered with depictions of Indian elephants, chariots and archers, but lacking the official markings that would render them usable as coinage.[11]

As well as the carrot of pay and rewards, any army must apply the stick of discipline and punishment. In the Greek world generally, military discipline was by modern standards somewhat lax; citizen soldiers did not take well to being ordered around by their fellow citizens, and discipline could only be enforced through the law courts. Macedonians, serving in a monarchy and with aristocratic officers, appear to have followed a more familiar modern pattern, though the only direct evidence we have for military discipline is from the Antigonid kingdom and takes the form of fines for missing equipment. There was, however, probably also corporal punishment – the king could have members of the Royal Pages flogged, so it is likely that officers could do the same to the common soldiers. The death penalty was also available for serious offences. At the mutiny at Opis, Alexander selected 13 ringleaders to be led away to summary execution, but as Arrian says, 'Alexander had become by this time quicker-tempered, and courted as he now was in the barbarian manner, had ceased to be so kindly as in old times to the Macedonians' (Arr. *Anab.* 7.8.3). The relationship between a Macedonian king and his army was essentially a personal one, based on mutual esteem, so strict punishments do not necessarily fit easily in this model.[12]

Since there are no memoirs written by ordinary Macedonian soldiers, and the closest we can come to their thoughts are the speeches composed by later historians and put into the mouths of kings and senior generals, it is difficult to gain insights into what motivated the men of Alexander's army. Regular, or at least regularly promised, pay meant that, for most of the army, soldiering was simply a way of life, a way to earn a living while also enjoying the usual perks of the soldier – enhanced status back home, foreign travel, plunder, sex and violence.[13]

Pay, bonuses, and plunder would provide much of the motivation for the army, but in addition there are usually more intangible processes at work in motivating men to a life of hardship, danger and violence. These forces can be summed up as the combination of 'cause and comrades'. Many militaries have found that the primary force in determining soldiers' behaviour is peer group approval, and in particular, the small peer group of the squad or equivalent, the immediate comrades of the soldier and the men among whom he lived and fought. For the Macedonian phalanx in particular, this body will have been the *dekas*, or file, of 16 men in Alexander's time. As well as forming a tactical unit, the *dekas* will have shared a tent or tent group, a

---

11 Holt (2003); Karunanithy (2013) pp.154–7.
12 Carney (1996).
13 Lloyd (1996) on combat motivation. Karunanithy (2013) pp.152–4 for examples of enhanced status at home (e.g. front row seats at the theatre).

campfire and servant, and eaten their meals together, which will have helped in the formation of the close personal bonds that most soldiers form with their immediate comrades. As the phalanx was, at least at first, recruited by region, men will also likely have served with men from their own locality, very likely men they already knew in peacetime life, which will have further strengthened the bonds between them. When these bonds became weakened as, later in the campaign, reinforcements were added without reference to their origins, and (even worse) Asians were admitted to their units, the backlash contributed to the mutinies on the Hyphasis and at Opis.

Bonds within the unit were strengthened by professional pride in their own abilities and supposed invincibility. Rigorous training helped to build and promote this self-confidence. Macedonians were later said to 'glory in war', but this was not true in their days as ineffective light infantry; pride in their equipment, formation, training and skills developed along with the new formation, the Macedonian phalanx. We can compare with the similar situation in Achaea, in southern Greece, at the end of the third century, when the Achaeans too adopted Macedonian arms and tactics; '[T]he new order of battle pleased them wonderfully, since it seemed to secure a close array that could not be broken, and the armour which they used became light and manageable for them … [they] wished to get into action with it and fight a decisive battle with their enemies as soon as possible' (Plut. *Philop.* 9.7–8).

As for the cause, Alexander made much of the official purpose of the expedition, punishing the Persian Empire for the invasion of Greece 150 years before. It is possible that this cause motivated some of the allied Greeks, but unlikely that it had much influence on the Macedonians themselves (whose ancestors had, after all, sided with the Persians). For most of the Macedonians, the cause to be fought for was something altogether simpler; the aggrandisement of Macedon and the enrichment of themselves.

The Macedonians in the army were also in a special position; as *Macedones* they were citizens of the Macedonian state and had a privileged status above that of the lowest classes in Macedon or the non-Macedonian members of the army. The role of the *Macedones* in a supposed Macedonian constitutional monarchy has been overstated by some modern historians. Clearly, Macedon was an absolutist monarchy, and the king had tremendous personal power, but even so, custom and tradition gave the *Macedones* an important role in the state and meant that they expected to be persuaded and led by their rulers, not simply commanded. Affirmation of a new king by the assembled *Macedones*, in the form of the army, was an important element of the succession, and *Macedones* also had a tradition of outspokenness and direct access to the king (they could appeal to him in legal disputes for example). Greek thought saw a distinction between free citizens with political power and the slavish subjects of an absolutist monarch, which is how they saw the subjects of the Persian Empire. Macedon, as an absolutist monarchy, was in an outlying position in the Greek world, but the *Macedones* would have found, in their customary rights and traditions, enough to set them apart, in their own minds, from the Asian subjects of the Persian king. This, aside from ordinary racism, is why Alexander's orientalising efforts after Gaugamela, and his attempts to adopt some of the outward forms of the Persian kingship, were so badly received by the Macedonians. It seemed not just an adoption of 'foreign ways', but also an attempt to erode their own special status.[14]

Many armies throughout history have been motivated by some degree of religious fanaticism, or at least by the idea of a just cause in religious terms, and have also been comforted by the prospect of an afterlife. Greek religion did not provide a particular emphasis on these factors, but there certainly was a belief that the gods could and did intervene directly in human affairs to promote the interests of those who had pleased them (as depicted in Homer's *Iliad*), and there was also a strong belief in omens and auguries. For the whole of the army, correct religious practice in terms of making sacrifices and following the correct ceremonies, while avoiding irreligious acts like plundering the temples of friendly gods, would have been the primary factor in winning divine approval, and the pre-battle sacrifice to ensure good omens was an important element of army preparation before combat. Alexander was particularly meticulous in such matters, with an official seer, Aristandros, tasked with performing and interpreting the proper ceremonies and also providing a positive spin on the various natural phenomena encountered during the campaign as indications of future Macedonian victories. As one example among many, there was a lunar eclipse on the night of 20–21 September 331, shortly before the battle of Gaugamela; 'Alexander sacrificed to the Moon, Sun and Earth, who are all said to cause an eclipse. Aristandros thought that the eclipse was favourable to the Macedonians and Alexander, that the battle would take place that month, and that the sacrifices portended victory to Alexander' (Arr. *Anab*. 3.7.6).

Personal loyalty to the king was also a powerful factor. Macedonians were to show remarkable loyalty to the institution of monarchy, even when the occupant of the throne was a man with little to admire. In the case of Alexander, the combination of personal charisma, his sharing in hardship and risk-taking, his technical ability, and his record of success will have provided sufficient motivation to many. Alexander was particularly careful to present himself to the army as sharing in their dangers and privations and also noted and celebrated their individual successes. For example, after Issus, Alexander

> …heaped with praise every man he had seen perform some distinguished deed in action or of whom he received a reliable report to that effect, and he honoured them all with commensurate rewards. (Arr. *Anab*. 2.12.1)

Something as simple as remembering the names of officers and men (for example, Arr. *Anab* 2.10.2) would help to reinforce this personal connection, and this applied not only at the top; Alexander expected the same level of personal leadership to extend all the way down through the officer corps (Arr. *Anab*. 3.9.6–8).

---

14 Hammond (1995) for the 'constitutional monarchy', Taylor (2020) pp.131–43.

There will have been an element of what we would now call patriotism, of pride in the status and success of Macedon, but personal loyalty to Alexander was probably of even greater importance. Even this was not sufficient, in the end, to drive the army on indefinitely, and eventually they became so exhausted by constant campaigning and so keen to return to their Mediterranean homelands that on the Hyphasis they refused to continue. The record of success they had up to this point, however, proves how well-motivated and, therefore, how effective the army of Alexander was.

9

Minor Actions and Sieges

The final chapter of this volume will consider the 'big four' major battles (Granicus, Issus, Gaugamela, Hydaspes) in which Alexander's army was engaged. This chapter will look at a selection of minor actions and sieges that illustrate the capabilities and *modus operandi* of the army. Naturally, during a long campaign, many such actions were fought, and any selection is somewhat arbitrary; I hope, however, that the following will provide useful illustrations of the army in action and will help to make the point that Macedonian success depended on far more than the abilities of the army on the field of pitched battle.

Minor Actions

Mount Haimos
In 335, in the first full year of his reign, Alexander launched a campaign against the Triballians and Illyrians, peoples on the northwest frontier of Macedon, with the intention of securing the homeland prior to the invasion of Asia. Advancing from Amphipolis, on the coast, with an unspecified force that included Companion cavalry, archers, Hypaspists, Agrianians and at least a portion of the phalanx (Pezhetairoi and/or Asthetairoi), Alexander met the first organised opposition from the 'free Thracians' (as opposed to those who had been subdued by Philip) at Mount Haimos (Arr. *Anab.* 1.1.7–13). The Thracians (a force of unspecified size and composition) occupied some high ground and had formed a stockade of wagons to fight behind. Their plan was to launch at least some of the wagons down the hill onto the approaching Macedonians to break up their formation. Alexander ordered his hoplites (that is, the men of the phalanx) to break formation and allow the wagons to pass through where possible (compare with the Persian chariots at Gaugamela), and where this was not possible due to the lie of the land, to lie down under their shields and allow the wagons to bounce over them. In this way, the wagons, when unleashed, caused no losses among the phalanx. This episode has caused some perplexity and indeed incredulity among modern writers, largely caused by the erroneous modern insistence that the Macedonian phalanx carried small shields (though it is doubtful that

if a shield of 60 cm diameter did not provide protection against a rolling wagon, that one of 90 cm diameter would). At any rate, the actual instances of wagons rolling over men under their shields were probably very few, and we need not imagine whole formations forming a Roman *testudo*-like roof for the wagons to cross; the primary means of defence was to get out of the way, and only those unable to do so were to cluster together behind their shields. The evasive actions undertaken must, of course, have caused considerable disorder, as men must have moved rapidly out of the way or lain down, all of which would break up the Macedonian formation. But the training, discipline and confidence of the phalanx were sufficient to overcome this disorder, and the men reformed once the wagons were safely past and continued their uphill advance. Alexander ordered the archers (Macedonians, presumably) to advance on the right, while he himself led 'the agema' (meaning, in this case, the Agema of the Hypaspists), other Hypaspists and Agrianians on the left. Once the phalanx came to close quarters, it easily defeated the lightly armed Thracians. The precise nature of these movements in Arrian's account is obscure, but we see a number of features that were to be typical of many later actions: the discipline of the phalanx; the use of light forces ahead of the attack to soften up the enemy with missiles; the use of a strike force of Hypaspists and Agrianians under Alexander's personal command; and the superiority of the Macedonian phalanx in close combat.[1]

Lyginos River

Alexander then advanced against the Triballians, whose king, Syrmos withdrew to the Ister (Danube), leaving a large force of Triballians in Alexander's rear on the river Lyginos (Arr. *Anab*. 1.2.4–7). The Triballians formed line in a narrow wooded valley with the river at their backs, so Alexander formed the phalanx deep, and therefore narrow, and sent slingers and archers ahead to try to provoke the Triballians into attacking and leaving the protection of the valley. The plan worked, the Triballians charged out to chase off the light infantry, upon which Alexander ordered the Companion cavalry, divided into two parts on each flank (respectively the 'cavalry of Upper Macedonia' and the 'cavalry from Bottiaia and Amphipolis', so we may guess that each force contained two *ilai*), to charge the Triballians in the flanks. Further cavalry were deployed (unusually) in front of the phalanx, and the cavalry and phalanx overcame the Triballians at close quarters, the phalanx in close formation (*pykne*), and the cavalry barging the tribesmen with their horses. The Triballians lost 3,000 men, while the Macedonian losses were 11 cavalry and 42 infantry killed.[2]

Sagalassos

In the winter of 334–333 Alexander was campaigning in Pisidia, in south western Asia Minor, capturing or taking the surrender of successive cities. The inhabitants of Sagalassos, the 'most warlike' of the Pisidians, occupied

---

1 Bloedow (1996), Heckel (2005) (cf. Heckel and Jones (2006) plate F), English (2009) pp.122–3, English (2011) pp.22–5, Howe (2015).
2 Fuller (1960) pp.221–2, English (2009) pp.123–4, English (2011) pp.26–8.

a hill in front of their city with an unspecified force (Arr. *Anab.* 1.28.2–8). Alexander stationed the Hypaspists on the right under his own command and the Pezhetairoi (and Asthetairoi?) 'each battalion under the commanders in the order of precedence for the day' (1.28.4). Archers and Agrianians were placed in front of the right wing, and Thracians under Sitalces in advance of the left. Cavalry were not deployed on this occasion as the ground, hilly and rough, was not suitable for them. As the Macedonians advanced, at the steepest part of the hill, the Pisidians in *lochoi* (meaning in distinct small units, rather than as a single mass) attacked on each flank. The archers were driven back, but the Agrianians resisted, allowing the phalanx to come up and easily defeat the lightly armed Pisidians, who fled with 500 dead.

The Persian Gates

Following the victory at Gaugamela (330), Alexander was pressing forward into Persis, the Persian heartland (Arr. *Anab.* 3.18.1–9). The Persian Gates, a mountain pass, was held against him by a force of 40,000 infantry and 700 cavalry, according to Arrian, or, barely less plausibly, 25,000 infantry and 300 cavalry, according to Diodorus (Diod. 17.68). Alexander had left a portion of the army under Parmenion to follow the main road into Persis, while he led the Macedonian infantry, the Companions, Prodromoi, Agrianians and archers against the pass. An initial assault on the pass, which was also defended by a wall, was driven back by missiles, including from catapults ('machines'). So, as is usually the case with defended passes, prisoners offered to show him an alternative route around. Alexander divided his force into four parts. Krateros was left in the camp with two *taxeis* of infantry, some archers, and 5,000 cavalry, with orders to attack the wall when a trumpet signal indicated Alexander was in position. Alexander himself led the Hypaspists, one *taxis* of infantry, the fittest of the archers, the Agrianians, the Royal Squadron of the Companions, plus another *tetrarchia* of cavalry (see Chapter 3). Ptolemy was left with 3,000 infantry to take the defending walls once the Persians abandoned it (it is unclear how his task differs from that of Krateros). Finally, Amyntas, Philotas and Coinos took 'the remainder of the army' (their *taxeis*, presumably) and marched into the plain to prepare a bridge. Alexander's night march proceeded as planned, crossing difficult country at speed, falling on the rear of the Persian position and rapidly overwhelming their outposts. He then attacked the Persian main force at dawn, with Krateros, summoned by trumpet, assaulting from the other side, and Ptolemy's force seizing the wall when the Persians abandoned it. The episode demonstrates the extreme difficulty of holding a pass against a determined and aggressive enemy acting with local knowledge.[3]

River Tanais (Jaxartes)

'Tanais' is a name given by the Greeks to several Asian rivers, most notably the Don. This Tanais, called Jaxartes (Iaxartes) by other Greek authors, the modern Syr Darya, marked the boundary between the Persian provinces of

---

3   Fuller (1960) pp.226–34, Speck (2002), English (2011) pp.162–3.

Bactria and Sogdiana and the Scythian territories beyond. Alexander was engaged in founding a city on the southern side when a large Scythian force gathered on the opposite bank, shooting arrows and insults across the river (Arr. *Anab*. 4.4.1–9). Alexander ordered hides to be prepared for a river crossing and set up catapults (again, 'machines') on the river bank. A volley from the catapults, while killing only one man, dismayed the Scythians, who had thought themselves out of reach, and they fell back a little from the river bank. Alexander then used trumpet signals to order the crossing to begin. The archers and slingers were first across, and they kept the Scythians at a distance while the heavy infantry and cavalry crossed. Alexander then ordered a hipparchy of mercenary cavalry and four squadrons of lancers to charge the Scythians; these were met by the usual horse archer tactics of evading the charge while shooting at the attackers. So, Alexander mixed archers, Agrianians and 'other psiloi' (javelinmen?) with the cavalry as *hamippoi* and advanced again, ordering three hipparchies of Companions and the hippakontistai to charge, then the rest of the cavalry with squadrons in column. The precise nature and impact of these manoeuvres are unclear, and various interpretations have been suggested. The usual view is that the two waves of attacking Macedonian cavalry broke up Scythian attempts to circle around and surround the leading wave, trapping them between the two forces, a tactic that was adopted centuries later by Byzantine cavalry against their steppe opponents. The overall effect was that the Scythians were unable to carry out their usual evasive wheeling tactics, whether because of the intermingled light infantry, the division of Alexander's force into two waves, or the column formations. Either way, the Scythians fled, with 1,000 dead and 150 prisoners. It was around the same time as this action that the Macedonian army suffered one of its rare defeats, the force under Pharnuches, Caranos and Andromachos being shot down by mounted archers under Spitamenes (Arr. *Anab*. 4.5.2–9), an indication of how dangerous a mounted, missile-using army could be to a slower force (even one with cavalry support), without an Alexander present to balance the scales.[4]

Massaga

The Indian campaigns of 327–326 saw numerous minor actions and city assaults (which will be considered below), but our accounts contain few details of the tactics involved. Only a few tactical details stand out, such as the battle between Ptolemy's division of the army and an Indian force (Aspasians) on a hill, where Ptolemy led his force on in columns (Arr. *Anab*. 4.25.2), a tactic familiar from Xenophon (Xen. *Anab*. 4.8.9–15) where columns were used to attack a defended hilltop. Columns had the advantage over a linear (phalanx) formation that they were less easily broken up by difficult terrain. Alexander then led the whole army against Massaga, the chief city of the neighbouring Assacenians, who, according to Curtius (8.10.23), could muster 38,000 infantry, including 7,000 mercenaries from lands deeper into India (Arr. *Anab*. 4.26.1). The Indians drew up near their

---

4   Fuller (1960) pp.236–42.

city walls, but Alexander wished to draw them further out so that a defeat and pursuit would be more catastrophic for them, so ordered his force to face about and retire to a hill just over a kilometre away. The Indians gave chase, but as soon as they were within bowshot (maybe 200 metres), the phalanx ('at a signal', 4.26.3) about-faced and counterattacked, led by the hippakontistai, Agrianians and archers. When the Indians fled back to their city, the fight became a city assault and will be recounted below.[5]

Sangala

Following the victory over Poros at the Hydaspes, Alexander continued his advance deeper into India, subduing (massacring) the peoples he encountered. Another combined battle and siege took place at Sangala, where the local people, the Cathaioi, attempted resistance (Arr. *Anab*. 5.22.3–24.5). They were drawn up on a hill in front of the city and had formed a triple palisade of wagons about the hill. Alexander sent the mounted archers to harry the defences and prevent any sally while he made his preparations. He formed the phalanx of Asthetairoi in the centre, along with Perdiccas's hipparchy, while on the right he led the Agema of cavalry and Cleitos' hipparchy, the Hypaspists and the Agrianians. Archers were posted on both wings. Further cavalry coming up were posted to either wing, while additional infantry were used to 'increase the solidity of the phalanx' (5.22.7), presumably by forming a second line, although Arrian's words suggest it was by forming closer order, so perhaps the extra numbers allowed the already-present Asthetairoi to close their order, with the reinforcements occupying the resulting gaps. Alexander initially led a cavalry advance, but as the Indians remained behind their wagons, shooting, the actual attack was left to infantry. The first line of wagons was quickly carried but then formed an obstacle to the order of the phalanx as it attacked the Indians formed up between the first and second rows. However, discipline and determination were sufficient to carry the second line also, and the Indians abandoned the third line, fleeing back to the city, which was then assaulted (see below).[6]

Sieges and Assaults

An essential part of Alexander's campaign was the capture of fortified centres of population in the lands that he traversed. As was noted in antiquity, an army that marches through a country without capturing its fortified places and cities no more controls that country than a sailing ship controls the sea. If Alexander was to make himself ruler of the Persian Empire, he had to capture, or receive the surrender of, its population centres. This was also necessary in order to secure his rear as he marched on, to remove centres of resistance and bases for hostile armies, and to secure supplies for his army. Alexander's army was therefore equipped with a siege train containing various siege engines, including stone and bolt shooting catapults, siege

---

5 Fuller (1960) pp.245–7, English (2011) pp.178–9.
6 Fuller (1960) pp.255–8.

towers and rams, and the army was also capable of conducting siege works – digging trenches and mounds, for example – and of launching assaults, with ladders if necessary, against lower or more lightly defended walls. The army also contained large contingents of missile-armed troops capable of suppressing defensive shooting and clearing walls of defenders. Unlike earlier Greek armies, which generally had limited siege capability, Alexander's (and Philip's) army was, therefore, well capable of besieging and assaulting any fortified position, and the various sieges that mark the campaign are in some ways more important than the pitched battles. The following accounts cover some of the more important and typical of such sieges and assaults, selected from a very large number for which there is often no more information available than 'he took the city by assault'.

It must be remembered also that many cities, especially in the Greek areas of western Asia Minor, surrendered voluntarily rather than face a siege (and ensuing massacre). It was normal practice in the ancient world that a city that resisted and was carried by assault would be subject to the massacre and enslavement of its population, something that served as a deterrent to such resistance, though it is striking just how many cities were willing to take their chances against even so demonstrably capable an army as Alexander's. Alexander's campaigns, being lengthy and geographically extensive, were marked by numerous such massacres of civilian populations, but, in the context of warfare, this in itself would not have been thought unusual or blameworthy by his contemporaries, and ancient attitudes were comparable to, say, many contemporary views of the Allied bombing campaign against the civilian population of Germany in the Second World War – unfortunate perhaps, but justifiable in the circumstances.

The sieges and assaults that follow are selected to illustrate particular aspects of the business of capturing a city.

Thebes
While Alexander was on Macedonia's northwest frontier in 335, the city of Thebes rebelled against his control, besieging the Macedonian garrison in the citadel, the Cadmeia (Arr. *Anab.* 1.7.7–8.8). Alexander made a rapid march south and appeared unexpectedly before the walls of the city, delaying any attack to give the Thebans time to reconsider their position. However, the Thebans opted to continue their resistance, so Alexander moved his army to the south of the city, near to the Cadmeia (citadel), where the Thebans had built an outer palisade to prevent any support from being given to the Macedonian garrison. Here, two *taxeis* of the phalanx, those of Perdiccas and Amyntas, launched a premature attack on the palisade, which succeeded in breaking through, and Alexander was obliged to follow up this success. The Agrianians and archers were sent through the captured palisade to support the attacking *taxeis*, while Alexander himself retained the Hypaspists in reserve outside. The Thebans then rallied and drove the attacking Macedonians back but lost formation in the pursuit; Alexander counterattacked with the Hypaspists and, in turn, drove the Thebans back. As so often happened, when the fugitives, closely pursued, pushed through the gates into the city proper, the pursuers were able to penetrate the gates

along with them, while the garrison in the Cadmeia broke out and entered the city from within. There followed a wholesale massacre, as Alexander had determined to make an example of the city, and the neighbouring Greek allies who joined in the assault worked off old grudges against the Thebans. Thebes, despite its defences, had been captured almost by accident, as the result of an engagement outside the walls.

Halicarnassos

After the victory at the Granicus, Alexander attacked and captured Miletos with help from his fleet (Arr. *Anab.* 1.19.1–6). He then marched on into Caria, where a large enemy force had gathered at Halicarnassos (modern Bodrum) under the command of the Rhodian mercenary Memnon (Arr. *Anab.* 1.20.2–23.4). Alexander drove back an initial sally by the defenders and then settled in for a siege. An initial diversion was an attempt to take the nearby town of Myndos, where an internal faction had sent an offer of surrender. However, when Alexander approached by night as agreed, there was no sign of surrender, and he had not brought ladders or 'machines', as he was not expecting a siege. The phalanx was sent in to undermine the wall, and succeeded in bringing down one tower but not in creating a breach, and as reinforcements were arriving by ship from Halicarnassos, Alexander abandoned the attempt.

He then returned to besieging Halicarnassos, filling in the moat (which was around 15 metres broad and seven deep) so that he could bring up siege towers and other machines – likely stone-throwing catapults. A defensive nighttime sally was easily repelled, and the attackers, over several days, brought down two towers and an intervening section of wall. The defenders responded by building a crescent-shaped inner wall of brick behind the damaged section. At this point, Perdiccas' *taxis* was involved in another unscheduled assault, fighting defenders who had sallied out from the wall and coming close to forcing one of the gates. The following day, Alexander brought his siege engines up against the inner replacement wall, the defenders sallying out with torches and setting light to one of the siege towers before being driven off. Flanking shooting from the standing towers of the wall, however, succeeded in halting this attack.

A few days later, Alexander attacked the brick wall again and was met by another sally in force, attempting to set light to the siege engines. This sally was driven back by missiles from the siege towers and in hand-to-hand fighting. Another strong sally was made from the main gates (Tripylon, Triple Gate), which was driven back by two *taxeis* of the phalanx and supporting light infantry. The gates were shut early due to the defenders' fear that the Macedonians would force their way in with the fugitives, and so many of the defenders were killed outside the walls. Alexander's losses are given as 40 men, though given the high number of officer casualties (Arr. *Anab.* 1.22.7), they could well have been higher.

Memnon and the Persian commander Orontobates now decided the city was indefensible and so abandoned the main part of the city, some retreating to the nearby island citadel, others to Cos, setting fire to the defences around the fallen part of the wall. Alexander, having now captured the main part of

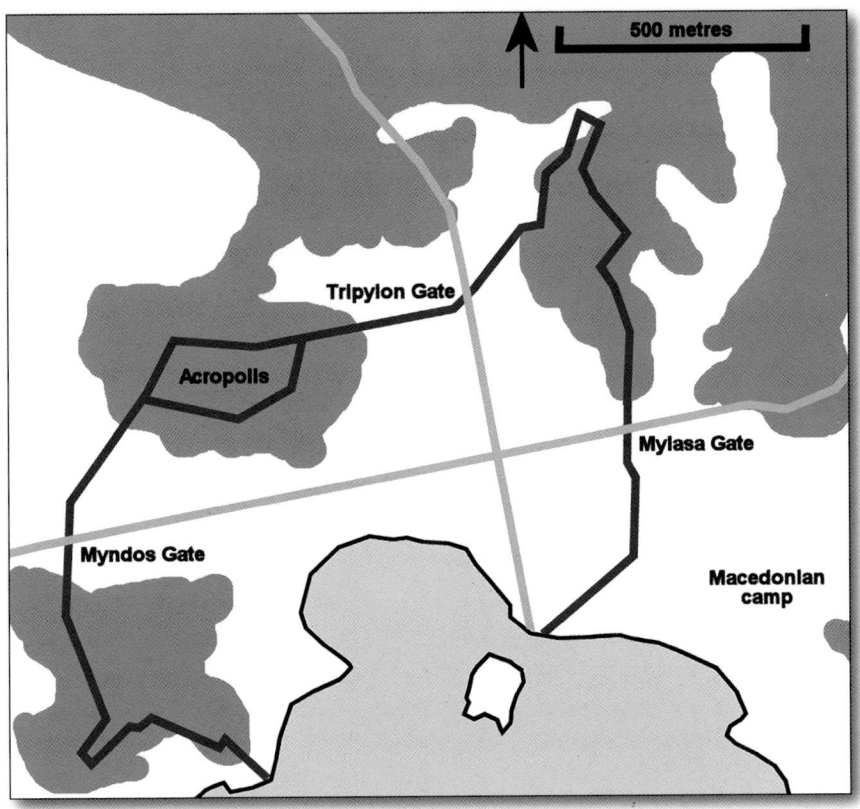

The siege of Halicarnassos

the city and without a fleet (he had disbanded the Greek fleet shortly before, trusting in his ability to defeat the Persian navy by capturing its land bases), decided not to remain to conduct the siege of the citadel, and marched on into Phrygia, leaving a strong force (3,000 mercenary infantry and 200 cavalry) to control what was left of the city. This force eventually captured the citadel (though with heavy losses) the following year (Arr. *Anab*. 2.5.7).[7]

Tyre

The siege of Tyre (332), modern Sūr in Lebanon, was the longest, hardest and most well-known of Alexander's sieges (Arr. *Anab*. 2.16–24). Alexander, having defeated Darius at Issus, was continuing his policy of securing the Mediterranean coast and defeating the Persian navy by capturing its bases. He had already taken the surrender of Sidon and Byblos, which had been reluctant providers of ships to the Persian fleet. Tyre, however, in an excellent defensive position on a fortified island off the coast of Phoenicia and, still with an advantage in numbers of ships, hoped to follow a policy of neutrality, admitting neither Macedonians nor Persians within its walls.[8]

Alexander opened the siege by starting the construction of a mole to cross the straits between the mainland and the island, a distance of some 700 metres (Diod. 17.40.4). This was obviously a vastly greater

---

7 Fuller (1960) pp.200–6; English (2010) pp.41–55.
8 Fuller (1960) pp.206–16, Romane (1987), English (2009) pp.140–8; English (2010) pp.56–85.

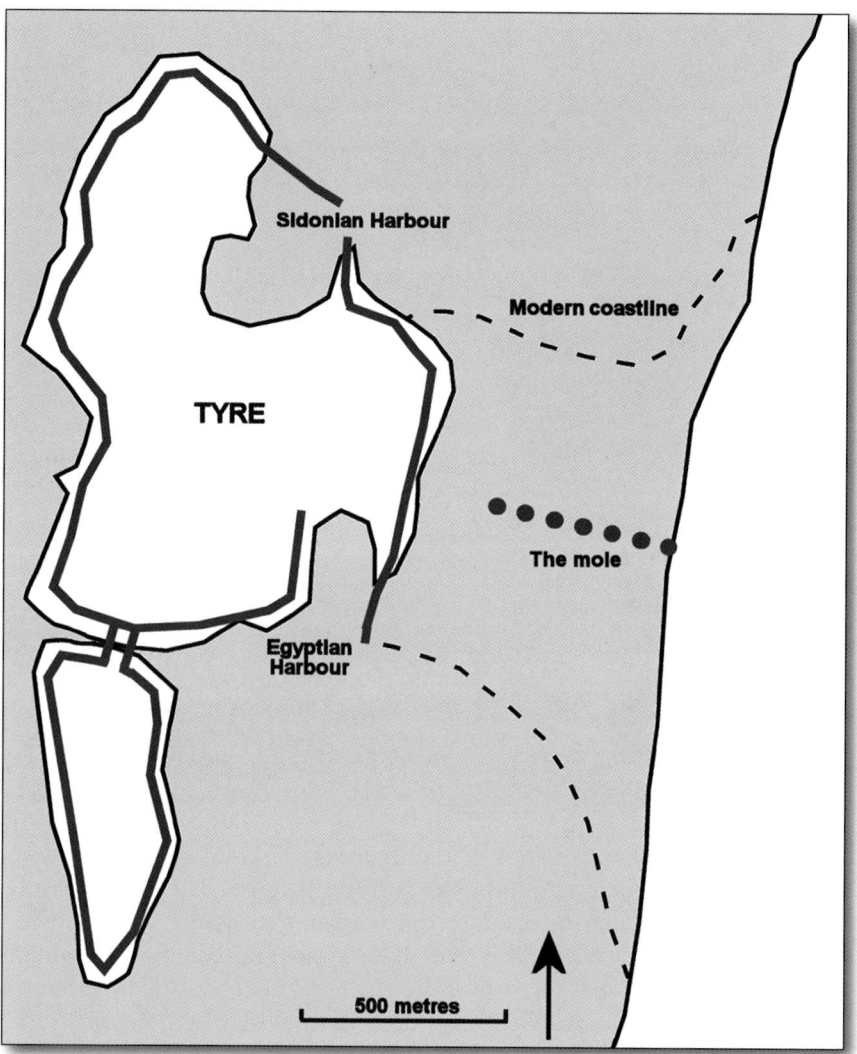

The siege of Tyre.

undertaking than the crossing of the moat at Halicarnassus, and indeed the whole siege was to last six or seven months (Diod. 17.46.5). Most of the crossing was not deep sea but shoals, crossable on foot, only the channel nearest the island was deep (about six metres). The mole was built (by the Macedonians themselves, not by slave or pressed labour) by piling stones and timbers into the sea mud, with stakes being driven into the mud to provide a footing. While the mole advanced rapidly at first, it slowed when it came into missile range of the walls, to deeper water, and when Tyrian ships harassed the builders. Two towers were built on the end of the mole, protected by hides and equipped with catapults, to provide covering fire. The Tyrians, however, built a fireship (from a horse transport) and used their triremes to tow it onto the end of the mole; this set alight the Macedonian towers, and more Tyrians sallied out in small boats to burn the other machines.

Alexander ordered the mole to be rebuilt wider, to hold more machines, and also went to Sidon to recruit the Sidonian fleet, which was joined by the ships from Byblos and Arados, as well as various Greek and Ionian ships, and crucially 120 from Cyprus, which now, following news of the Persian defeat at Issus, decided to throw in its lot with the Macedonians. Alexander was therefore able to organise a fleet considerably stronger than that of the Tyrians, and when it sailed against Tyre, with the Hypaspists loaded aboard as marines, the Tyrians refused battle and shut themselves up within their two harbours (the Sidonian and Egyptian harbours).

Alexander also recruited many local engineers (*mechainopoioi*) from Cyprus and Phoenicia and built large numbers of machines (presumably mostly catapults), which were deployed on the mole, horse transports, and slow triremes. The Tyrians countered with wooden towers to increase the height of the wall opposite the mole (the walls were already 50 metres high, according to Arrian), with fire arrows to shoot at the ships, and by dropping stones into the sea at the base of the wall to prevent the ships making a close approach. There followed a battle of ingenuity, with Alexander setting boats to dredge the stones out of the sea, the Tyrians sending out protected ships to cut the anchor ropes of these ships, Alexander setting guard ships to protect the ropes, the Tyrians sending divers to cut the ropes underwater, and finally, chains being used to anchor the ships in place. The stones were then dredged out and deposited in open water by machines (probably cranes of some sort – it is highly unlikely that the large stones were flung away by stone-throwers).

The Tyrians now launched a naval sortie of three quinqueremes, three quadriremes and seven triremes to surprise the Cypriot squadron outside the Sidonian harbour. This achieved some success, but Alexander quickly brought up ships from the other side of the island. Though these were seen by the Tyrians in the city as they passed it proved impossible to get a warning to the attacking Tyrian ships, which were caught outside the harbour, with many being sunk. With the Tyrian fleet largely neutralised, Alexander renewed the attack from the mole and with machines (stone-throwers most likely) mounted on ships. These had little success by the mole or on the Sidonian side but succeeded in breaching the wall on the Egyptian side. An initial assault on this breach was repulsed, but two days later, the attack was renewed. Engine-carrying ships were first sent in to widen the breach, then two troop transports with gangways (boarding ramps) were sent in, one manned by Hypaspists, which Alexander accompanied in person, the other by Coinos' battalion of Asthetairoi. Other ships meanwhile patrolled the walls, looking for any lapse in the defence. The assault was successful, with the Hypaspists seizing a section of wall but losing their commander, Admetos. Meanwhile, the Phoenician and Cypriot fleets were able to force their way into the harbours as the defence of the city collapsed. There followed the usual massacre of the inhabitants, with the survivors sold into slavery. Intriguingly, Carthaginian envoys were present at the fall of the city and were spared by Alexander (Arr. *Anab*. 2.24.5). There had been some hope that Carthage might assist Tyre (one of its mother cities), according to Diodorus and Curtius (Diod. 17.40.3; QC 4.3.19), but a confrontation between Carthage and Macedon was avoided, as Carthage was embroiled in conflict on Sicily.

Gaza

With the Mediterranean coast secured, Alexander continued his march toward Egypt but found the city of Gaza, built on a mound with a strong wall and defended by Arab mercenaries, held against him. There followed another long (two-month) and difficult siege, the last of the large-scale formal sieges of the campaign (Arr. *Anab*. 2.26–27). Alexander began by constructing siege engines (probably those that had been used at Tyre, dismantled and transported by sea) and building a mound to raise the height of the machines to that of the walls, mainly on the south side. Once the mound was high enough (over 80 metres, according to Arrian 2.27.3), siege engines were brought forward to attack the walls, and the defenders launched a sally to set light to the engines. Alexander brought up the Hypaspists to push back the sally but was himself shot in the shoulder through shield and armour by a catapult from the walls. As well as assaults from the mound, the walls were undermined in several places by tunnels. Three assaults on these breaches were beaten back, but a fourth, using ladders to cross the broken and partly collapsed walls, succeeded in entering the city and opened the gates from within to the rest of the army. The defenders were massacred, with the women and children sold as slaves.[9]

A nineteenth-century depiction of the city of Gaza by David Roberts, 1839, in The Cleveland Museum of Art. (Cleveland Museum of Art, CC0)

Seven Cities in Sogdiana

The years 332–329 were taken up by the occupation of Egypt, the final defeat of Darius at Gaugamela, and the capture of the Persian heartland. While Alexander was campaigning on the Tanais (Jaxartes) in 329, the Sogdianians and Bactrians rebelled and killed their Macedonian garrisons, taking refuge in seven cities (or fortified towns). The rapid capture of these places by Alexander's force is typical of the fate of many mud-brick-walled cities in central Asia around this time (Arr. *Anab* 4.2.1–3.5). Alexander ordered the phalanx to prepare ladders, a specified number for each *lochos*. Crateros was

---

9   Fuller (1966) pp.216–8, Romane (1988); English (2010) pp.85–103.

sent against the city of Cyropolis, the largest of the cities, to enclose it in a ditch and stockade and build siege engines. Alexander meanwhile marched on Gaza (a different Gaza from the Arab city); the walls were cleared of defenders by the slingers, archers, javelinmen and catapults, allowing the phalangites to set up their ladders and go over the wall. The inhabitants were massacred and enslaved. The next two cities were captured in rapid succession in the same way. The cavalry were meanwhile sent on to the next two cities to prevent the escape of their populations when they saw the smoke from the destruction of the captured cities. Note that in these cases, the objective was not the capture and use of the cities themselves (Alexander frequently preferred to destroy native cities and replace them with new foundations of his own) but the subjugation or killing of the population. Alexander's purpose would not be served if the populace escaped out into the surrounding countryside, where they would be able to raise further revolts, and he preferred to contain them where they could be killed if they did not surrender, removing the immediate threat of revolt and encouraging greater obedience in other nearby populations. Alexander then joined Crateros at Cyropolis, proposing to batter the wall down with stone-throwing engines. However, he spotted a watercourse under the walls, which was currently dry, permitting access, and led an assault force of Hypaspists, archers and Agrianians through this opening into the city, opening the gates from within while the defenders were distracted by the approaching siege engines. Survivors of the initial massacre took refuge in the citadel but were forced to surrender due to lack of water. The seventh and final city either surrendered or was taken by assault also (Arr. *Anab.* 4.3.5).[10]

Three Rocks

Further campaigning in Sogdiana in 328–327 was required to subdue ongoing resistance, with many of the natives taking refuge in the apparently impregnable Sogdian Rock (Arr. *Anab.* 4.18.4–19.6). This Rock was a citadel surrounded by steep cliffs and (at the time of the attack) winter snows, and provided with provisions for a long siege. The Sogdians boasted that the Rock could only be captured by men with wings which, along with its strategic importance as a centre of resistance, provoked Alexander into even greater determination to capture it. He, therefore, gathered 300 men with rock-climbing experience and issued them with ropes and pitons made from tent pegs. The men succeeded in climbing the steepest, and so least well-guarded, part of the Rock, at night. Alexander offered cash prizes to those who made the climb, with the first up to receive 12 talents – a fortune. Thirty of their number fell to their deaths in the ascent. Once on the summit, they waved flags to signal their success, and Alexander's herald called on the Sogdians to observe the 'men with wings'. The Sogdians, unaware of the small numbers or lack of weapons of the climbers, immediately surrendered. Amongst the prisoners was the family of Oxyartes, who was leading the Bactrian resistance, including his daughter Roxane, who was to become Alexander's first wife.

---

10 Fuller (1960) pp.234–6; English (2010) pp.104–112.

Alexander now marched against another rock, the Rock of Chorienes, that was held against him, Chorienes being either the local commander (called Sisimithres by Curtius, QC 8.2.19) or the title of this commander (Arr. *Anab.* 4.21.1–10). This was another steep-sided rock with a single approach path and surrounded by a ravine. Alexander divided the army into day and night shifts and set them to work felling pines and using them to fill in the ravine, first making ladders to climb to the bottom of the ravine, then fixing stakes in the base of the ravine, binding these together with wickerwork, and infilling with soil to make a solid platform. Once the ramp had advanced within arrow shot of the defences, the defenders could see the writing was on the wall and surrendered to Alexander on favourable terms. Chorienes retained his position and supplied the Macedonians from his stockpiled stores.

The following winter, campaigning in India, Alexander encountered another rock, called Aornos ('Birdless', a name used for several high places) held by the inhabitants of Bazira and other neighbouring towns (Arr. *Anab.* 4.29.1–30.40). This was another high place with access along a single path, with a good supply of water on the summit, and enough flat land to grow crops. Alexander tasked Crateros with stockpiling supplies in the nearby city of Embolima, in case of a long siege, while himself advancing on the rock with the archers, the Agrianians, Coinos' taxis of Asthetairoi, 'the most nimble but best armed' from the rest of the phalanx, 200 Companions, and 100 mounted archers (Arr. *Anab.* 4.28.7–8). Hypaspists were also present. Some local people offered to lead Alexander to a subsidiary height, which could serve as a base for the main assault, and Ptolemy was sent to occupy this position with the Agrianians, unspecified *psiloi* and selected Hypaspists. Ptolemy took the place and defended it with a stockade, indicating his success with a fire signal, which, however, alerted the Indian defenders of the main rock to his presence. The Indians then attempted to throw Prolemy's force off the height, while Alexander was unable to fight his way through to relieve him. Alexander sent an Indian deserter with local knowledge with a letter to Ptolemy coordinate to a combined attack the following day and succeeded in fighting through to link up with Ptolemy's position. They were still unable, however, to attack the main rock itself, so Alexander set the men to work building a mound to link the two positions. As the mound progressed over the following days, slingers and catapults were able to shoot at the defenders and prevent them from sallying out. When the Macedonians took a hill close to the top of the rock, the Indians opened negotiations for surrender. Alexander supposedly learned (how is not specified) that these negotiations were just a ruse to buy time and allow the defenders to scatter in the night, so while the defenders' guard was lowered, he led an immediate assault with 700 bodyguards and Hypaspists which succeeded in capturing the summit of the rock.[11]

---

11 Fuller (1960) pp.247–54; English (2010) pp.113–142.

MINOR ACTIONS AND SIEGES

The landscape near Pir Sar, the ancient Aornos Rock, Pakistan. (CC0)

Massaga

We have already seen above the initial fighting outside the city of Massaga. When the Indians fled back into the city, Alexander led an assault (Arr. *Anab*. 4.26.4–27.4). Siege engines were brought up, which brought down a section of wall, but an immediate assault on the breach was repelled. A second assault the next day, supported by a siege tower containing archers, catapults and (perhaps) stone-throwers, also failed to penetrate the breach. The next day, another 'machine', presumably a siege tower, was brought up from which a bridge was thrown over the breach, and an assault was launched across it by the Hypaspists. However, the bridge collapsed under the weight of the attackers, and the survivors were bombarded with missiles and attacked by Indians sallying from the walls. Alcetas' *taxis* was sent forward to retrieve the wounded. The following day, another attempt was made by a siege engine and bridge. The commander of the defenders was then killed by a catapult, and the defenders lost heart, offering to surrender. In a perhaps uncharacteristic act of bad faith, Alexander allowed the mercenary defenders to leave the city under terms, then attacked and massacred them and captured the now undefended city.[12]

---

12 Fuller (1960) pp.245–7.

Sangala

The Indian campaign was marked by numerous assaults on walled towns, most of which were defended by mud brick walls of modest height and were simply stormed by Alexander's army with ladders. The capture of Sangala in 326 was more complex (Arr. *Anab*.5.23.3–24.5). We saw above how the initial defence was formed outside the walls behind lines of wagons. Once the Macedonians captured this position, the Indians retreated into the city. Alexander surrounded the city so far as he was able, given its size, with a remaining gap where there was also a lake covered by cavalry. When the defenders attempted to flee the city at night, the cavalry prevented their escape and drove them back into the city. Alexander then built a double stockade around the city, with a gap for the lake, which was covered by outposts. Deserters from the city informed him that there would be another attempted breakout, so Ptolemy was assigned three *chiliarchiai* of Hypaspists (which presumably means all of them except the Royal Hypaspists), the Agrianians and a *taxis* of archers and tasked with preventing the breakout and alerting the rest of the army by trumpet signal. Note again how capturing the city was not the main objective, but rather the subjugation or killing of the inhabitants. Ptolemy used the wagons from the earlier engagement along with the partially completed stockade to block the escape route, and when the inhabitants duly made their attempt, cut down large numbers of them. The rest fled back to the city. Alexander then brought forward siege engines, and the army undermined parts of the walls and used ladders to go over other parts, capturing the city by assault, with many of the defenders massacred and the rest captured.[13]

The Mallians

Following the mutiny on the Hyphasis, where the army refused to march any further into India, Alexander was forced to turn back and march down the Indus toward the sea (326–325). However, this was not an end to his conquests, as he subjugated the peoples the army passed through on the march. Particular resistance was shown by the Mallians, whose towns were captured in a number of assaults, chiefly by ladder. The centre for resistance was the main city (unnamed in Arrian, Arr. *Anab*. 6.8.4–11.2), which also contained refugees from the other cities. The Mallians initially made a stand outside the city on the banks of the Hydraotes river, but when Alexander crossed the river with his cavalry, with light infantry and the phalanx following behind, the Mallians fled within the walls, and Alexander surrounded the city. The following day, with the army divided into two parts, Alexander assaulted the outer wall and forced entry through a small gate while the defenders fled back to the citadel. The second division of the army, under Perdiccas, was slow in following up, having not initially brought up their ladders as they had seen the outer wall abandoned. The Macedonians set about undermining and scaling the citadel wall, but Alexander, feeling the assault lacked enthusiasm (something he had complained of on other

---

13 Fuller (1960) pp.255–8.

occasions since the mutiny), set up a ladder himself and mounted it with two companions, Peucestas and Leonnatos, and a half-file-leader, Abreas. The Hypaspists following up had the ladders break under them, leaving Alexander and his party isolated on the wall, where they were a target for archers on the nearby towers. Alexander therefore jumped down into the city, and held off all attackers until shot through the chest. Abreas, too, was killed, and Peucestas and Leonnatos defended the now unconscious Alexander. The ladderless Macedonians outside the wall managed to get over, driving pegs into the mud bricks or climbing on each other's shoulders, and, having got in, managed to open the gate from the inside. There followed a more than usually brutal massacre, the women and children being killed along with the men rather than being enslaved as was usual. Alexander himself recovered in due course, though his health may have been permanently damaged by the wound.[14]

Throughout all of these sieges and assaults, we see the ingenuity of both Alexander and the army in devising methods of capturing the most apparently impregnable positions, and the energy and determination with which the army carried out their orders, as well as the benefits of the siege engineers and their machines in overcoming walls of any size. However, the best-known actions of the army of Alexander were not minor actions, sieges or assaults, but the major pitched battles against equivalent opposition, and it is to those battles that we will turn in the next chapter.

---

14 Fuller (1960) pp.259–63.

10

The Major Battles

The comments on sources in previous chapters apply particularly to the major battles. The best accounts are to be found in Arrian. The accounts in Diodorus and Curtius contain many differences of detail which are often irreconcilable with the accounts in Arrian, and in some cases (particularly Granicus, as will be noted below) major differences, which require one source to be rejected and another accepted – in such cases, Arrian's account is always to be preferred. It is common practice to cherry-pick details from Diodorus or Curtius (or other sources – Plutarch contains some relevant snippets), but the poor quality of the battle accounts in Diodorus in particular, and the confusion displayed by Curtius in his account of Gaugamela, make it apparent that it is unsafe to use information from either of these sources, especially if it differs from that found in Arrian. The following accounts are, therefore, based almost exclusively on Arrian, with other information only included in a few cases where it may expand what we know.

It is worth also making some general comments about the possibility of 'reconstructing' any ancient battle. Expanding and elucidating the existing source accounts to provide a more detailed and (ideally) coherent account of the course of a battle has always been a major component of ancient historiography, but questions have been raised as to the real value of this exercise. Even the best of our ancient battle accounts are incomplete, unclear and imprecise, and it is doubtful whether it is really possible to improve on them, as the many differences in modern accounts of even the best-documented battles show. Battles were inherently confused and confusing affairs, and even accounts written very shortly after the battle took place must have contained many points of dispute or uncertainty. Two millennia later, usually without any surviving first-hand accounts and with little inherent understanding of the military systems and practices in place at the time, we have little chance of ever really understanding what took place in any ancient battle or of clearly describing its course.

Nevertheless, I will here attempt an account of each of the major battles of Alexander's army, keeping in mind at all times that there is far more uncertainty than certainty in such accounts. The diagrams that accompany the text are inevitably schematic and should not be taken to represent the precise positioning and movements of the forces involved; I have, however, endeavoured to show the units in the correct scale, in terms of depth and frontage, as the large blocks traditionally used in such diagrams tend to obscure the difficulties inherent in manoeuvring such large formations. Absolute accuracy is impossible since there are too many unknowns, such as the intervals between units (which, particularly for cavalry, I may have underestimated).[1]

I will generally refer to the forces of the Achaemenid Empire that faced Alexander as 'Persians' though it should be noted that only a small proportion of the Achaemenid army was actually made up of ethnic Persians. Where a unit consists of actual Persians, I hope this will be clear from the context. Similarly, Alexander's army will generally be referred to as 'Macedonians', though as we have seen only a third of the army was ethnically Macedonian.

Granicus

Introduction

The battle on the River Granicus (identified as the modern Biga Çayı in northwest Turkey) was the first significant battle of the campaign, taking place in May or June 334, shortly after Alexander's army had crossed over to Asia. The order of battle of Alexander's army is, therefore, reasonably easy to compile since it will have been largely the same as that of the army at the time of the crossing – although, as we saw earlier, even here, there are discrepancies between the various accounts. Alexander was keen to seek out a victory over the local defending forces that would establish the superiority of Macedonian arms and free him to campaign along the Ionian coast. The Persian command was divided. Memnon, the Greek mercenary commander, advised a scorched earth policy, not risking an engagement with the Macedonian army as it was superior in infantry but retreating and destroying provisions. The other Persian commanders, led by Arsites, satrap (or 'hyparch') of Hellespontine Phrygia and Spithridates, satrap of Lydia and Ionia, refused to abandon or despoil the territories over which they ruled and insisted on facing Alexander in battle (Arr. *Anab.* 1.12.8–10). They were encamped near the city of Zeleia in an advanced position, and after the council of war in which their strategy was decided, advanced to the River Granicus. Alexander, aware that a Persian force was in the vicinity, was advancing in battle order with his heavy infantry in two lines, cavalry on the wings, baggage train behind, and a scouting force of Prodromoi/Sarissophoroi and light infantry ahead; these spotted the Persian army on the opposite bank of the river and reported back to Alexander (Arr. *Anab.* 1.13.1–2).[2]

---

1   Whatley (1964) for the problems; Sabin (2007) offers an alternative methodology (a wargame simulation), pp.1–15 for further discussion.
2   Granicus: Badian (1977); Foss (1977); Bosworth (1980) pp.114–24; Hammond (1980b); Devine (1988); Bosworth (1988) pp.39–44; Hammond (1989c) pp 67–77; Lane Fox (2004) pp.119–22; Sabin (2007) pp.129–133; English (2011) pp.33–60.

Orders of Battle

The main difficulty with the Macedonian order of battle is that Arrian describes the deployment of the main Macedonian units but (characteristically) does not mention the allied infantry forces, and in his account of the actual fighting, only the forces immediately around Alexander are described at all, as if the rest of the army played no part in the battle. However, as the whole Macedonian army was present, it is reasonable to assume it was deployed and took some part in the fighting, at least in a supporting role. The units described by Arrian (Arr. *Anab*. 1.14.1–3), with their likely strengths (as discussed in earlier chapters), are as follows:

Companion cavalry	1,800
Thessalians	1,800
'Sarissophoroi' (Prodromoi)	800
Paionians	200
Thracians (Odrysians)	200
Greek allies	600
Hypaspists	3,000 (or 2,000)
Pezhetairoi/Asthetairoi	9,000 (or 12,000)
Archers	500
Agrianians	500

Missing are the allied and mercenary infantry, and the Thracian infantry other than Agrianians:

Greek allied infantry	7,000
Mercenaries	5,000
Thracians	7,000

The location of the first of these, the allied hoplites, is surely given by Arrian's description of the approach march (1.13.1), with the hoplites (that is, the heavy infantry) drawn up in 'double phalanx'. This suggests that, as at Issus and Gaugamela, the allied infantry formed a second line behind the Macedonian phalanx and, therefore, at this battle, will not have been actively engaged. The missing mercenaries and Thracians may have formed a part of this second line or might perhaps have been assigned as a guard for the baggage train (by comparison with arrangements at Gaugamela).

The Persian order of battle presents greater difficulties. Arrian just gives an overall figure (Arr. *Anab*. 1.14.4): about 20,000 cavalry and 'little short of the same number' of foreign (that is, Greek) mercenary infantry. Diodorus gives the lower number of 10,000 for the Persian cavalry (Diod. 17.19.4–5) and breaks this down into units: Paphlagonians, Hyrcanians, Medes, Bactrians and unspecified 'other national contingents'. Since many of these peoples are from the east of the Persian Empire, it is surprising to find them as part of what should be a local force in the west, though it is just possible that they were military settlers established in Anatolia by earlier kings. Diodorus adds the fantasy figure of 100,000 Persian infantry, but this can be disregarded, as can

Justin's even more fantastic 600,000 infantry (Just. 11.6.11) – such numbers have no historical value whatever. It is hopeless attempting to determine the precise size and composition of the Persian army. If they really mustered 20,000 cavalry, this is a very large force indeed, dramatically outnumbering Alexander's 5,000 or so cavalry, and half the size of the maximum effort force of 40,000 or thereabouts supposedly raised for Gaugamela from the entire Empire (see below). At the same time, if the Persians had nearly 20,000 Greek infantry, they would not have considered themselves much inferior to the Macedonians in infantry, as Arrian (Arr. *Anab.* 1.12.9) states they did, nor would the subsequent massacre of the mercenaries (Arr. *Anab.* 1.16.2) have been so straightforward. Perhaps the suggestion in Plutarch (Plut. *Alex.* 16.12) and in Diodorus that Persian infantry (that is, in all probability, locally recruited Anatolian infantry, rather than ethnic Persians) were present can be accepted – it would be odd if the local satraps mustered no locally recruited infantry at all. Diodorus also records that Memnon was originally sent to Asia Minor with a force of 5,000 Greek mercenaries (Diod. 17.7.3) so it is conceivable that this was the entirety of the Greek mercenary force at this battle. Combining the various figures, we might very tentatively suggest the following totals:

Cavalry (Paphlagonians, Hyrcanians, Medes, Bactrians and others)	10,000
Greek mercenaries	5,000
Anatolian infantry	15,000

This would give a plausible size of force to defend the western satrapies, not so small that it would be madness to oppose Alexander's army, but not absurdly large. We can, however, only speculate, and the true totals will remain forever unknown.[3]

Terrain

As with most battles in antiquity, the precise location of the Battle of the Granicus is not known, though there have been several reasonable suggestions. The usual identification of the River Granicus is the Biga or Kocabaş river, and the battle is thought to have taken place somewhere north of the modern town of Biga in Turkey. However, even if we could identify the precise river and the location on the river, we cannot know for certain how much the landscape has changed over the intervening millennia. Rivers have particularly dynamic processes and can alter course dramatically and, perhaps most importantly, the vegetation and ground cover may well have changed greatly. The modern river has tree-lined banks, but none of our sources mentions any obstruction from trees or vegetation, so presumably, the ground was more open in the fourth century than it is today (this observation also applies to many other battles). All we really have to go on are the descriptions in the sources. Arrian describes Parmenion giving a

---

[3] See the various guesses of Bosworth (1980), Hammond (1980b); Devine (1988); Badian (1977) pp.284–6; discussion in Sabin (2007) pp.130–1.

The Granicus river (Biga Çayı) today. (Kızıldeniz, CC BY-SA 4.0)

speech advising Alexander not to attack across the river as 'many parts of it are deep; its banks, as you see, are very high, sometimes like cliffs.' We can suspect more than a little rhetorical exaggeration in this description. During the actual fighting, the Persians were initially advantaged by the river bank (Arr. *Anab* 1.15.2), but the advantage was not so great as to prevent the Macedonians from pushing up out of the river onto the level ground. The banks of the modern river, with a height of two or three metres and a slope of around 45 degrees, seem to fit this description well enough. The Persian and Greek infantry was posted behind the cavalry, possibly on higher ground, though it may be that this just means ground higher than the bed of the river. No tactically significant hills are mentioned, at any rate, and the nearest hills to the proposed battle site today are up to two kilometres to the rear, which seems too far even for a reserve force.[4]

---

4   Foss (1977); Badian (1977); Hammond (1980b).

THE MAJOR BATTLES

Deployment

The tactical problem facing the Persians was straightforward – they needed to oppose the advance of Alexander's army deeper into their territory and, ideally, to defeat that army. The forces at their disposal were a body of cavalry that was large by any standards and between two and four times larger than that available to Alexander, but they were relatively weak in infantry. The defence of a river line appears to have been a common Persian tactic. Some modern commentators have expressed incredulity that the Persians would defend the river bank with cavalry (rather than infantry), but we see a similar defence by Persian (Carduchian) cavalry, with infantry held on higher ground to the rear, in Xenophon (Xen. *Anab.* 4.3.3). The Persians were to follow similar tactics (but with more infantry) at Issus, and the ancient historians, including Arrian, who had military experience, do not seem surprised by this tactic, so there are no grounds for doubting that this is what the Persians did. We do not know how long the Persian army had been in position on the Granicus when Alexander arrived. It is possible that they had only just arrived themselves, and so the battle was very much a meeting engagement, which could explain why all the infantry, moving more slowly, were still in the rear. Diodorus (17.19.4–5) provides the only details of the Persian deployment, which is speculatively depicted in the diagram. Arrian (Arr. *Anab.* 1.14.4) notes that the strongest (presumably both numerically and in terms of quality) of their forces were massed against Alexander, who was conspicuous at the head of his own forces, which suggests that rather than forming a solid immobile line on the river bank, the Persians retained some freedom of movement, with units able to manoeuvre on the ground behind the river, and with pickets or advance forces on the bank itself. This also indicates the second main element of the Persian plan – they hoped to kill Alexander himself, which could well have stopped the invasion in its tracks. Without any clear succession, the Macedonian kingdom could have fallen apart in the scramble to succeed Alexander, as was indeed to happen 11 years later. This was a good plan, and it came within a literal hair's breadth of working.

Alexander wanted an immediate engagement with the Persian army that would allow him to establish local superiority in Asia Minor. The greatest danger, as throughout the campaign, was that the Persians would refuse battle and retreat into the interior while supporting uprisings in Greece. An immediate attack across the river would also surprise the Persians with its speed and aggressiveness, as Alexander was to do throughout his career. The reply Arrian says that Alexander gave to Parmenion's advice to wait and cross at dawn, that this 'would encourage the Persians to think themselves equal to fighting the Macedonians' (Arr. *Anab.* 1.13.7) is plausible – Alexander's need now was for a rapid attack and immediate victory that would establish psychological superiority over his opponents.

This is one of several reasons why the detailed account of this cross-river attack to be found in Arrian, with all its technical details of the deployment and measures taken for crossing the river, of the nature of the fighting on the banks of the river, and of the casualties suffered, is to be preferred to the single sentence in Diodorus' account which suggests that Alexander took Parmenion's advice –

'But Alexander at dawn boldly brought his army across the river and deployed in good order before they could stop him' (17.19.3). Diodorus' battle accounts, in general, are so vague, formulaic and unreliable (see further comments on Issus and Gaugamela below) that no particular weight need be given to this single sentence here. Although at 17.23.2 Diodorus also notes that 'they say' that Alexander placed the river at his rear deliberately to prevent the possibility of flight, we might also note that although the account of Curtius, who used the same sources as Diodorus, is lost, Curtius later notes that Alexander was able, due to his recklessness, to 'cross the Granicus while thousands of cavalry and infantry stood on the far bank' (QC. 4.9.22). Inexplicably, some modern accounts expand this sentence of Diodorus into a dawn or overnight up- or down-stream river crossing by Alexander followed by a battle fought at right angles to the river on the following day, which is incompatible with the accounts both of Arrian and Diodorus. The only motivation for this strange invention seems to be the assumed impossibility of Alexander attacking across the river, an attack which did not remotely perplex Arrian, who had considerably more experience of the operations of ancient armies than any of his modern critics. This 'alternative Granicus' still, sadly, attracts adherents to this day. The battle, we must assume, took place much as Arrian described it, and it is pointless inventing fantasy alternatives or attempting clumsy hybrids of Arrian's and Diodorus' accounts.[5]

So, Alexander needed to force an opposed river crossing against cavalry positioned to defend a difficult but not insurmountable obstacle. The primary tactical problem is described in the speech Arrian says Parmenion gave: 'As we emerge [from the river] in disorder and in column, the weakest of formations, the enemy cavalry drawn up in phalanx will attack' (Arr. *Anab.* 1.13.6). River crossings, and the passage of difficult terrain of any kind, were conducted in column, whereas the proper fighting formation was the 'phalanx', that is, a linear formation. The problem for Alexander then was to get his army across in column without being thrown back by the enemy in line and to deploy his forces into line as rapidly as possible. Compare this with a similar situation earlier when fighting the Taulantians, where the infantry was ordered to cross a river and then extend to the left to form the phalanx (Arr. *Anab.* 1.6.6).

The way in which this was achieved at the Granicus will be described below, but Alexander's initial deployment was intended to set up this attack. The first requirement was to establish a bridgehead at one point on the river and drive back the immediate defenders at that point. Once this was achieved, the rest of the army would have its crossing made easier by the fact that the Persian defenders could no longer count on secure flanks. Alexander posted the Companions, archers and Agrianians on the right wing. Next to these (on their left) were the Sarissophoroi (Prodromoi), Paionians, and one *ilē* (Socrates') of Companions. This, as Plutarch (Plut. *Alex.* 16.2) noted, amounted to thirteen *ilai* of cavalry. Next were the Hypaspists in their usual position on the right of the phalanx, then the main phalanx, in sequence

---

5 The most extreme version of the 'alternative Granicus' is that of Green (1991) pp.489–512 (retracted in second edition); contra, Badian (1977).

THE MAJOR BATTLES

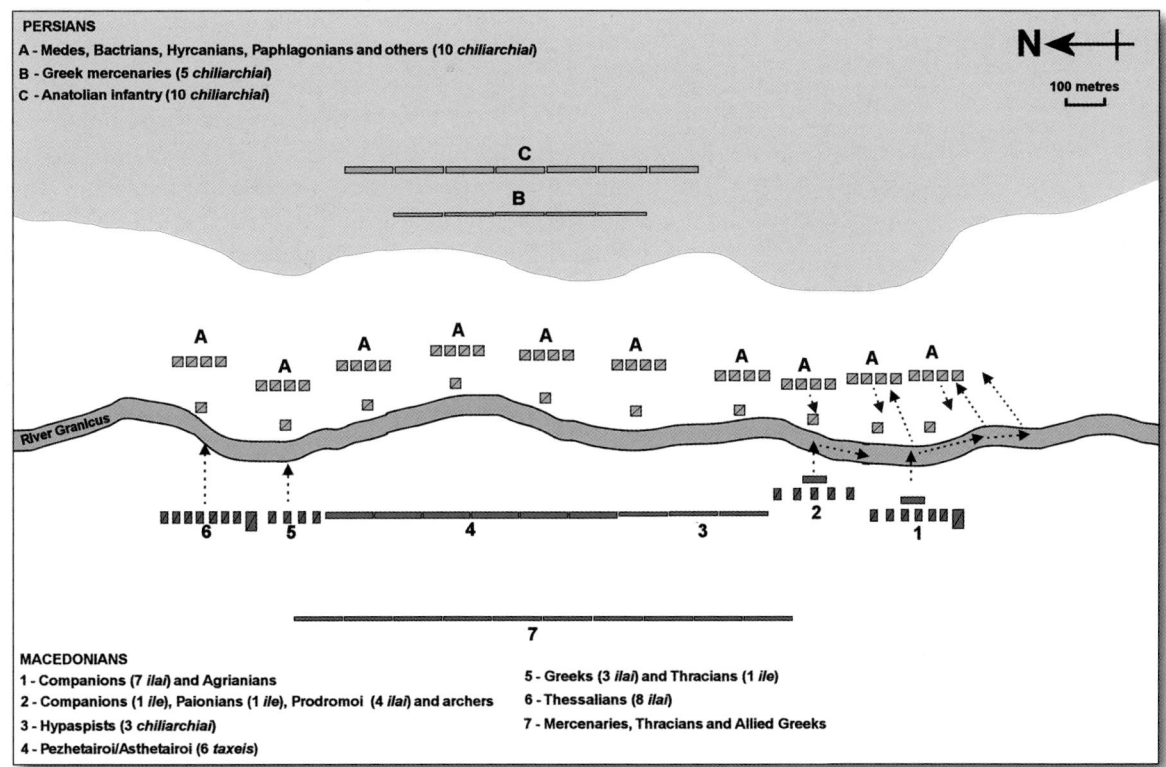

The Granicus, deployment and initial attack.

the *taxeis* of Perdiccas, Coinos, Amyntas, Philip, Meleagros and Crateros. On the left of the phalanx were Thracian and allied cavalry, and finally, the Thessalian cavalry.

As noted above, strangely missing from accounts of the battle are the mercenaries, the Balkan infantry (Thracians and others) and the allied League hoplites. The silence of the sources on some of these units is a common theme in all of Alexander's battles. Possibly they were not present, performing some detached duty elsewhere, or possibly (most likely in my view, since Alexander had every reason to keep his army together at this point) they were formed behind the Macedonian phalanx as a second line, which was not engaged at all on this occasion.

The Course of the Battle

The battle opened with Alexander ordering forward the vanguard units, the Prodromoi (characteristically, Arrian calls them Sarissophoroi at 1.14.1 and Prodromoi at 1.14.6, without noting that this is the same unit) and Paionians, under the command of Amyntas, son of Arrabaios, (a different Amyntas from the phalanx commander) and Socrates' *ilē*, commanded on the day by Ptolemy, son of Philip (not the historian and future king, who was the son of Lagos). With them was one *taxis* of infantry (Arr. *Anab.* 1.14.6) – it is unlikely that this was a phalanx battalion since the Hypaspists lay between the cavalry and the phalanx, so, in this case, Arrian probably means a unit of light infantry, the Agrianians or archers who were posted with the cavalry. Then Alexander led forward the Companions into the river, performing a manoeuvre the nature of which is obscure in Arrian's account and which has caused some perplexity to modern commentators: 'continually extending his troops obliquely in the direction in which the current was pulling them' (Arr. *Anab.* 1.14.7); the current was running from Alexander's right toward his left. The precise nature of this manoeuvre is opaque, not least because there is debate as to whether the extension was actually with the current (to the left) or against it (to the right), but its intent is clear: 'so that the Persians should not fall on him in column as he emerged, but that he himself might attack them, as far as might be, in phalanx' (Arr. *Anab.* 1.14.7). So, the Companions entered the river in column, and once in the river, they extended into line (phalanx) toward their left or right; if to the left, this will have meant deploying behind the point on the bank assaulted by the vanguard units (Paionians, Prodromoi, Socrates' *ilē* and the archers/Agrianians), who had been sent forward first to 'fix' the Persian defenders in place; if to the right (as I think more likely), it offered a chance to outflank the Persian defenders, as suggested by Polyaenus (Polyaen. 4.3.16). This allowed the Companions to march in column but to fight in line, as was ideal (note that there is no indication of the Companions or any of the cavalry fighting in wedge formation on this occasion, for whatever reason).[6]

The vanguard units themselves were having a difficult time, met by volleys of javelins from the Persians and with some Persian units advancing to the bank itself (meaning that others were posted a little way back) to engage them hand to hand (an '*othismos* of horses', as Arrian calls it, 1.15.2). At this point, 25 Companions were killed, and the vanguard was forced back into the river, but Alexander was now close behind, or alongside, with the main force of the Companions, and he counterattacked the massed Persian cavalry on the bank. There followed a close hand-to-hand fight in which the Macedonians were advantaged by their cornel wood lances (*xystois*) against the javelins of the Persians and by the light infantry fighting as *hamippoi* amongst them, and in which Alexander himself was in the thick of the action in a series of Homeric single combats. As the fighting developed, Alexander's force must have made it out of the river onto the level ground since Alexander first attacked Mithridates, who was 'riding far ahead of the line and leading on a "ram" [*embolon*] of cavalry' (1.15.7). This suggests a more open type of combat than the 'othismos' on the banks, with cavalry now having room to manoeuvre. The 'ram' of the Persian cavalry probably just means a strong, deep formation in this case rather than a wedge, as the word *embolon* is also used in this sense to mean an attack column (similar to the ram of a trireme). The Persian plan to kill Alexander was almost successful at this point, as he was struck a penetrating blow on his helmet by Rhoesaces and was about to be attacked from behind by Spithridates when Cleitos the Black saved him by cutting off the Persian's arm with a blow from his *kopis* (1.15.6–8). More *ilai* of Companions, as they made their way across the river, joined in the fighting (Arr. *Anab.* 1.15.8 – a repetition of the description of further Macedonian *taxeis* crossing, 1.15.4), and the Persians turned to flight, first from the point where Alexander was (which Arrian 1.16.1

---

6   Hammond (1980b) p.75; wedges, Devine (1983) but see also Buckler (1985).

confusingly calls the centre, though it was not the centre of the whole line), and then the whole cavalry force.

As is unfortunately typical of Arrian's battle descriptions, nothing whatever is said of what the rest of the army (the Hypaspists, main phalanx and left wing cavalry, including the Thessalians) was doing while this combat was taking place on the right although Diodorus notes that the Thessalians 'won a great reputation for valour because of the skilful handling of their *ilai* and their unmatched fighting quality' (Diod. 17.21.4). It is a common theme in Alexander's battles for Arrian, and presumably his sources, Ptolemy and Aristoboulos, to ignore or downplay the actions of the Thessalians and other allies, and for Diodorus and Curtius (representing their 'Vulgate' sources) to emphasise the Thessalian contribution (but without any tactical details). We must assume that the Thessalians and allies fought their way across the river in a fashion similar to Alexander, while the rout of the Persian cavalry meant that the Macedonian infantry were able to cross the river largely unopposed – there is no trace in any source of Macedonian heavy infantry fighting Persian cavalry on the bank. At any rate, the phalanx was now free to attack the Greek, or Asian and Greek, infantry, who were now without cavalry support and were 'stunned by the unexpectedness of the situation' (Arr. *Anab.* 1.16.2), a vindication of Alexander's decision to attack at once. Alexander brought his infantry up to attack frontally while 'bidding the cavalry fall on them from all quarters' (1.16.2), killing all but 2,000 who were taken prisoner. Given the likely small size of the mercenary force (assuming the figure of 20,000 is not correct) and the unsuitability of any Asian infantry to stand up to the heavily armed Macedonians, together with the cavalry being free to attack their flanks and rear, this massacre was entirely to be expected, though Alexander's implacability will have served more to strengthen the resolve of the Greeks in Persian pay than to intimidate them.

Outcome

The Macedonian losses given by Arrian (1.16.4) are the 25 Companions of the vanguard, of whom Alexander ordered bronze statues to be set up at Dion, the Macedonian religious centre, and 60 of 'the rest of the cavalry' (presumably this includes Prodromoi, Paionians, Thessalians and allies – it is not clear if all the Companion losses are included in the 25, or if these are only from Socrates' *ilē*), and 'about 30 infantry'. Plutarch (*Alex.* 16) notes that Aristoboulos recorded nine infantry losses, so this may be nine Macedonian infantry and 21 other infantry. Such light losses are not totally implausible for a victorious army, in comparison with other ancient battles, and there would also have been many more wounded. The losses given for the Persians are no more reliable than the figures for the size of their army, but Arrian's 1,000 cavalry dead (1.16.2) is not wholly impossible. Whatever the numbers, the battle had achieved exactly what Alexander wished, ending resistance in the field for the rest of the campaign through Asia Minor and inducing a succession of cities to surrender. The next two years could be spent reducing those cities which continued to hold out and installing garrisons and governors in the captured provinces until Darius himself was ready to oppose Alexander's march out of Asia Minor at Issus.

Issus

Introduction

We have already seen in Chapter 7 the strategic movements that led to the battle of Issus; how Darius, at the head of the Persian grand army, waiting in the plains of northern Syria for Alexander to emerge from the Cilician passes, eventually lost patience and marched through the passes to seek battle, and how Alexander's army, after a long delay while Alexander recovered from sickness, marched out into Syria through a different pass, the two armies passing like ships in the night. Discovering what had happened, Darius marched south along the coastal plain and took up a defensive position on the river Pinarus, while Alexander turned his army about and marched back through the pass into the plain to confront the Persians. Alexander's position was a dangerous one, with the Persians between him and all contact with friendly territory, although modern conceptions of the Persians 'cutting his line of supply' should not be overstated since ancient armies did not operate long supply lines but depended on the local area for their supplies. The basic strategic position was unchanged by the reversal in facing of the two armies. Alexander needed a victory over Darius' army to free him up to continue the conquest of the Mediterranean coast and remove the risk of Persian intervention in Greece, while any defeat would leave the Macedonians, deep in potentially hostile territory, in an extremely dangerous situation.[7]

In terms of sources, we are better off than for the Granicus; Arrian contains a reasonably detailed account of the battle (but with some frustratingly vague sections). We have both Diodorus' and Curtius' versions of the 'Vulgate' tradition, which does not differ in any major way from Arrian's account, though there are differences of detail, and both authors embellish their accounts with extremely doubtful, if colourful, details of the fighting, Diodorus' version of the battle in particular being reduced almost to nonsense. We also have the second-century historian Polybius' critique of the account by Callisthenes, Alexander's official historian. While Polybius' criticisms are, in many cases, not valid, we do, through them, get to see some details of Callisthenes' account. Minor snippets of information in Plutarch, Justin and Polyaenus add little to the sum of our knowledge.[8]

Orders of Battle

None of the sources give a detailed account of the army of Alexander at Issus. As we can see from Polybius (12.19), even Callisthenes provided no order of battle, nor even a total figure for the size of Alexander's army, and Polybius is reduced, like so many modern accounts, to trying to guess the size of the army from what we know of the size of the invasion army, adding and subtracting more or less arbitrary numbers to account for losses and reinforcements. Polybius arrives at a total of 42,000 infantry and 5,000 cavalry.

---

7 Issus: Bosworth (1980); Devine (1985a), Devine (1985b); Hammond (1992), Sabin (2007) pp.133–6, English (2009) pp.132–40; English (2011) pp.71–109.

8 Bosworth (1980) pp.203–4; Devine (1985b); Hammond (1989c) pp.98–102; Hammond (1992); Sabin (2007) pp.133–136.

From the accounts of the battle we can discern the presence of most of the core units of Alexander's army, and the safest procedure would seem to be to assume (in the lack of any definite information) that these had approximately the same strengths as at the invasion, losses and reinforcements having broadly cancelled out, though there may have been more Macedonian infantry, given the reinforcement of 3,000 that arrived at Gordion (Arr. *Anab.* 1.29.4), and the Companions and Thessalians too will have been reinforced. As usual, there is no mention in any accounts of the allied infantry and only a passing reference to mercenaries. It is possible that both were absent from the battle, perhaps still guarding the passes, as they had been sent ahead with Parmenion for this purpose (Arr. *Anab.* 2.5.1), though the Thessalian cavalry who were also detailed for this mission, and Parmenion himself, had certainly rejoined the main army before the battle. It is likely that, if the allies were present, they again formed a second line to the Macedonian phalanx, as at the Granicus. As such, the Macedonian order of battle will be similar to that at the Granicus with some minor additions:

Companion cavalry	2,000
Thessalians	2,000
'Sarissophoroi' (Prodromoi)	800
Paionians	200
Allied cavalry	600
Mercenary cavalry	400
Hypaspists	3,000
Pezhetairoi / Asthetairoi	9,000 (or 12,000)
Archers	500
Agrianians	500
Allies	7,000?
Mercenaries	10,000?
Thracians	7,000?

For the Persian army we have the usual problem that none of the sources are able to give remotely plausible figures. Arrian (*Anab.* 2.8.5–6) suggests at least 30,000 cavalry, 20,000 light infantry, 30,000 Greek mercenary hoplites, 60,000 Cardaces (more on these below), another 20,000 probable light infantry, and assorted worthless masses to bring the total to 600,000. Diodorus (17.31.1) offers 400,000 infantry and 'not less than' 100,000 cavalry. Curtius (3.2.4–9) provides lists of units of various nationalities, totalling 250,000 infantry and 62,200 cavalry. Clearly, little useful can be learned from these figures. The total of 30,000 mercenaries is common to Arrian and Curtius, and may come ultimately from Callisthenes, who, according to Polybius, credited Darius with '30,000 cavalry and 30,000 mercenaries' (Pol. 12.18.1). It is possible that Darius had recruited this many Greeks, since Greek mercenaries were undoubtedly plentiful and continued to be so under Alexander; yet, as Polybius points out, there are enormous difficulties in assigning such a huge force (just of Greeks, let alone all the other forces) to Darius, since the battlefield was too narrow (see below) to accommodate them unless they formed in great depth, and there is little trace in the battle accounts of such a massive, deep phalanx of Greek hoplites on the Persian side. Attempting to guess more plausible figures is a forlorn task. The following extremely tentative proposal halves Arrian's figures (and disregards the worthless masses, since if they existed, they had no impact on the course of the battle), still allowing Darius a significant numerical advantage, but with some chance of fitting such an army into the coastal plain.[9]

Cavalry	15,000
Greek mercenaries	15,000
Cardaces	30,000
Light infantry (archers, slingers, javelinmen)	20,000

Curtius is the only source to provide any detail on the identity of the Persian units (3.2.4–9). He lists Persians, Medes, Barcanians (with axes and shields), Armenians, Hyrcanians and Tapurians (?), Derbices (?) (the reading of these last two is unclear in the manuscripts), and some 'lesser known peoples'. As Curtius notes, no Bactrians, Sogdians or Indians were present. This then represents the cavalry from the central regions of the Empire, lacking those from the western satrapies already overrun by Alexander, and from the east, which would not yet have had time to respond to Darius' summons. Curtius also (3.9.4) credits Darius with a guard of 3,000 cavalry – that there was such a guard is certain, its strength less so; at Gaugamela, Diodorus (17.59.2) gives them a strength of 1,000 men.

The Cardaces (Persian 'Kardaka') are an enigmatic unit, and various proposals have been made as to their identity, none of them conclusive. The designation may be ethnic, or it may indicate a selected body of men or new recruits equivalent to Greek ephebes or mercenaries. Given the size and importance of the unit in Darius' battle line, it is possible that it was composed of ethnic Persians or Medes from the heart of the Empire and so constituted the bulk of the ethnic Persian infantry. As to its equipment, Arrian (2.8.6) calls the Cardaces 'hoplites', while Polybius (12.17.7) reports Callisthenes as placing 'peltasts' alongside the mercenaries. Perhaps the truth is that these men fought in close order and hand to hand with spear and shield, but that their shields were smaller and lighter than the heavy Greek aspis, and they were unarmoured or only lightly armoured. Thus, they were armed like peltasts but fought like hoplites and so were equivalent to 'Iphicratean' peltasts. These may be the men depicted on the Alexander Sarcophagus, some with round and some with crescent-shaped shields.[10]

Terrain
As at the Granicus, the Persian army was drawn up behind a river, the Pinarus. In this case, none of our sources suggest Alexander performed anything other than a direct frontal attack across the river, although this has not prevented some armchair warriors, convinced of the absolute impossibility of such an

---

9 See Sabin (2007) pp.134–5, on whose findings these figures are largely based. On the size of Persian armies in Greek tradition, Manning (2021) pp.319–331.
10 Head (1982), Head (1992); Sekunda (1992) pp.51–4.

The battlefield of Issus, as depicted in 1836. (PD)

attack, imagining that Alexander's right wing at least marched upriver to a conveniently unguarded ford, crossed there, and marched back again to the battle. Such fantasies can be disregarded, and instead, we must make the best of the evidence we have. A century or more of scholarly endeavour has failed to identify the Pinarus with certainty. All such efforts seem to be predicated on the idea that identifying the modern river will help us to understand the events of the battle (which seems doubtful) and that the modern river, and indeed the modern coastal plain, will not have changed significantly in the intervening 2,300 years (which seems profoundly unlikely). As at the Granicus, the most important features of the battlefield will have been ground cover (vegetation) and the nature of the river banks. Polybius (12.22.4) notes that Callisthenes claims that they were 'precipitous and thorny' – and this will certainly have changed completely since Alexander's day, especially given the impact of human activity (road building, construction, quarrying). The three rivers proposed as candidates for the Pinarus (Deli, Kuru or Payas) all have their pros and cons; the first two are both longer than Callisthenes records, and the last is closer in length but very rough. The best bet seems to be to stick to the ancient descriptions (modified by scepticism) and accept that, in common with the vast majority of ancient battlefields, the precise location cannot be determined with certainty. The accompanying diagram depicts the course of the modern Payas and should be regarded as schematic, but will hopefully provide a reminder that, unlike the depictions in some modern maps of this battle, rivers tend not to flow in straight lines.[11]

---

11   Bosworth (1980) pp.203–4; Devine (1985b) pp.5–6; Hammond (1992) p.395.

In terms of ancient testimony, Callisthenes (via Polybius 12.17.4) tells us that:

> The width of the ground from the foot of the mountain to the sea was not more than fourteen stades [2.5 km], through which this river ran diagonally. On first issuing from the mountains its banks were broken, but in its course through the level down to the sea it ran between precipitous and steep hills.

Polybius criticises the stated width of the plain on the grounds that neither the Persian nor Macedonian armies could fit in this space. In the case of the stated figures for the Persian army he has a point, but for the Macedonians, he makes the mistake in his calculations (Pol. 12.21) of assuming that the Macedonians deployed at least 32,000 men in a single line and that they were all deployed at four-cubit (two-metre) intervals, neither of which assumptions are sound. As to the nature of the ground, Polybius complains that Alexander would not risk the Macedonian phalanx on such precipitous and wooded river banks (Pol. 12.22), but as there is no doubt that the phalanx did engage across the river, we must conclude that the banks were not quite as rough and impassable as Callisthenes suggests (but still rough enough to cause the phalanx some difficulties). Stories (Arr. *Anab.* 2.10.1) of the Persians reinforcing the banks with fieldworks must also be treated with caution; if these fieldworks existed, they played no part in the fighting. The other feature of note is that the landward hills, on the Macedonian right and Persian left, formed a curved 'bay' (Arr. *Anab.* 2.8.7); this higher ground was suitable for light infantry and allowed Persian forces posted there to curve around the Macedonian flank.

Deployment

Arrian records (2.8.3) how Alexander, during his approach march, steadily deployed his army from column of march into line (phalanx) formation, by *paragoge* of units, that is, each marching up to the side of the unit in front, as space became available. At first, this applied just to the infantry, but as the plain opened out, the cavalry too were brought up into line, at first on the right (2.8.9). Polybius criticises Callisthenes' description of this deployment on the ground that space was not available to deploy the whole army and that the army could not march any distance deployed in line without suffering disorder, but in the latter case, at least the criticism is unfounded since there is no reason to suppose the army marched very far in line. Even so, Arrian (Arr. *Anab.* 2.10.1, 3) records Alexander advancing with frequent halts to dress the line and keep the phalanx in order.[12]

We can roughly estimate the amount of ground that would be required for the Macedonian army. Taking the phalanx and Hypaspists, assuming their strength stood at 15,000, and that they deployed eight deep (as Callisthenes states) and in normal close order (two cubits, one metre, per file), with insignificant gaps between units, they would occupy a frontage

---

12   Taylor (2020) pp.246–50.

of 1,875 metres (reduce this to 1,500 metres if there were only 9,000 men in the main phalanx). Calculations for the cavalry are harder, since we do not know precisely what formation they adopted (wedge, rhombus or square), nor what depth, nor what intervals they had between files, nor between units. Polybius assumes that the cavalry had two-metre intervals and that gaps must be left between cavalry squadrons equal to the frontage of each squadron. This latter point, at least, may be doubted since such gaps would be needed for cavalry performing charge-and-withdraw attacks, but less so for heavy cavalry, like the Companions, who intended to charge into contact. We can best give a range of values, assuming an average of eight ranks in depth (whatever the formation, but Thessalian rhomboids may have taken a little less space), in which 2,000 men would occupy as little as 250 metres (one-metre file intervals, no gaps between squadrons) or as much as 1,000 metres (two-metre file intervals, squadron-sized gaps between units). The median value (625 metres) would mean that the two main units, Thessalians and Companions, would together require around 1,250 metres of frontage. Added to the infantry phalanx, this gives some 3,125 metres. This already well exceeds Callisthenes' 14 stades (2,520 metres) and leaves no space for the other front-line Macedonian units (which included Prodromoi and Paionians and the allied cavalry). However, remembering that the river flowed 'diagonally' across the plain and that Callisthenes' figure is for the width of the plain, not the length of the river, which may have been a stade or two longer, we can see that it might just be possible for Alexander's army to fit into the space available, especially as the right wing, on the hills, did not have a definite edge, but could and did extend up into the hills.

Arrian (Arr. *Anab*. 2.8.3–4) describes the deployment of the Macedonian army on the approach march but also lists a number of last-minute changes made by Alexander as he neared the Persians and was able to react to their deployment. In particular, the Thessalians, who started out on the right, were later (2.9.1) sent across to the left, behind the phalanx, to hide their movement. It is not clear why they needed to be hidden since all the Persian cavalry were already on the Macedonian left. Alexander also deployed, then repositioned, several units to oppose, chase off and then screen the Persian outflanking force on the hills (2.9.3–4). The result of these various moves is described here.

On the right were the Prodromoi under Protomachos and the Paionians under Ariston, supported by two *ilai* of Companions; these were either in front of the other cavalry or beside them (to their right), Arrian throughout his work using the verb *protattein* in both senses. Since they would have been in the way of the attack of the main body of Companions if they were in front, in this case, they were probably on the right. The Companion cavalry were next, and the archers under Antiochos (perhaps in front of the infantry). The infantry phalanx consisted of the Hypaspists under Nicanor on the right, then Coinos' *taxis* (of Asthetairoi), followed by Perdiccas, Meleagros, Ptolemy, Amyntas and Crateros (Arrian 2.8.4 slightly obscures this order, but see also QC 3.9.7). On the left were the Cretan archers and Sitalces' Thracian javelinmen (again, these could be 'in front of' or 'next in order'). The strength of Sitalces' unit is not given – it is unlikely that it was all of the Thracians present, and I have assumed a strength of 2,000. Next came the cavalry – the Thessalians, and Greek allied cavalry, all under Parmenion. Behind and at an angle to the Macedonian right was a flank guard, at first consisting of the Agrianians and 'some' cavalry (either mercenaries or Odrysians) and archers. When the Persian flanking force withdrew, Alexander redeployed the archers, the Agrianians, and the cavalry to the extreme right of his line, leaving just 300 cavalry as the flank guard. This redeployment, and the retreat of the Persian flanking force, meant that the Macedonians outflanked the Persian left wing (2.9.4). The main force of mercenary infantry were 'drawn up in support of the whole line' (Arr. *Anab.* 2.9.3), forming a second line to the phalanx. If the allied League infantry were present at this battle, then they too would have formed part of this second line.

There are two versions of the Persian deployment, Arrian's and Curtius' accounts differing in the placement of the Greek mercenaries. I will follow Arrian here, in the absence of any compelling reason not to do so, and given Curtius' confusion on other points, such as the redeployment of the Thessalians (QC 3.11.3). The initial Persian deployment was screened by cavalry and light infantry, sent forward over the river (Arr. *Anab.* 2.8.5). These were withdrawn when the deployment was complete, and most of the cavalry were placed on the Persian right (2.8.10). The Persian right wing, then, consisted of almost all of the Persian cavalry, as the land near the sea was considered better going for cavalry. An initial Persian cavalry force deployed on the left was mostly withdrawn (for lack of space on the left) and joined those on the right (2.8.11). This resulted in the unusual phenomenon of the Persian army having almost no cavalry on its left wing and allowed the Macedonians to outflank them there. The Persian centre was held by infantry, the Cardaces forming two bodies to either side of the Greek mercenaries who held the centre – Arrian notes that the Greeks were intended to face the Macedonian phalanx, in the centre. Incidentally, Arrian notes that the 60,000 Cardaces was 'the number which the ground where they stood allowed to be posted in one line' (2.8.6). If they had been eight deep and with one-metre file intervals (neither of which is a given), 60,000 men would have required 7,500 metres, over 40 stades (Polybius' criticism here has considerable merit). The Greeks alone would have needed 3,750 metres in their normal deployment. In order to fit 90,000 men even into around 16 stades (around 2,800 metres), they would have to be formed 32 deep, and this would leave no room for the cavalry. Even the reduced numbers I proposed above, if formed 16 ranks deep, would fill the width of the battlefield, and remember that the Macedonian line outflanked the Persians on the right, so the battlefield width is not the only constraint – the Persian line was overall shorter than the Macedonian. It is possible that Persian numbers should be reduced still further, or else we must assume that they formed up in even greater depth. Arrian tells us that Darius stationed himself in the centre of the line (2.8.11). This would appear to place him in the centre of the mercenaries, though as there was cavalry only on the right wing, the geometric centre may have fallen at the boundary between right-hand Cardaces and the mercenaries. Curtius, however, states that Darius stationed himself on the left (QC 3.9.4), perhaps

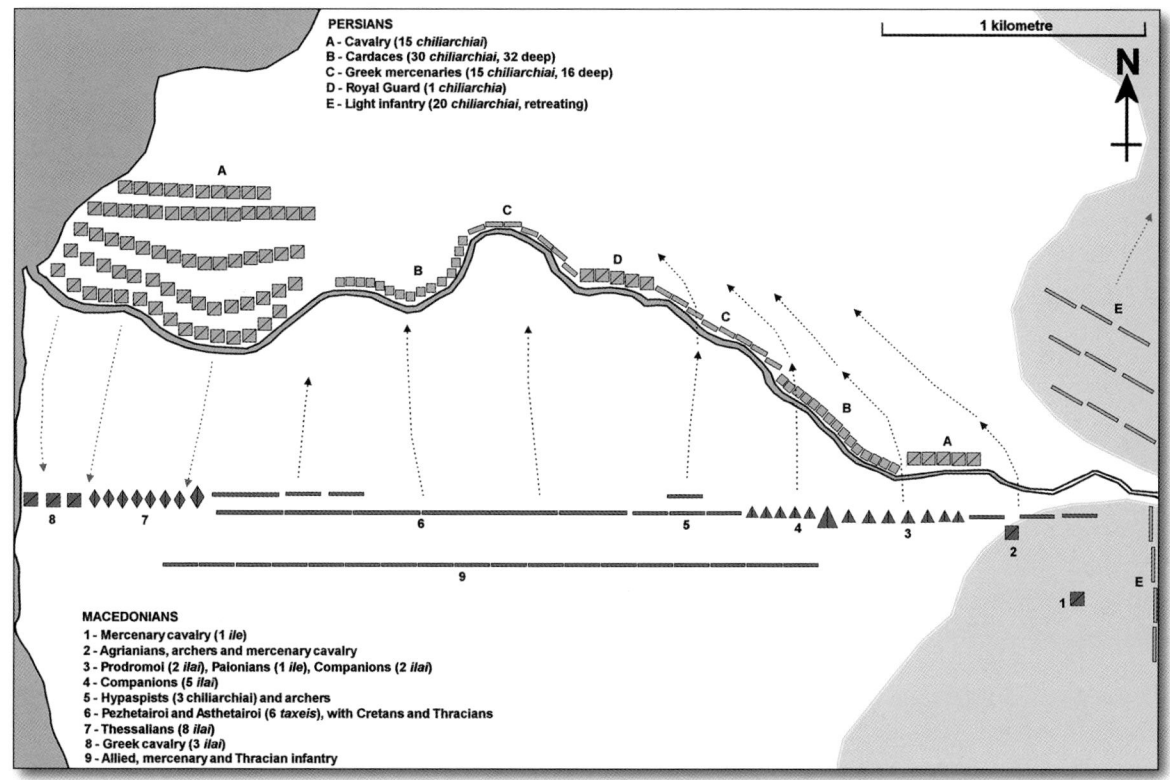

Issus, deployment and initial moves.

between the mercenaries and the left-hand Cardaces. Around Darius will have been the guard. Curtius (3.9.4) credits this guard with a strength of 3,000 cavalry, though there is no mention during the battle of such a large cavalry force in the centre of the Persian line, so they were perhaps 1,000 strong, as at Gaugamela. Large numbers of light infantry were available, initially used to screen the deployment of the main army. When these were withdrawn, some may have formed a skirmish line in front of the main army, though most of them formed the flanking force that Darius deployed forward onto the hills above the plain, which bent around Alexander's right wing as he advanced.

The main problem with the Persian deployment is, as usual, fitting the numbers of Persians into the available space. Whatever the total width of the battlefield, the space on the Persian right was constrained by the sea on one side and the infantry phalanx on the other. Into this space, Alexander deployed something not much over 2,000 cavalry (the Thessalians and the Greek allies). Opposing them was the entirety of the Persian cavalry, at least 30,000 according to Arrian, 15,000 according to the guess I gave above. To fit into the available space, these must have either been deployed in great depth or in multiple separate lines. Just how deep depends on the question of file intervals and inter-squadron gaps discussed above, but allowing 500 metres for the Thessalians and Greek allies, even 15,000 Persian cavalry would have formed 30 deep at one-metre intervals and without squadron gaps, a vast and impractically dense mass of horsemen. This highly suboptimal deployment may provide the explanation for how they were defeated by a Greek force with barely one-eighth their numbers (or else, of course, there may, in reality, have been far fewer of them).[13]

The Course of the Battle

Although Arrian provides a detailed account of the deployment of the two sides and the preparations for battle, his account of the fighting itself is particularly laconic, to the point almost of incomprehensibility. Diodorus and Curtius both provide more detailed, colourful descriptions of the fighting, but they are details culled largely from their imaginations, and, with their accounts of hurled javelins and drawn swords, are written by Romans or for a Roman audience, and add little to our understanding of the battle. The briefness of Arrian's account may be due simply to the fact that in the swirling confusion of two large armies engaging in a very narrow space, nobody present had a clear view of events, and it was simply impossible at the time (and even more so centuries later) to explain or describe all the small-scale tactical moves that may have taken place. The modern tendency to invent tactical niceties to augment the sparse ancient accounts serves only to confuse, not clarify, the course of the battle.

The opening movements saw Alexander sending the Agrianians and some archers against the Persian outflanking force on his right. The Persian light infantry fled before this advance further up onto the hills, so it was at this point that Alexander redeployed the archers, Agrianians, some of the mercenary or Odrysian cavalry, and two *ilai* of Companions to his right, allowing him to overlap the Persian left (Arr. *Anab*. 2.9.3–4). According to Arrian the army still had some way to march at this point to reach the river, though the distances cannot have been great, perhaps a few hundred metres. Alexander had time to pass down the line, delivering a few final encouraging remarks and receiving the ovation of the army (Arr. *Anab*. 2.10.2) – we may doubt that he covered the whole 2.5 kilometres of the line in this exercise. The entire army then recommenced its advance at a steady pace to avoid any fluctuations or breaks in the line (Arr. *Anab*. 2.10.3). Once within missile range – perhaps around 100 metres – Alexander and 'those about him' (the Companions, presumably) charged directly at the Persian line across the river 'in order to strike panic into the Persians by the rapidity of the attack', and to avoid losses from archery (Arr. *Anab*. 2.10.3). Arrian's account of what happened is a model of brevity: 'The moment battle was joined hand-to-hand, the Persian left gave way; and here Alexander and his followers won a brilliant success.' (Arr. *Anab*. 2.10.4). Exactly how and why 2,000 cavalry were able to overcome at least 15,000 'hoplites' (assuming it was the left-hand Cardaces that Alexander charged) has been left to readers' (or later historians') imaginations. Diodorus and Curtius have nothing to add on this crucial incident. In the absence of any hard evidence, it is futile to invent more complex tactical moves to explain the situation, but a few observations can be made. The Macedonian army outflanked the Persians on the right, with the Agrianians, mercenary cavalry and perhaps two *ilai* of Companions

---

13   See comments in Sabin (2007) p.136 n.49 on the lack of space in most modern reconstructions.

being free to wheel inwards and charge the Persian infantry in the flank – this may well have been the decisive move. It was also not just the Companions attacking, as aside from the flanking forces, the Hypaspists no doubt followed the cavalry charge and lent their weight to the attack. The speed of the attack, stressed by Arrian, also compares with Alexander's decision to attack rapidly over the Granicus. Persian infantry doctrine was traditionally based on a preliminary period of shooting to soften up an enemy before any close engagement, and Alexander's rapid charge, expressly intended to avoid the effects of archery, will have had a similar psychological impact as the Athenian charge at Marathon, or the charge of the Ten Thousand at Cunaxa (in the latter case also the Persians fled without even coming to close combat). That a sudden attack, pressed home with determination, could cause the collapse and rout of even a large infantry force was not unprecedented, and the addition of the flanking attack by the Macedonian right will only have made it more likely. The collapse of the Persian left wing appears to have been total, to have been won at very little cost, and in a very brief interval of time.

On the other wing, however, the Persian cavalry had, in their turn, charged over the river to attack the Thessalians (Arr. *Anab.* 2.11.2). Arrian classes this as 'a desperate cavalry fight', without going into the details of how the Thessalians and Greeks held off an allegedly vastly stronger force of Persian cavalry. Diodorus and Curtius (and Plutarch) provide more colourful accounts, and Curtius (QC 3.11.14–15) adds some tactical details: one *ilē* of Thessalians was ridden down, and the rest fought a wheeling battle, retreating, turning and attacking again, in which the more heavily armoured Persian cavalry were at a disadvantage. Arrian (2.11.3), too, mentions the armoured cavalry, but only to note that the armour impeded their subsequent flight. Most important in this combat must have been the limited space available, which prevented the Persians from outflanking the Greeks or bringing their superior numbers to bear.

Now, in the centre, the third act of the battle was under way. Here, the phalanx of Pezhetairoi and Asthetairoi attacked the Greek mercenaries across the river. The banks here, perhaps steeper than those in the upper or lower reaches of the river, turned out to be a more serious impediment, and the order of the phalanx was broken up. The mercenaries attacked, trying to exploit these gaps, and there was a severe struggle, which was exacerbated by the rivalry between Greeks and Macedonians. Here 120 Macedonians were killed, including one of the taxiarchs, Ptolemy son of Seleucos, which suggests that one *taxis* of the phalanx at least must have come very close to defeat. However, Alexander's victorious right wing, and perhaps the rightmost *taxeis* of the phalanx (if the Macedonians outnumbered the mercenaries, as is likely), were now able to wheel inward and attack the mercenaries in the flank. This saved the day for the struggling phalanx, although the mercenaries themselves appear not to have been decisively routed, and according to Curtius, they got away in good order (QC 3.11.18). Most likely, the Macedonians were content to pursue the fleeing Persian units and not take any further risks against well-formed and determined opponents.

The last controversial point in the battle is the action of Darius. According to Diodorus and Curtius, Alexander, as soon as he had routed the Persian left, made for Darius' position. Arrian states that Darius fled as soon as the left wing began to collapse (Arr. *Anab.* 2.11.4), but Diodorus (17.34.1–7) and Curtius (3.11.7–12) describe a hard-fought battle between elements of the victorious Macedonian right and Darius' guard. Only after several of Darius' officers had been killed did Darius turn his ceremonial chariot in flight, a moment possibly captured in the Alexander Mosaic from Pompeii. In this case, Diodorus and Curtius may be preferred to Arrian, but it is unclear why Arrian or Ptolemy would underplay such a dramatic moment in this way. This would mean that the Macedonian right, in order to get at the right-hand group of mercenaries and attack their flank, had to go through Darius' guard, and it was the flight of Darius and his guard that signalled, and triggered, the final collapse of the Persian army, the right wing cavalry somehow getting wind of the turning of the tide of the battle, and making their escape.

Outcome

The Macedonian pursuit was pressed vigorously. However, the casualty figures for both sides are worthless. Those for the Persians at least show some consistency (110,000 men), but this makes them no more believable, while the Macedonian losses vary between all the sources. We can only say that while the victor's losses were, as was often the case in ancient warfare, comparatively light, the phalanx did suffer higher than usual losses in its fight with the mercenaries. Darius himself got away, though his family was captured (and treated honourably) by Alexander. Many of the mercenaries also escaped, though all but 2,000 made their way home to Greece rather than sticking with what was increasingly obviously a lost cause. The Persian army itself was severely mauled, but not destroyed. Alexander was free now to complete his capture of the Mediterranean coastline, but a final reckoning with Darius, and the largest Persian army yet, was still to come.

Gaugamela

Introduction

It took a further two years for Alexander to secure the Mediterranean, encompassing the sieges of Tyre and Gaza, the triumphal entry into Egypt, and the pilgrimage to the Siwa oasis. Then Alexander turned north and east, and struck inland from Syria to reach the Euphrates. Darius had not been idle for these intervening years, gathering his forces from all remaining parts of the Empire, including the Upper Satrapies bordering on India. With this army, he waited in Babylon at first for Alexander's approach, not attempting this time to contest either the Euphrates or Tigris river crossings other than with token forces. As Alexander continued to march inland, Darius marched out to meet him, selecting a broad plain east of the Tigris on which to fight the battle. Alexander still had reason to fear that the Persian king would not offer battle but would finally adopt Memnon's original advice, fighting with scorched earth and guerilla actions, but the Persian tradition of fighting pitched battles to determine the outcome of wars was as strong as the Greek, and Alexander had also tauntingly challenged Darius to fight for his kingdom in a series of diplomatic letters. The result would be a formal engagement to decide the outcome of the first half of the campaign and, as the Greeks saw it, the lordship of Asia.

On this occasion, however, unlike at the Granicus and Issus, Alexander was to show a little caution. He initially marched directly for the Persian army's location as soon as firm intelligence was brought in by his scouts, but on cresting a range of hills and seeing the Persian army deployed on the plain, he paused to take stock, reconnoitre the battlefield, and revise his plans. This also allowed the army to rest from its approach march, while the Persians stood to arms all night for fear of a night attack (as was proposed, allegedly, by Parmenion). The following day, Alexander led his army out of camp in battle array.

It is interesting to note that, unusually for any ancient battle, there exists a near-contemporary though very brief account in the form of a Babylonian cuneiform tablet (now in the British Museum), recording astronomical events leading up to the day of battle. The events of the battle itself are summarised as 'The twenty-fourth [day of the month], in the morning, the king of the world [Alexander] … his standard. Opposite each other they fought and a heavy defeat of the troops … The king [Darius], his troops deserted him and to their cities … They fled to the land of the Guti.'[14]

Orders of Battle

Arrian, for the first time, gives a total size for the Macedonian army (Arr. *Anab.* 3.12.5), stating that it amounted to 'some 7,000 cavalry and 40,000 infantry'. This matches well enough with the numbers we have for the crossing of the Hellespont, and though losses were suffered and garrisons detached, reinforcements were also received. In the absence of hard information to the contrary it is best to conclude that the various individual contingents – the locations, but not the numbers, of which Arrian describes in his account – again had more or less the same strength as they had earlier in the campaign. However, some specific reinforcements are known, notably that the Agrianians appear to have increased in number, perhaps to 1,000 men (Curtius 3.9.10 mentions newly-arrived Agrianians 'from Greece', usually amended to 'from Thrace', before Issus), and there appear also to be more archers, perhaps also now up to 1,000 in number. The Companions and Thessalians had also received reinforcements earlier in the campaign, and 500 Thracian cavalry joined the army in Egypt (Arr. *Anab.* 3.5.1). Given the large size of Alexander's infantry force, it seems also that the allied League, mercenary Greek and Balkan contingents were definitely present at this battle, and were given a specific tactical role. We do not, however, have definite information as to the size of these contingents, and they must be deduced from what is left over when other named units are accounted for.[15]

---

14 Gaugamela: Marsden (1964); Devine (1986) and (1989a); Sabin (2007) pp.136–9; English (2011) pp.110–157; Babylonian text – Bernard (1990).
15 Macedonian numbers largely based on Marsden (1964) pp.24–30, table on p.38 and App.2, pp.68–73.

The Macedonian order of battle can be summarised as follows, based on Arrian (Arr. *Anab*. 3.11.8–12.5). These details are based on good evidence for the Macedonian and main line forces, but become more speculative for the Greeks, mercenaries and Thracians. The total that Arrian gives: 'some 7,000 cavalry and about 40,000 infantry' (Arr. *Anab*. 3.12.5) is likely to be accurate.

Companion cavalry	2,000
Thessalians	2,000
'Sarissophoroi' (Prodromoi)	800
Mercenary cavalry	1,000
Allied cavalry	750
Thracians (Paionians, Odrysians)	700
Hypaspists	3,000
Pezhetairoi / Asthetairoi	12,000 (or 9,000)
Macedonian archers	500
Cretan archers	500
Agrianians	1,000
Javelinmen	500
Veteran mercenaries	2,000
Other mercenaries	9,000
Sitalces' Thracians	2,000
Other Thracians	3,000
Allies	7,000

For the Persian order of battle, we have an unusually complete list of unit names together with their locations in the line, thanks to the capture after the battle of a written deployment plan (Arr. *Anab*. 3.11.3), at least according to Aristoboulos. Arrian's other main source, Ptolemy, apparently did not mention this plan, and Arrian provides a second, slightly vaguer, catalogue of Persian units (Arr. *Anab*. 3.8.3–6), which may come from Ptolemy and which has some discrepancies with Aristoboulos' list. Curtius (QC 4.12.6–12) provides a third variation, together with strengths for some of the units. This chaotic situation cannot be resolved with certainty.

Total strengths given for the Persian army are also the usual fantasy numbers: 40,000 cavalry and 1,000,000 infantry according to Arrian (Arr. *Anab*. 3.8.6), 45,000 cavalry and 200,000 infantry in Curtius (QC 4.12.13), and 200,000 cavalry and 800,000 infantry in Diodorus (Diod. 17.53). Arrian's figure of 40,000 cavalry is not totally incredible, as Darius had two years to prepare for the battle and could call on the cavalry-producing eastern satrapies of the kingdom, and Alexander clearly expected his army of 47,000 men to be comprehensively outflanked. This is a truly vast cavalry force, however, and it may be that the true number should be revised considerably downwards (for comparison, at Waterloo, Napoleon deployed around 15,000 cavalry). On this occasion, the terrain does not provide any helpful clues as to the length of the line, and ingenious attempts to compare the total Persian line length to that of the Macedonians fail on the simple fact that we do not know at what depth the Macedonians deployed (eight or 16 deep), which clearly makes a huge difference to the length of their line. For the purposes of making a guess, I will assume the Persians deployed around 20,000 cavalry, around 10,000 infantry of reasonable quality and value, with maybe another 40,000 poor-quality infantry deployed to the rear. The order of battle given below combines the best guesses of modern commentators with the figures of Arrian and Curtius and my own estimates.[16]

Royal Kinsmen	1,000
Bactrians	3,000
Dahai and Arachotians	2,000
Persians	2,000
Susians	1,000
Cadusians	1,000
Syrians	1,000
Mesopotamians	1,000
Medes	3,000
Parthians and Sacae	2,000
Tapurians and Hyrcanians	2,000
Albanians and Sacesians	2,000
Indians	1,000
'Apple-bearers' (Guard)	1,000
Greek mercenaries	2,000
Persians	4,000
Carians	1,000
Mardian archers	2,000
Uxians	10,000
Babylonians	10,000
Red Sea peoples	10,000
Sittacenians	10,000
Scythed chariots	200

Terrain

The battle was fought, according to current best estimates, on the open plains around 20 kilometres either northeast or east of modern Mosul, perhaps near the modern towns of Karemlash or Darweshan, in Iraqi Kurdistan. This location is not particularly conducive to scholars pottering around in search of ancient battlefields, and this, along with the fact that the battlefield was selected specifically because it was devoid of any natural features (Arr. *Anab.* 3.8.7), means that debates about the location of the battle have not taken place to the same extent as for Alexander's previous battles. The ground was flat and featureless, aside from the low hills from which Alexander first viewed the Persian army, and unless archaeology is some day to reveal evidence of weapons or casualties, it is unlikely we will ever know exactly where the battle took place nor does it much matter. Around October, when the battle took place, at the tail end of the summer season, the ground would

---

16 Compare calculations of Marsden (1964) pp.32–9; Devine (1986) pp.100–3; Hammond (1989c) pp.140–3.

THE ARMY OF ALEXANDER THE GREAT

View of the possible site of the battle of Gaugamela, Kurdistan. (Calvin D. Sun, MD of The Monsoon Diaries, monsoondiaries.com | nstagram.com/monsoondiaries)

have been dry, brown and dusty, and whether the plains were (as now) given over to agriculture or still had natural ground cover, there would have been little vegetation to impede army movement, and such as there was may have been removed by the Persians to ensure smooth running for their cavalry and chariots (Arr. *Anab.* 3.8.7).[17]

Deployment

The Persian army standing to arms in order of battle meant that Alexander had a chance to study its deployment and plan his own accordingly. The resulting formation is described in detail by Arrian (3.11.8–12.5), though unfortunately some points of detail and a couple of fundamental features remain obscure. The main battle line was formed in conventional fashion, with the Companions on the right, led by the Royal Squadron, followed (going right to left) by the Hypaspists, then the six *taxeis* of Asthetairoi and Pezhetairoi, then a unit of allied Greek cavalry, and finally the Thessalians. Parmenion, as usual, was given the command of the left, with Alexander personally commanding the right.

Unlike in the previous two battles, Alexander fully expected to be outflanked in this battle – he was heavily outnumbered in cavalry and there

---

17   Location and terrain – Marsden (1964) pp.11–23; Fuller (1960) pp.163f. There are some willing and able to visit the possible battlefield – see for example, <youtu.be/guw1huK73EE?si=cud8mI bHWPNpnrSx> and <https://monsoondiaries.com/2018/05/08/the-battle-of-gaugamela-is-in-iraq/>.

were no terrain features on which he could anchor his flanks. It might be thought in these circumstances that the line would be made as long as possible, so as to reduce the chance of encirclement, but in fact Alexander posted over half of his army as flank and rearguards, thus shortening the line and making outflanking even more certain. There are a number of reasons for this. Facing a superiority of cavalry, no length of line would have been sufficient to prevent outflanking completely, so it was better to provide flank and rear guards than to extend the line. The forces used for the rearguard, probably the allied Greek infantry and mercenaries, were not considered the best quality and, as at the previous two battles, Alexander preferred to fight the battle with his most capable and motivated units, chiefly the Macedonians and Thessalians, even though this meant using only a part of his available force, a clear indication of the perceived superiority of quality over quantity. Finally, Alexander accepted being outflanked as part of his plan, intending to draw Persian cavalry around his flanks to clear the way for the decisive charge of the Companions in the right centre.

So, to guard the rear Alexander posted the allied Greek and some mercenary infantry as a second line behind the phalanx, as he may have done also at Issus and perhaps the Granicus, though at Gaugamela they had a definite tactical function, to face about and protect the rear of the phalanx against encircling enemy cavalry. Arrian's wording – that Alexander 'posted a second line, so that the phalanx would be two-fronted' (3.12.1) does not make it clear whether this second line was immediately behind the main phalanx, effectively doubling its depth (this is the meaning of 'two-fronted', *amphistomos*, given in the Tacticians (Asclep. 11.3–4, specifically says that file-leaders formed the outside rank on both sides of a column), or was a separate formation posted at some distance to the rear. Most likely it was the latter, since there needed to be room for two flank guards, posted 'at an angle' (*es epikampen*) to the front line. The phrase 'at an angle' has been interpreted in various ways, and the Greek word used does not have a fixed meaning in terms of what angle is meant, but it is most likely that these flank guards were posted at roughly right angles to the front line, so that as the army faced the front they formed deep columns. The formation as a whole would therefore have been a vast hollow rectangle. These flank columns contained a mixture of cavalry and light infantry, as Alexander intended once again to take advantage of the function of light infantry as *hamippoi*, supporting the cavalry, though in this case the cavalry would also be required to charge out ahead of their supports to intercept Persian outflanking movements. The right-hand column (Arr. *Anab.* 3.12.1–4) consisted of, from front to back, half the Agrianians, the Macedonian archers, and the 'old' mercenaries ('old' probably in the sense that they had been with the army from the outset, rather than being formed from one of the drafts of new reinforcements). This mercenary unit was unlikely to have been all the mercenaries present and, perhaps, was a single unit of 1,000. 'In front of' these were further units, the Prodromoi and Paionians, and then a unit of mercenary cavalry. As usual, Arrian uses *protattein* to mean both 'in front of' and 'next in line to', in this case further complicated by the fact that these formations being columns, units 'in front of' the main column would also be to their right. The usual interpretation is that these units were posted in multiple lines (or columns, as deployed). The other half of the Agrianians and archers and a unit of javelinmen were also deployed as a skirmish line in front of the Companions, specifically to deal with the Persian chariots. A similar flank guard formation was deployed on the left, made up of Sitalces' unit of Thracians (as at Issus) along with allied cavalry, the Odrysian cavalry and another unit of mercenary cavalry. A further unit of Thracian infantry (of unknown strength) was posted as a guard for the baggage animals, well to the rear.

The Persian deployment was also unusual, in that almost the whole of the front line was made up of cavalry, rather than the usual arrangement of an infantry centre with cavalry on the wings. The left wing was formed primarily of Bactrians, heavy, partially armoured cavalry, supported by Dahai, mounted archers, and Arachotians, who were probably heavy cavalry. Next, working left to right, was the Persian national contingent, a mixture of cavalry and infantry (but in separate units since there is no mention of Persian infantry and cavalry closely cooperating the way Alexander's light infantry did with his cavalry), along with other cavalry from the central Empire. The centre contained the 'Kinsmen' (guard cavalry), the 'Apple-bearers' (the Persian infantry guard), various other infantry, and a small force (perhaps as few as 2,000) of Greek mercenaries, the remnants of the force that fought at Issus. The right wing was another mix of cavalry units of various nationalities, most importantly Medes (heavy cavalry), and Sacai and Parthians, mostly light cavalry and horse archers. In the rear were formed large (but apparently useless) bodies of infantry. In front of the whole line was the Persian secret weapon, 200 scythed chariots, a traditional Persian weapon with a mixed record of success, but which Darius hoped would break up the formation of the Macedonian phalanx, allowing his much smaller force of heavy infantry to fight them with some hope of success. Arrian (3.11.6–7) also mentions a small force of Indian elephants, but as they do not appear in the battle accounts and Arrian also notes that they were captured in the Persian camp along with the baggage (3.15.4) it is most likely that they played no part in the battle.[18]

Darius' army was undoubtedly strong in cavalry, but it lacked any strength in infantry. His best hope was to use his cavalry superiority to outflank and overwhelm Alexander's cavalry, while breaking up the Macedonian phalanx with his chariots and then surrounding and destroying it with his cavalry. The plan required that his cavalry manoeuvre around Alexander's flanks rather than confronting the Macedonians frontally, and as it turned out, this was its greatest weakness.

The Course of the Battle
Arrian (Arr. *Anab.* 3.13.1–15.7) provides a reasonably detailed and comprehensible account of the course of the battle, though as is often the case he is vague on some of the key movements and on events on the Macedonian left, and a few uncertainties and controversies remain. Diodorus (17.57–

---

18 On scythed chariots see Heckel, Willekes and Wrightson (2010).

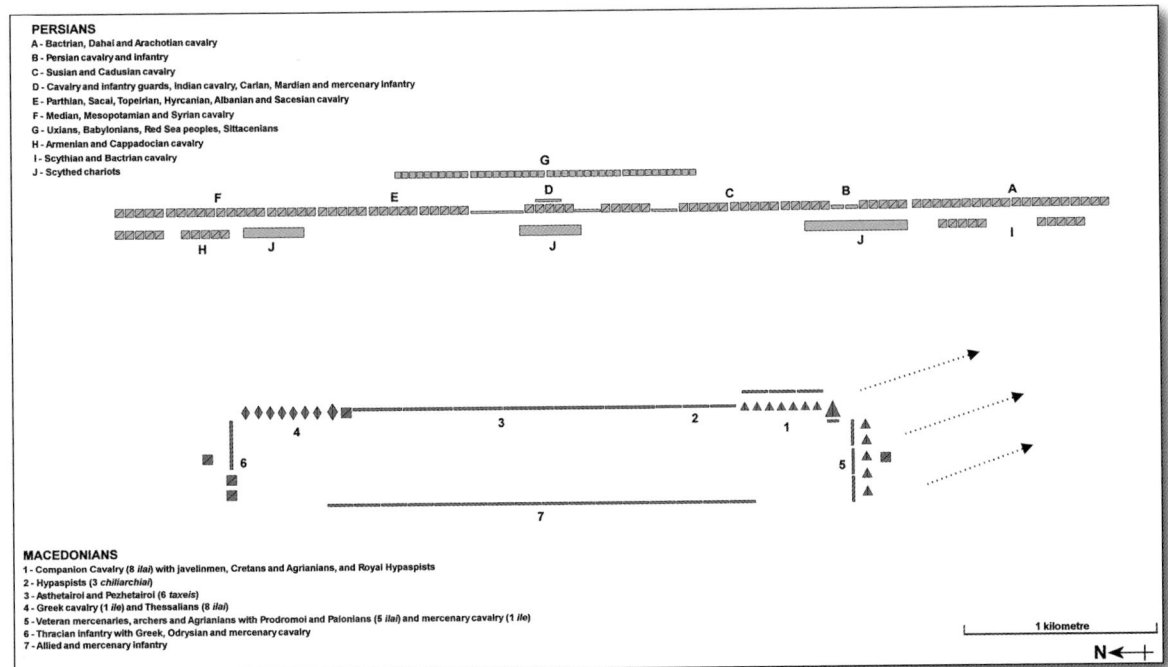

Gaugamela, deployment.

61) provides a colourful account with particular emphasis on the scythed chariots and, along with Curtius (QC 4.13–16), on events in and around the Macedonian camp, with which both are fascinated. Curtius muddles commanders, contingents, camps, infantry with cavalry, and left with right, though some still believe that useful information can be extracted from his account. Plutarch (*Alex* 32–3) adds nothing of value. So as usual, we are primarily reliant on the account of Arrian.

Alexander's camp was about 5.4 kilometres away from the Persian army, on the hills from where Alexander had his first sight of its deployment (Arr. *Anab*. 3.9.3–4). From there, the army advanced over the intervening ground in battle array. As they drew closer (perhaps a few hundred metres), the Persian centre was opposite the Companions, on the right of the shortened Macedonian front line (Arr. *Anab*. 3.13.1). At this point Alexander began to march 'more towards his right' (Arr. *Anab*. 3.13.1), usually interpreted as an oblique advance (as suggested by QC 4.15.1) but, given the closeness of the two armies at this point, it may be that the movement was directly to the right, the whole battle line switching from an advance in line, by a half turn to the right, to an advance in column (the flank guards, previously advancing in column, would now be moving rightwards in line). The Scythian cavalry advance guard in front of the Persian left was already 'in contact with' (perhaps meaning in shooting range of) the Agrianians and archers posted in front of the Companions (Arr. *Anab*. 3.13.2). Arrian records that the Macedonian movement threatened to take them off the levelled ground in front of the Persian army, although this can hardly have been so unless the Persians only levelled narrow lanes in front of the chariots – the Persian army must still have outflanked the Macedonians on both flanks. Anyway, Darius wished to halt the rightward movement, so ordered his left wing advance

THE ARMY OF ALEXANDER THE GREAT

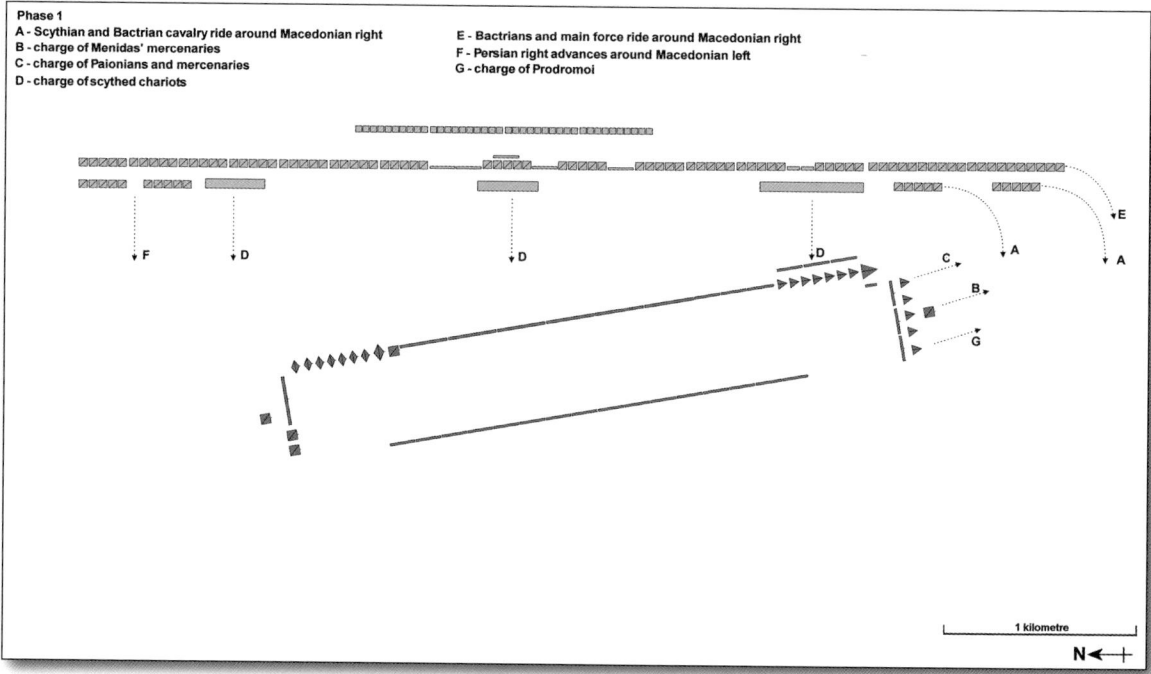

Gaugamela, initial moves.

guard (Bactrian and Scythian cavalry) to ride around the Macedonian right wing. Outflanking movements of this sort, easy to draw on a battle map but much more complicated to conduct on a battlefield, were usually made in column, the original lines making a half turn in place to the left (in this case), advancing in column and wheeling forward to form a new line at right angles (more or less) to the original line, which would then turn in place again to face inward. While conducting such a manoeuvre a force was vulnerable, out of combat formation and probably in some disorder, depending on experience and training. Alexander seized the opportunity and ordered Menidas with the mercenary cavalry to attack; the Scythians and Bactrians, however, were practised horsemen and were able to recover their formation and counter-charge, supported by their main line, and Menidas' men were driven back. Alexander sent in reinforcements – the Paionians, supported by the mercenary infantry – and this combined arms force held and broke up the Bactrians and Scythians, despite their heavier armour (Arr. *Anab.* 3.13.4).

Darius now ordered forward the scythed chariots; there were 100 in advance of the Persian left, now opposite the Companions, and smaller groups of 50 each in front of the Persian centre and right. Despite the colourful accounts of Curtius and Diodorus, these chariots seem to have been completely ineffective, the Agrianians and Balacros' javelinmen breaking up their charge with javelins and dispersing to pull down drivers and horses. Those that did get through passed through gaps in the line (the line of Companions, but the central chariot unit may have attacked the phalanx, Diodorus, 17.58) and were brought down by the grooms and the Royal Hypaspists, who had been posted behind the Companions to act as *hamippoi* for them (3.13.6 – the Hypaspists proper were stationed to the left of the Companions).

Darius now ordered a general advance (previously only the advanced forces had been committed), still directed toward encircling the Macedonian line as it continued its march in column to the right (Arr. *Anab.* 3.14.1). This committed the main force of Bactrian cavalry on the Persian left, along with their supports, to riding around the Macedonian right, and again Alexander sent his flank guards out to intercept them, the Prodromoi joining the units already committed. These Persian movements meant that the main Persian left wing cavalry units were now fully committed to encircling the Macedonian right, where they were being held by the flank guards, while, with the neutralisation of the scythed chariots, there was little direct opposition in front of the Companions. It is not accurate however to talk of a gap, since several units in this sector remained uncommitted, including probably the ethnic Persian mixed infantry and cavalry force. Alexander seized his chance, and ordered forward the Companions, Hypaspists and the main phalanx. Arrian refers to these forming 'like a ram' (3.14.2), but as at the Granicus we should not interpret this as actually forming a wedge, still less a gigantic wedge of mixed cavalry and phalanx infantry, as there was no need and no time for the complex drill manoeuvres that would have been required to create such a formation. Rather, the Companions will have wheeled their individual squadron-strength (or smaller) wedges to the front, while the Hypaspists, Asthetairoi and Pezhetairoi will have half-turned to their left, back into line, and advanced straight ahead. As at Issus, Arrian provides sparse details of this advance and subsequent combat – 'for a little time it became a hand-to-hand fight' (3.14.3), but the 'thrusts' (*othismois*) of the Companions, and the close order and bristling sarissai of the phalanx, evidently quickly overcame Persian and Greek resistance, and Darius himself again made good his escape. The Persian centre appears to have immediately and rapidly collapsed, while the Persian left was also broken by the charge of the Prodromoi – perhaps this time the Persians did not reform their order as quickly as the advance force had and also became aware of the collapsing centre.

These were the events on the Macedonian right and centre-right. However, the Persian right had also attacked the Macedonian left, though Arrian supplies no details of what happened, merely noting (3.15.3) that the Thessalians 'fought brilliantly' and put to flight the forces opposed to them. Curtius (in the midst of his garbled account of the battle) adds some details: Mazaios, commander of the Persian right, sent 1,000 men (3,000 in Diodorus, 17.59.5) far around the Macedonian left to raid the camp in an attempt to free the Persian royal family, held captive there (QC 4.15.5), while also encircling and attacking the Macedonian left (QC 4.16.1, as also in Arrian 3.14.6). Both Arrian and Curtius (and Diodorus, 17.60.7) record the story that Parmenion sent a messenger to Alexander begging for assistance, forcing Alexander to turn back from his pursuit. According to Diodorus, the message was sent but never reached Alexander. Modern historians have reasonably doubted that such a messenger could ever have reached Alexander if he had been in hot pursuit. Whether or not the messenger is real, all sources agree that Parmenion successfully defeated the Persian right without Alexander's help, but that Alexander did turn back (in what may have been a planned move) and encountered retreating cavalry from the Persian centre and centre-right.

THE ARMY OF ALEXANDER THE GREAT

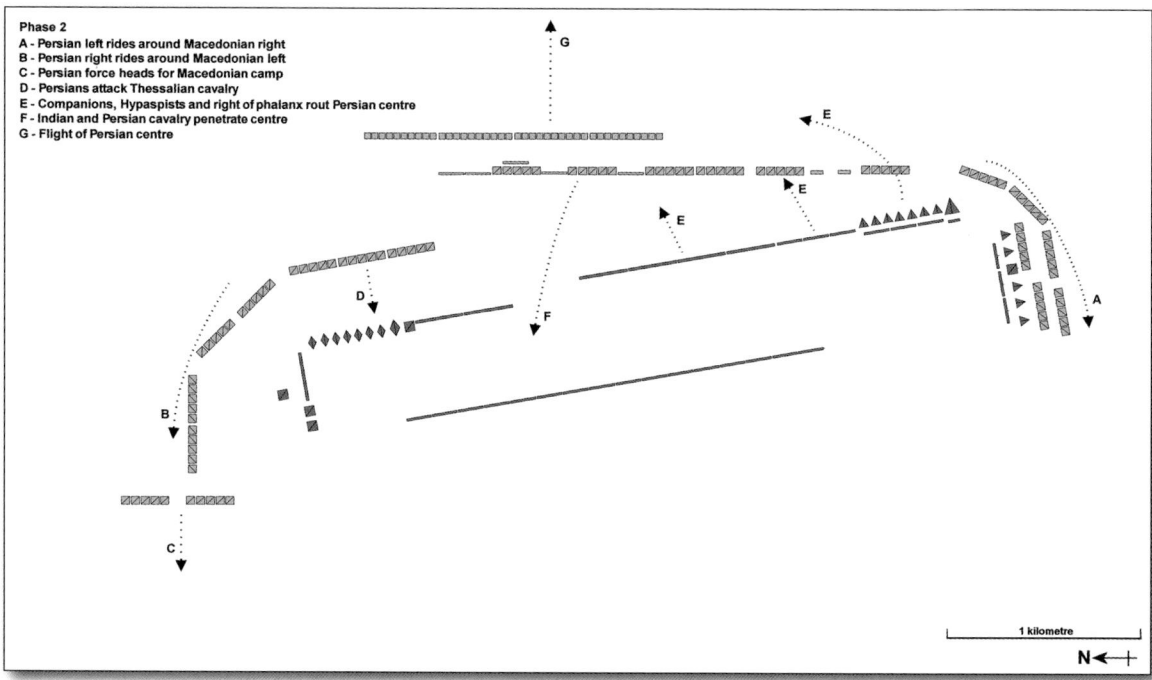

Gaugamela, Alexander's attack.

This cavalry had taken part in one of the more mysterious moves of the battle. When the Macedonian phalanx made its advance on the Persian centre, the two left-hand *taxeis*, those of Simmias and Crateros, were unable to join the advance but remained in place to assist the Thessalians in opposing the Persian cavalry assailing the Macedonian left. This left a gap, into which 'some Indian and Persian cavalry' advanced, 'right up to the Macedonians' baggage animals' (Arr. *Anab*. 3.14.5). The second line phalanx 'turned about face, according to previous orders, [and] appeared in rear of the Persians', driving them off (3.14.6). Several perplexing points arise here; are these Macedonian baggage animals the same as the Macedonian camp, allegedly attacked by Mazaios' outflanking cavalry, and distant some 5.4 kilometres from the battlefield? This is hardly possible, if the rear phalanx was able to about face and march to engage them while the battle was ongoing, so we must assume this was a forward area of baggage (and prisoners) immediately behind the line. Arrian (3.14.5) states that the baggage handlers were mostly unarmed, though he had earlier (3.12.5) noted that the Thracian infantry had been posted to guard the baggage. He states also that they 'had never expected that anyone would cut through the double line of the phalanx' to attack them, though surely the whole point of the double phalanx was to protect against encirclement, from which the baggage, apparently posted behind the rear guard, would have been completely unprotected. An attack, far from unexpected, was almost inevitable, and only the direction of the attack might have come as a surprise. Finally, it is not clear how the attackers got through the second line of the phalanx unless the same gap opened in the second line as in the first. This is certainly possible if the second line, usually depicted in modern reconstructions as a single, shorter block, was in fact composed of separate units, each matching one of the front-line *taxeis*, and mirroring their movements. Many of these problems are resolved if we assume that the baggage was posted between the first and second lines of the phalanx, rather than behind the second line, and so inside the hollow rectangle formed by the army as a whole – this was the normal place for baggage to be placed in a marching square in enemy territory. Arrian may have misunderstood the description of the attack on the baggage in his sources, and the second line, rather than facing about, simply advanced to drive off the Persian attackers. The question then is why the baggage was brought forward rather than being left in the protection of the camp. At any rate, this Persian breakthrough had no effect on the outcome of the battle, though the Persian and Indian cavalry, returning from their raid (back through the same gap in the phalanx?), along with Parthians from the Persian right, encountered the Companions as they swung round on their move to support the Macedonian left, and fought one of the hardest-fought engagements of the battle (Arr. *Anab*. 3.15.2), with heavy losses on both sides and 60 Companions killed, until the remaining Persians broke through and made their escape.

Outcome

With the battle won all across the field, Alexander resumed his pursuit of Darius, suffering heavy losses from exhaustion of horses as he did so (Arr. *Anab*. 3.15.6). The stated casualty figures are worthless, varying significantly between the sources; Arrian's estimate of 'up to a hundred' Macedonian dead can hardly be accurate if the Companions alone lost 60 men, but no more accurate figure can be obtained. As usual in ancient warfare, the victors' losses were relatively light, with no lasting impact on army strength, while the Persians will have suffered heavily in the pursuit, especially the infantry, the bulk of whom played no part in the battle.

With Darius finally defeated and the last Persian army dispersed, Alexander was now undisputed ruler of the Persian Empire, though it would take many years of hard campaigning for him to establish even partial control over the Empire's eastern provinces.

Hydaspes

Introduction

Alexander's march through the Upper Satrapies and into India brought him, in the spring of 326, deep into Indian lands and to the river Hydaspes (the modern Jhelum), where he was to fight the last of his major battles (if indeed it was a major battle, the numbers present on both sides are unknown but probably rather modest). The local Indian rulers were divided on whether to oppose Alexander or join him; Taxiles (or Ambhi), ruler of the city and kingdom of Taxila, had joined him, bringing a welcome addition of men and elephants to what was now the Imperial army. Taxiles' old enemy Poros, however, on the other side of the Hydaspes, resolved to oppose the invader and drew up his army accordingly to defend the river bank. Unlike the previous battles against the Persians, the river, in this case, was wide and deep and could not easily be forded, especially in the face of a determined enemy with numerous elephants. Alexander had to resort to stratagem, carrying out a series of feints, fake crossing attempts, and night-time alarms until Poros relaxed his guard. Alexander then divided his army into three sections: one to guard his camp (and maintain the pretence that the army was still present at full force); one to watch an intermediate section of the river and cross when able; and an assault force under his own command to conduct a night crossing of the river.

The crossing, using a combination of the usual stuffed hides and flat-pack boats that were carried to the required point and constructed in place, was conducted successfully, despite a thunderstorm, and a misjudgement of the terrain that left an extra channel, which the army had to ford, between the initial crossing place and the far bank. Alexander then formed his assault force ready to march against Poros' army. For his part, receiving news of the crossing, Poros initially sent a rapid response force of chariots (heavy Indian chariots with a crew of six men) and cavalry to oppose the crossing, but these arrived too late, became mired in mud, and were easily overwhelmed by Alexander's cavalry. Poros then led out his whole army to oppose Alexander, choosing drier, firmer ground on which to deploy, and the resulting battle was fought as the two forces encountered one another.

The main source for the battle is, as usual, Arrian (5.15–18), but unfortunately, he is more than usually vague on some of the key tactical points and on the forces engaged, and, as a result, the Hydaspes is one of the least satisfactory of Alexander's battles, it being impossible to construct any coherent course of events, resulting in numerous, mutually divergent speculative reconstructions from modern historians, any or none of which may be close to the truth. Curtius (QC 8.14) provides a fairly lengthy account of the battle but with few tactical details, concentrating mostly on the terrifying spectacle of the elephants. Diodorus' account (Diod. 17.87–9) is worthless, and Plutarch (*Alex* 60) adds nothing of interest, nor does a single stratagem in Polyaenus, 4.3.22. We are, therefore, largely stuck with Arrian's account, with all its ambiguities.[19]

Orders of Battle
Arrian provides a breakdown of Alexander's forces prior to the battle, but the main problem with his account is that he does not make it clear exactly which of these forces crossed the river and took part in the battle. Crateros was left in command of the camp with one hipparchy (his own), the Arachotian and Parapomisadai cavalry, and two *taxeis* of the phalanx (those of Alcetas and Polyperchon), together with 5,000 Indians. His orders were to cross only if Poros moved all his elephants away to face Alexander. The intermediate force was under Meleagros, Attalos and Gorgias with the mercenary cavalry and infantry (strength unknown) and, presumably, though Arrian does not say so, with these commanders' own *taxeis*, since they were all taxiarchs. These too were ordered to cross once the Indians were engaged by Alexander, though Arrian never mentions them again. The key question then is whether

---

19   Hydaspes: Hamilton (1956), Devine (1987); Hammond (1989c) pp.210–3; Bosworth (1995) pp.265–9; Sabin (2007) pp.139–143; English (2011) pp.192–215.

they crossed and joined Alexander for the battle, or crossed only once battle was joined, in time to take part in the pursuit, as is strongly suggested by Arrian (5.18.1) referring to 'Crateros and the others who had been left behind as commanders of Alexander's army on the banks of the Hydaspes' crossing after the battle was decided. This would mean that the battle was fought only by Alexander's strike force, which Arrian states consisted of 5,000 cavalry and 6,000 infantry, made up of the Agema of the Companions, three hipparchies (those of Hephaistion, Perdiccas and Demetrios), and the Bactrian, Sogdianian and Dahai cavalry, together with the Hypaspists, two *taxeis* of Asthetairoi (Cleitos and Coinos), the archers and the Agrianians. As the strength of a hipparchy is not known, and neither is the strength of the Asian cavalry units, it is easy enough to make the forces listed total 5,000 cavalry, but the infantry present, if all units were at full strength, should come to well over 6,000 (3,000 Hypaspists, 1,500 or 2,000 each in the two phalanx *taxeis*, and 1,000 each Agrianians and archers), so either the infantry units were not at full strength (perhaps due to the limits of available transport at the crossing), or Arrian has miscounted (both strong possibilities), perhaps counting only the heavy infantry. The following table lists one possibility, assuming there were 6,000 heavy infantry plus 2,000 light infantry.

Agema of Companions	500
Three Hipparchies (each of 500)	1,500
Bactrians	1,000
Sogdianians	1,000
Dahai	1,000
Hypaspists	3,000
Two understrength *taxeis* Asthetairoi	3,000
Archers	1,000
Agrianians	1,000

Arrian also mentions javelinmen (5.13.4) so they might have been present also, although he might just mean the Agrianians (an 'and' is missing in Arrian's text between 'Agrianians' and 'javelinmen'). There remains a problem with the cavalry, since at least one, and perhaps as many as four, hipparchies are unaccounted for – see further the discussion below, and in Chapter 6.

For Poros' army, there is the usual wide variation of estimates, though none of the ancient historians' imaginations ran as wild as they did for the Persian armies. Arrian (5.15.4) proffers 30,000 infantry, 4,000 cavalry, 300 chariots and 200 elephants. Curtius (8.13.6) agrees on the number of chariots and infantry, but gives only 85 elephants, and states that Poros sent 4,000 cavalry and 100 chariots as the advance force to oppose Alexander's crossing. Arrian, after some debate and in evident frustration at the various numbers in his sources, makes this force 120 chariots and 2,000 cavalry, on the authority of Ptolemy. Diodorus (17.87) gives an even larger total for the infantry (50,000) but only 3,000 cavalry and 130 elephants (but 1,000 chariots), while Plutarch (*Alex.* 62) suggests 20,000 infantry and 2,000 cavalry, numbers which, because they are smaller, have gained some adherents.

The number of infantry can only ever be a guess. Plutarch's 20,000 may be accepted in the absence of anything better, though it is probably still too high for a single Indian kingdom. Indian infantry fought as archers or javelinmen, with long swords as secondary weapons (Arr. *Ind*. 16.8–9). The archers used long bows, which were difficult to string on muddy ground; Arrian reports that the bows were placed on the ground to shoot, but this may be a misunderstanding, although Macedonian coins do depict very long Indian bows which may touch the ground. As the battle was fought on dry ground, this would not matter in this case anyway. The chariots were placed, according to Arrian (Arr. *Anab*. 5.15.7), ahead of the Indian cavalry. Arrian gives their number as 300, although 120 were included in the advance force so these should perhaps be subtracted from the total, giving 180 – still a sizable number. Arrian's 4,000 cavalry may be correct, as there were enough cavalry present for Alexander to need to make special plans to counter them, but still few enough that Alexander had cavalry superiority. Indian cavalry were armed with javelins and small shields (Arr. *Ind*. 16.10). The elephants are the main difficulty; Arrian states that the elephants were drawn up a *plethron* apart, about 30 metres, while Polyaenus suggests 50 feet, about 15 metres. If Arrian's numbers and intervals are correct, the line would have stretched for six kilometres, which seems absurdly wide. We may be forced, therefore, to accept Curtius' numbers (85) for the elephants, though Arrian's intervals still give an extensive line of 2.5 kilometres. Even if Alexander's 6,000 heavy infantry formed only eight deep, they would occupy just 750 metres of frontage, leaving them massively outflanked by the Indian army. Curtius' numbers with Polyaenus' intervals would give a more manageable elephant line of 1.2 kilometres. Behind them, 20,000 infantry would have to form 16 deep in close order (as Arr. *Anab* states, 5.16.2) to match the elephant line, though Arrian (5.15.7) tells us that they overlapped the elephants on each end. Even allowing for overlaps, this would seem to be unusually deep for a formation of archers and javelinmen, so the infantry numbers should perhaps be revised still further downwards to allow them to form less deep and possibly in more open order. The following table summarises these findings:

Infantry (archers and javelinmen)	10,000
Chariots	180
Cavalry	4,000
Elephants	85

Terrain

Although the river Hydaspes played a crucial role in the buildup to the battle, it played no part in the battle itself, which was evidently fought far enough back from the banks that it had no impact on the fighting. However, it was close enough that Crateros and the other reinforcements, crossing over, were able to join in the pursuit of the defeated Indians. Much of the ground around the river was muddy from the overnight rain, which impacted negatively on the Indian chariots in the initial skirmish, but Arrian reports that Poros found a place to draw up his army that was 'sandy and therefore

THE MAJOR BATTLES

View of the south shore of the Hydaspes river (Jhelum), Pakistan. (Xishan01, CC BY-SA 3.0)

all level and solid for cavalry to charge and retire' (3.15.5), so the actual terrain of the battle appears to be a featureless, flat and reasonably dry plain. There might have been some folds in the ground to allow concealment (see below). Attempts to fix the exact location on the river seem hopeless, given that broad rivers prone to monsoon flooding flowing across shallow plains can change course dramatically even in short time periods – maps of the proposed location from just 70 years ago are impossible to match up with modern aerial photographs. The approximate location was somewhere on the modern Jhelum River, about 40 kilometres southwest of the modern town of Jhelum, in Pakistan. As usual, we know nothing about the crucial question of vegetation and ground cover. Arrian's description implies a completely featureless plain, though this must surely have been agricultural land and covered in fields, as it is today. The modern fields are lined with scattered trees and thin hedges, though there is no mention of such features in the battle accounts.[20]

Deployment

The overall picture of Poros' deployment is clear enough in Arrian (5.15.5–7). Having reached his chosen dry battlefield, he formed a front line from his elephants, stationed at intervals as discussed. Behind these, the infantry were drawn up, with their individual units matching ('more or less') the intervals between the elephants (5.15.7). The infantry line overlapped the elephant line (we do not know by how much), extending outward on each wing. On each extreme wing, Poros drew up chariots in front, backed up by cavalry.

Alexander's plans and dispositions present more of a problem. Alexander was advancing ahead with the cavalry, following the successful skirmish with the Indian advance force, when he spotted Poros' army drawn up for

---

20 Fuller (1960) pp.180–5 for possible location, with map p.183.

battle. He halted the cavalry to allow the infantry time to come up and rest and to reconnoitre. The tactical situation was that Alexander had superiority in cavalry (Arr. *Anab*. 5.16.2) but that the elephants presented a formidable obstacle, primarily to the cavalry, whose horses would be afraid to approach the beasts, but also to the infantry. He, therefore, decided not to advance in the centre (that is, to hold back his own infantry) but to commence the attack by defeating the Indian cavalry, which would then leave his own cavalry free to operate against the Indian flanks and rear. Unfortunately, the means by which he planned to do this are hopelessly obscure in Arrian's account, and Curtius (still less Diodorus or Plutarch) offer little help. Alexander took command of 'most' of his cavalry, which appears to mean the Agema and the hipparchy of Hephaistion, plus the Dahai (Arr. *Anab*. 5.16.2 and 5.16.4), to attack the Indian left wing. Coinos, meanwhile, was sent 'to the right' (Arr. *Anab*. 5.16.3); the positioning of this statement straight after the description of Alexander moving against the Indian left suggests that Arrian meant Coinos moved against the *Indian* right, but it is also possible that he meant that he moved further to the *Macedonian* right. Coinos' forces are also unclear – he had 'the hipparchy of Demetrios and his own', but Arrian has not mentioned Coinos commanding a hipparchy before, and no such hipparchy is listed in the forces with which Alexander crossed the river, where the hipparchies chosen are those of Hephaistion, Perdiccas and Demetrios. Curtius, for what it is worth, has Alexander commanding the cavalry of Hephaistion, Perdiccas and Ptolemy (QC 8.14.14). Given the debate over the total number of hipparchies in the army at this period, this has led some to believe that Arrian has accidentally omitted several hipparchies, and perhaps more than he lists were present at this battle. However, it seems best to suppose that Coinos was acting commander of Perdiccas' hipparchy, and this is what is meant by 'his own', and that Arrian (or his source, Ptolemy) and Curtius have been more than usually careless.

This does not solve the problem of Coinos' orders: 'to close on the barbarians from behind when the latter saw the solid body of cavalry opposite to them and began to ride out against them' (Arr. *Anab*. 5.16.3). Curtius' version of these orders does not help: 'I [Alexander] am going to attack the enemy left wing. When you see me in the thick of the fight, set our right wing in motion and attack the enemy in confusion' (QC 8.14.15). Curtius does not have a good track record of telling left from right, and Alexander, in attacking the Indian left, would by any normal reckoning be in command of the Macedonian right himself. Furthermore, some deception is evidently intended in Arrian's version, if Coinos is to somehow appear behind the Indian cavalry as actually happened in the battle (see below), but it is not clear how such deception was achieved. Some modern commentators have supposed that Coinos' force was hidden either by the lie of the land or by moving behind the infantry phalanx. We may compare the manoeuvres before Issus, where Arrian (Arr. *Anab*. 2.9.1) explicitly says that the Thessalians redeployed behind the phalanx to avoid detection, although it is not clear in that case why they needed to do so. The problem is again insurmountable, and though various ingenious suggestions have been put forward, we cannot know what actually happened on the battlefield. In the account below, I will

THE MAJOR BATTLES

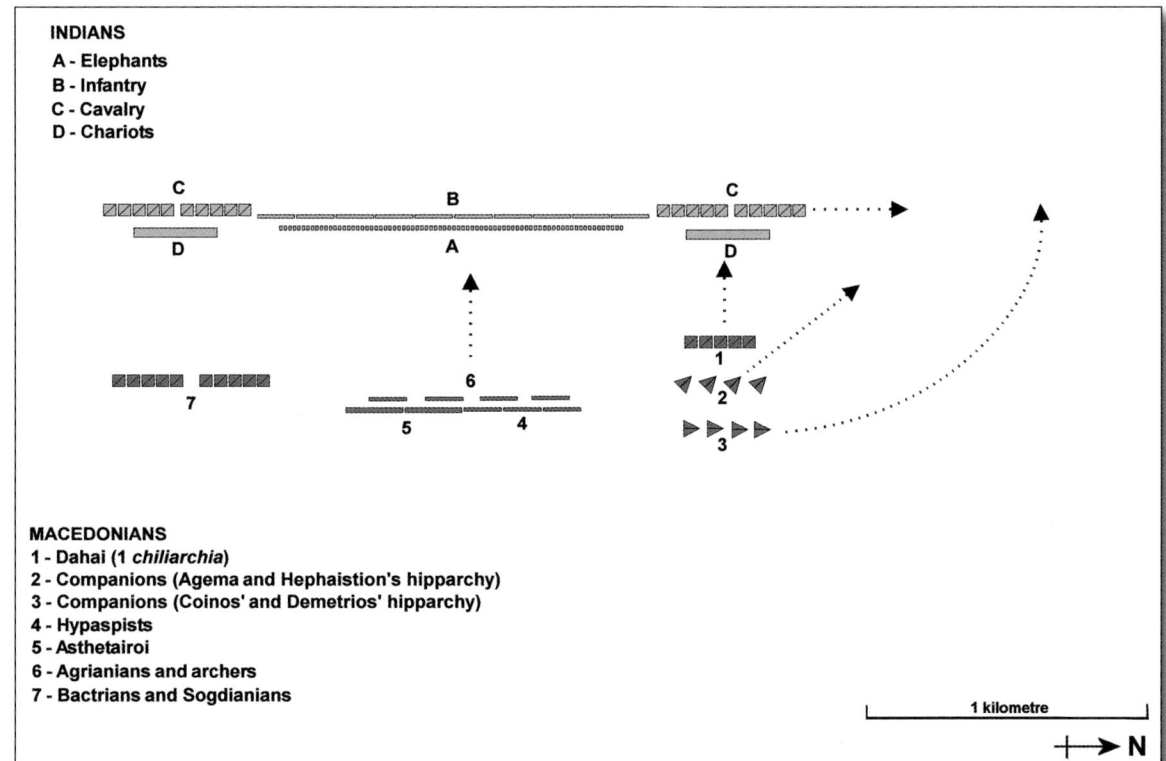

Hydaspes, possible deployment.

offer one possibility. The Bactrian and Sogdianian cavalry, meanwhile, are unaccounted for. Perhaps they formed the Macedonian left and held in check the Indian right wing cavalry, their role being simply ignored by historians much as that of the Thessalians had been in earlier battles.

Orders to the infantry were simpler; Seleucos (commander of the Hypaspists), and Antigenes and Tauron (perhaps stand-in commanders of the *taxeis* of Cleitos and Coinos) were ordered to avoid engaging the Indian main line until the cavalry action was complete, or at least well under way. Although Arrian does not say so, the Agrianians and archers were likely deployed ahead of the phalanx, to engage the elephants with missiles.

The Course of the Battle

Given the difficulties in understanding the Macedonian battle plan, any account of the course of the battle is necessarily speculative. Alexander opened proceedings by sending his mounted archers (the Dahai, 1,000 strong) against the Indian left (Arr. *Anab.* 5.16.4). We may guess that it was the chariots in advance that were the particular target of this arrow storm since chariots always proved particularly vulnerable to missile attacks. Alexander then rode to the attack with 'the Companion cavalry' (the Agema and Hephaistion's hipparchy). Arrian notes that Alexander wished to attack the Indians at speed 'while they were still in column, before their cavalry could be deployed in phalanx' (5.16.4), but it is not clear why the Indians were in column. At Gaugamela, the Bactrian and other cavalry were in column as they moved to outflank the Macedonian line, but this is not the case here, where if anyone is being outflanked, it is the Indians. Again, some tactical nuance must have dropped out of Arrian's account, and we must speculate. Alexander wished to keep his cavalry away from the Indian elephants, and he had an overall superiority in cavalry, so perhaps the outflanking movement here was being carried out by the Macedonians, moving out to the right and around the Indian left flank, thus moving away from the elephants in the centre. The Indians were forced to march to their left, in column, to match this movement, and Alexander, making use of the superior training of the Companions and the flexibility of their wedge formations, attacked before they could reorganise their line to face him. Arrian (5.17.1) states that the Indians were 'concentrating all their cavalry from every quarter' and were riding to match and oppose Alexander's movement. We get an impression of the Indians moving to match an outflanking movement; whether Arrian also means that the Indians moved their cavalry from their right wing to their left is less clear, though this is the usual modern interpretation. They may have done so if they were unable to see Coinos' force deploying to the (Macedonian) left behind the phalanx or in a fold of ground and thought they were unopposed by any cavalry on the Macedonian left. Even so, this would be a move of at least 1.2 kilometres and perhaps more, depending on the length of the infantry line, and it is hard to see how it could take place in the same timeframe as Alexander's 'full speed' attack, nor why they did not spot Coinos pursuing them. More likely is that Coinos manoeuvred to the Macedonian right and simply outflanked the Indians on their (the Indians') left, without any long approach march behind the Indian lines. At any rate, because of these moves, Coinos 'began to appear in their rear' (Arr. *Anab.* 5.17.1), and the Indians had to form on two fronts, most facing Alexander, the rest facing Coinos, which 'upset their formations and their minds', as Arrian puts it (5.17.2). Alexander immediately attacked, and the Indians broke without waiting for contact and fled back to the elephant line. Arrian writes as if there were two attacks: one while the Indians were in column not line, and one when the Indians were disordered by fighting on two fronts, and again, we cannot really make sense of his account. He adds a third engagement, the second by his reckoning (5.17.3–4) when the Indian cavalry return briefly to the attack once the infantry are engaged. It seems best to merge the initial two attacks – Alexander began his outflanking movement at speed, the Indians responded by marching in column to their left, Coinos appeared in the Indians' flank and rear, and Alexander attacked and broke the Indians. We are left then to account only for Coinos' movements; either he conducted an even wider outflanking move to the right, perhaps taking advantage of some dip in the ground, and appeared unexpectedly on the Indian flank, or he remained close to Alexander's force but concealed behind them, and was able to manoeuvre against the flanks of the Indian force when their flank-ward movement took them away from the infantry support. This latter is, I think, the least worst interpretation and is depicted in the diagram. We have then only to account for the activity of the Indian right wing cavalry, who may have been engaged in indecisive fighting with the Bactrians and Sogdianians.

The subsequent engagement of the infantry and elephant main lines is simpler, though not without its obscurities. The Agrianian javelinmen (and the archers, though they are not mentioned) will have been first to meet the advancing elephant line, 'hurling javelins at the drivers' and attacking from all sides (Arr. *Anab*. 5.17.3). Whether the elephants engaged the phalanx itself is unclear. Certainly, the phalanx eventually advanced 'with locked shields' to finally drive the elephants back (Arr. *Anab*. 5.17.7), but up to that point the fighting seems to have been entirely between elephants and light infantry, the latter 'giving way wherever [the elephants] charged, and shooting at them with javelins' (Arr. *Anab*. 5.17.6). The 1,000 Agrianians seem hardly an adequate force for this task; Curtius mentions Agrianians and Thracians (QC 8.14.24), so perhaps there were, after all, more light infantry present than Arrian records. It is also possible that the Hypaspists and Asthetairoi themselves were in their light infantry configuration, armed with javelins (which would have made the river crossing easier), and that they first engaged in open order, closing up later to drive back the elephants. Anyway, the Indian line was thrown into increasing confusion, as the cavalry were driven back on them and Alexander's cavalry, forced together by the fighting into a single mass (Arr. *Anab*. 5. 5.17.4), made repeated attacks first on the cavalry, then on the rear of the Indian infantry. Curtius (8.14.28–9) adds some implausible details on the nature of fighting elephants and adds that the Macedonians used axes and *kopides* against the unfortunate animals – most likely, these were just the regular sidearms of the light infantry, rather than special anti-elephant gear. After all the complex, if obscure, tactical manoeuvres of the cavalry combat, this was very much a soldiers' battle, devoid of any tactical subtlety at all, a straightforward, brutal slogging match. As the elephants lost heart and backed away into their own infantry, the Indians lost all order and many were cut down by the surrounding Macedonians, the survivors being pursued by the forces of Crateros and the others, which were now arriving from their own crossing of the river.

Outcome

Quoted casualty figures for the Indians are enormous but meaningless. Evidently the army was not totally destroyed, as Poros remained in command of his kingdom, his bold defiance of Alexander having attracted the latter's admiration (Arr. *Anab*. 5.18.4–19.3). So Poros, like his old enemy Taxiles (with whom he was reconciled), was set up as a proxy ruler for Alexander, with additional lands added to his kingdom. Figures for Macedonian losses range from Arrian's 80 infantry and 230 cavalry (Arr. *Anab*. 5.17.3), to Diodorus' 700 infantry and 280 cavalry (Diod. 17.89.3). Given the tough nature of the fighting, a higher number might be believed, but 700 is far too high if there were really only 6,000 infantry engaged.

The most lasting impact of the battle was the impression made by the elephants. In the short term, they helped toward the growing demoralisation of the Macedonian army. News of further armies ahead with even larger forces of elephants finally broke the Macedonians' enthusiasm for the campaign, and shortly afterwards, on the River Hyphasis, they staged the mutiny that ended Alexander's eastward march. In the longer term, the battle marks the start of the Hellenistic love affair with war elephants, which were to form a central component of so many Successor and Hellenistic armies in the centuries to come. Yet even at this first encounter, elephants had shown their weaknesses – effective against cavalry, but not manoeuvrable enough to be deployed aggressively against them, so they often had to be deployed spread out in a screen in front of infantry. Here, they proved vulnerable to missile weapons and to skirmishers able to dodge their attacks, while steady infantry that held formation could drive them back, where they could end up doing more harm to their own side than to their enemies.

Conclusions

All of Alexander's major battles display, so far as we can tell, similar features. They were fought primarily by the core Macedonian units of the army, ably supported by the Thessalians and Agrianians, with the other parts, except for the maximum effort at Gaugamela, having, at most, a supporting role. These core units – Companions, Hypaspists, Pezhetairoi and Asthetairoi – were first organised, armed and drilled by Philip II but were used to great effect by Alexander. In all the battles, the key to Alexander's tactics was a rapid offensive, putting the enemy off balance and giving them no time to adjust. This was achieved particularly by the decisive attack of the Companions, with Alexander at their head, providing inspiration and direction. But the other core units of the army were by no means limited to playing a passive role; the modern concept of 'hammer and anvil', often cited with reference to Alexander's army, should not obscure the fact that the infantry too took part in rapid offensive action, and though their exploits are sometimes underplayed in our sources, they were just as essential to the army's success. Alexander's rapid and decisive attacks were made possible by the training, drill and aggression of the whole army and their readiness to attack, undaunted by odds.

Alexander fought four major battles and won them all, as he won every battle, skirmish and siege at which he was present. The clearest defining feature of a military genius is success, so Alexander must deserve the very high reputation he had in antiquity and still has to the present day as a leader and commander in all types of warfare. It is true that the Persian armies Alexander faced seem to have put up a fairly poor performance, but even so, the Persians were themselves well regarded as a military force in their day and held together one of the largest empires of antiquity, so nothing should diminish Alexander's achievements. But on the whole, battles are won not by the tactical tricks of generals but by the skill, determination, discipline and fighting qualities of armies, and without a disciplined army to lead, no tactical nuances are possible. The general's role is largely one of preparation, ensuring that the army is trained and motivated before it even gets near the battlefield, and that officers at every level have a clear idea of the mission and their responsibilities. In this, Alexander was markedly successful. On the battlefield, Alexander displayed an ability for quick, decisive action, for spotting and acting on moments of perhaps fleeting opportunity, and for committing to the attack, when attack was called for, with energy and relentless determination. Alexander's rapid, aggressive actions could be called recklessness at times, and certainly on several occasions, if chance events had worked out differently (the melee at the Granicus, the catapult at Gaza), Alexander's career might have met a sudden and decisive end, and the army been left stranded deep in enemy territory with unknown but dangerous consequences. Perhaps, given their discipline and cohesion, they could have chosen a new leader and, like Xenophon's Ten Thousand, fought their way back home, or perhaps they would have fallen into civil war at the bidding of ambitious subordinates, as actually happened when Alexander died at Babylon, brought low not by a worthy enemy, but by disease. Alexander, however, rode his luck and carried fire and the sword throughout southwest Asia. In doing so, of course, Alexander was doing nothing admirable by modern standards. But there are still remarkably many today, in the early decades of the twenty-first century, ready to applaud and actively support their leaders' wars of aggression against their neighbours. The world of fourth-century Macedon was in some ways not so different from that of today, and a career of conquest would then have been regarded by most people as something to be aspired to. Alexander's conquests were among the most remarkable in the history of the world, and the credit for them, if credit is due, rests equally with Alexander and Philip and with the army they created and utilised with such success.

Notes to colour plates

1 – Alexander the Great
Based on the depiction of Alexander on the Alexander Mosaic, with a plumed and crested helmet as worn on the 'elephant medallions'. He wears ornate armour of the 'linothorax' type, apparently with metal scale reinforcement around the abdomen. The tunic is of the long-sleeved type also depicted on the Alexander Sarcophagus. The purple cloak with yellow borders is the inverse of the cloak of the Companions (below). A sword – in this case the curved kopis – is carried as a backup for when the usual long spear was broken in action. Note the cavalry in the background carrying shields – cavalry invariably fought shieldless in this period, but Arrian (*Anab*. 1.6.5) records an incident in Illyria where Companions and Hypasists took shields for a combined-arms assault on a hill, so Companions likely had shields for use when fighting dismounted (for example in city assaults).

2 – Companion Cavalry
This figure is based on a combination of the Alexander Mosaic and Alexander Sarcophagus. The elaborate armour ('linothorax') is similar to that of Alexander himself on the mosaic, while the plumed Boeotian helmet, perhaps a badge of rank, is also worn by a figure on the mosaic. Riders on the Sarcophagus are depicted with the same equipment but some are unarmoured, so it may be that armour was worn or not as a matter of personal choice. The cloak is the yellow cloak with purple border distributed to his Companions by Alexander later in the campaign and often depicted in art in the following years. The purple tunic has short sleeves, though long sleeves were also worn (as on the following figure). The long spear (*xyston*) carried a blade at both ends.

3 – Prodromoi Cavalry
This figure is inspired by the cavalry figure on the 'Kinch tomb' painting, which is often (though somewhat speculatively) identified as a Prodromos. Equipment is typical of the cavalry of northern Greece and Macedonia, with tunic and cloak, long spear with a blade at each end, and helmet (in this case, Thracian). These lighter-armed cavalry do without body armour. The long-sleeved tunic seems to have been typical Macedonian wear at the time,

though the bright colours of the depicted clothing may be an indication of high rank rather than being typical of the dress of the mass of Prodromoi, as may the leopard skin, replacing a probably more typical coloured blanket.

4 – Hypaspist

Depicted here is a Macedonian 'peltast' (in the later, Hellenistic, sense), inspired by figures on the Agios Athanasios tomb and the 'Ajax and Cassandra' painting from Pompeii. A sleeveless red tunic is the only protection for the body, though a plumed and crested Thracian helmet is also worn. The shield is the smaller type of Macedonian shield embossed with the distinctive patterning, while armament is a spear (shorter than the full sarissa of the bulk of the infantry, and of a size that could be wielded with either one or both hands) and/or javelins, as required.

5 – Pezhetairos

This figure is based on the infantry on the Alexander Sarcophagus, and wears body armour ('linothorax') and Thracian helmet, greaves, and a larger type of shield similar in size and shape to the Classical hoplite shield. The armour is basically white with red details, as is commonly depicted on tombs, with a lion insignia based on a figure on the Sarcophagus. The decoration of the shield is based on an example on the Agios Athanasios tomb – the Sarcophagus shows a variety of painted faces on shields probably of mythological figures, which may have been at the choice of the bearer, or may have indicated unit affiliation. The long sarissa would be carried in both hands in action, the handles of the shield permitting the bearer's left hand to extend beyond the shield rim. The Sarcophagus figures are shown barefoot (or in some cases, completely naked) but boots would certainly have been worn on campaign.

6 – Asthetairos

A more speculative depiction based on figures from the Sarcophagus and later Macedonian tombs, and bearing a Macedonian shield (rimless, and with the distinctive patterning embossed on the surface). This figure has been tasked with some special duty – a rapid march or assault on a town perhaps – so has replaced his sarissa with a set of javelins. The wearing of a single shoe was common Greek practice, it being thought that a single bare foot gave better grip on difficult ground.

7 – later Pezhetairos or Asthetairos

Again, based on figures from the Alexander Sarcophagus, but now equipped with the later-pattern pilos helmet, which could also be ornamented with crest and plumes as a sign of rank. The purple colour of the armour and its lion decoration is based on the Sarcophagus; such highly coloured armour may again have been an indicator of rank. The highly decorated shield (based on the Agios Athanasios tomb) and colourful armour may also reflect the greater resources available to the Macedonian army in the later stages of the campaign.

8 – Javelinman

This figure is depicted in the traditional Macedonian costume of tunic, cloak and *kausia*, as depicted on the door guard figures of the Agios Athanasios tomb, but he is equipped with the equipment typical of Macedonian infantry before the reforms of Philip II, that is a leather *pelta* and javelins. Shades of brown and white would probably have been typical. Open lattice boots could be worn with socks in cold weather. This figure is typical of peltasts or javelinmen of the period, and probably (though without the *kausia*) also resembles the dress of the Agrianian javelinmen. Long-sleeved tunics were worn by cavalry, and may also have been worn among the infantry, though short sleeves were no doubt also common.

9 – Archer

Almost nothing is known of the dress of archers of this period; the figure depicted wears a simple tunic and no other equipment, besides his bow and quiver. Macedonian archers will have worn a *kausia*, or a helmet if they could get one, while there are some indications that Cretan archers carried a small round *pelta* which could be strapped to the left arm while shooting (or perhaps more practically, slung on the back). A sword will have been carried if available, though archers will have hoped to stay out of reach of their opponents, so needed little hand-to-hand or defensive equipment.

10 – 'Iphicratean' peltast

This figure is representative of many of the mercenary Greek infantry in the army – all those who were not fully-equipped hoplites. He is armed as an 'Iphicratean peltast', with spear, javelins, a light but moderately large, round leather shield, and simple 'pilos' helmet. While Greeks often did go into battle barefoot, the 'Iphicratean boot', calf length and made of leather, might also have been worn, but there would have been little uniformity of equipment. Clothing colours would have been up to the individual, with whites and reds probably favoured, though it is possible that striped tunics of the type worn by Thracians were also popular among mercenaries.

11 – Thessalian cavalry

This figure, based on Thessalian coins and figures from the Alexander Sarcophagus, depicts typical Greek heavy cavalry, armoured in a short 'muscled' cuirass, though this particular individual has broken his spear and taken to his sword, and has also lost his helmet, which would have been of Thracian or Boeotian type. His cloak is blue with a white border as suggested by a figure on the Sarcophagus.

12 – Greek cavalry

Greek cavalry combined relatively heavy defensive equipment (a muscled cuirass) with light offensive arms (javelins). This example, inspired by Athenian tombs, wears his campaign-dress *petasos* or sun hat and a simple sleeveless tunic. Such cavalry are also depicted unarmoured.

NOTES TO COLOUR PLATES

13 – Thracian cavalry
Inspired by figures depicted on the Kazanlak and Alexandrovo Thracian tombs, this is a typical Greek or Thracian light cavalryman, armed primarily with javelins. A white tunic is depicted in the tomb paintings, along with a Thracian helmet, though considerable variety of colours and designs was possible, and the better-off would no doubt have worn body armour. The Kazanlak paintings suggest that leggings and long sleeves could also be worn, perhaps depending on season. The horse bears a simple, brightly coloured blanket – a rolled cloth or leather saddle might also have been used.

14 – Thracian infantry
Based on one of the figures from the Kazanlak tomb, and with equipment similar to that of the Greek peltasts. This figure wears a red tunic, though a variety of colours is depicted in tombs, including broad stripes of red, yellow or white. Thracian infantry will have favoured javelins, but seem to have carried bladed weapons more frequently than their southern Greek equivalents. Typically a curved Thracian sword is depicted, but here the sword has a long wooden handle – this is perhaps the weapon referred to as the 'rhomphaia'. The helmet is based on the Kazanlak paintings; it is similar in style to the Chalcidian type. Thracian helmets, like those of the cavalry, could, of course, also have been worn, along with a variety of other helmet styles.

15 – Greek infantry (Hoplite)
Greek hoplite equipment shows signs of becoming heavier in this period, with a muscled cuirass, as shown here, depicted on Athenian tombs and the Alexander Sarcophagus, replacing the linen or leather armour worn earlier in the fourth century. However, there was doubtless much variability, with Hellenic League contingents perhaps more likely to wear metal armour, and mercenaries more likely to wear textiles or to be unarmoured. The Attic style of helmet, uncommon in Greece, suggests the variety of equipment that might be worn by mercenaries. Thracian helmets would also have been common.

16 – Hippotoxotai (horse archers)
Precise details of the equipment or dress of Alexander's hippotoxotai are lacking, but this figure is intended to be typical of the mounted archers of the steppe and adjoining regions forming the Upper Satrapies of the Persian Empire. Clothing is richly coloured in reds and blues, while primary equipment is a recurve bow and quiver, backed up (in emergencies only) by a sword or axe. A pointed fabric cap or hat would often be worn.

17 – Hippokontistai (Arachotians)
This figure suggests the clothing of cavalry of the Upper Satrapies, such as the Arachotians, based on reliefs from Persepolis. The exact identity of the Hippokontistai is unknown, but if they were Asian they would have dressed in a similar fashion to other light cavalry from the region. The bronze helmet is a type worn by Persian invaders of Greece in the fifth century, which may

have still been in use, or else the usual fabric cap or head covering would be worn. Two javelins were normally carried, with one being thrown and one retained for hand-to-hand combat.

18 – Persian Companion
This figure is based on the Persian cavalry – probably Darius' 'kinsmen' – fighting on the Alexander Mosaic. Quilted textile armour, in red, is shown on the mosaic, and yellow caps. Offensive arms would originally have been javelins. Darius upgraded these to long spears to match those of the Macedonians, though it is mentioned as a point of contention for the mutineers at Opis that Alexander replaced Persian javelins with Macedonian spears among his cavalry, so a mix of spears and javelins may have been used before they were re-equipped. This figure brandishes a traditional axe as a backup weapon. It is unlikely that Persians were expected to adopt Macedonian clothing, since we have records of Persians around the court in traditional dress, so a mixed unit of Companions (the Fifth Hipparchy) would have presented a variable mix of Macedonian and Persian dress and equipment.

19 – Indian infantry
Based on a figure from an 'elephant medallion'; Indian infantry were typically dressed in a (white) linen quilt and head-covering, and carried a large sword on a baldric, along with either a long narrow rectangular leather shield with javelins, or as here, a long bow. This is the type of bow said to have been shot with one end on the ground braced by the foot, though here a more normal shooting pose is shown.

20 – Epigonos/Persian 'phalangite'
The Epigonoi proper are said to have been issued Macedonian equipment, though they may have retained their Persian clothes. Depicted here is a figure suggested by the proposed mixed phalanx of Macedonian hoplites and Persian javelinmen, based on the infantry figure shown being ridden down by a Macedonian cavalryman in the Kinch tomb painting. Pale greens and off-whites are the colours shown on the Kinch tomb, while the 'Macedonian star' on the shield indicates that this man is supposed to take his place in a Macedonian unit.

Further Reading

The texts mentioned here are by no means intended to be comprehensive, merely to allow interested readers to delve deeper into the modern literature on Alexander and his army (which is very extensive). It is also, and for similar reasons, limited almost entirely to English language works.

The first starting point for anyone wishing to read further about Alexander's army is the ancient texts, chiefly Arrian, Curtius, Diodorus and Plutarch. All these are available in editions from the Loeb Classical Library which, very importantly, allows the original Greek or Latin to be consulted alongside the modern translation. This is essential since translators are often not especially rigorous in their translation of technical or military terms and will (entirely reasonably) provide translations that match their interpretation of the facts, rather than a strictly literal rendering of the original. All these texts are also available online through the excellent Perseus Digital Library (www.perseus.tufts.edu/hopper/). Other useful websites are LacusCurtius (penelope.uchicago.edu/Thayer/E/Roman/home.html), which contains full translations of Diodorus and other texts, and Livius (www.livius.org), which contains many useful articles on ancient history.

Modern accounts of the life of Alexander are numerous, with more published seemingly every year. Robin Lane Fox's *Alexander the Great* (1973) is rightly considered a classic, though it is relatively weak on military matters. More recent titles include Adrian Goldsworthy's *Philip and Alexander: Kings and Conquerors* (2021). Goldsworthy is a military historian, so is stronger than other writers on the army and battles.

Books dealing specifically with the army of Alexander are perhaps surprisingly rather thinner on the ground. The starting point should still be Nicholas Sekunda, *The Army of Alexander the Great* (1984), from Osprey. The format of Osprey titles – brief text, heavily illustrated – does not allow Sekunda to go into great detail, but his approach of basing reconstructions strictly on archaeological evidence is well supported by the colour plates. Other useful Osprey titles are Sekunda's *Macedonian Armies after Alexander 323–168 BC* (2012) and Waldemar Heckel, *Macedonian Warrior: Alexander's Elite Infantryman* (2007). For a recent, more in-depth study of the army, there is Stephen English, *The Army of Alexander the Great* (2009), together with its companion volumes on the sieges and field campaigns. English provides a useful analysis of the army, though I disagree with him on a number of points of detail. Also valuable is David Karunanithy, *The Macedonian War Machine* (2013), which gathers an astonishing wealth of evidence for many of the more obscure aspects of Macedonian armies. The text of Gabriele Esposito, *The Macedonian Armies of Philip II and Alexander the Great* (2022) is of little value, but the book does contain numerous colour photographs of re-enactors, which may be of interest. Older but still classic titles aimed at the general reader are Peter Connolly, *The Greek Armies* (1979) and *Greece and Rome at War* (new edition 2016) – notable particularly for the quality of Connolly's archaeological reconstructions and imaginative recreations of ancient scenes.

Other titles worth noting are J.F.C. Fuller's classic *The Generalship of Alexander the Great* (1960) for an account of Alexander's campaigns written by an experienced soldier, and Philip Sabin's *Lost Battles: Reconstructing the Great Clashes of the Ancient World*, which takes an innovative approach (a wargame model) to the reconstruction of ancient battles. I must also include my own *The Macedonian Phalanx* (2020), which goes into far more detail than is possible in the present volume on matters specifically related to the phalanx, such as drill, equipment and organisation.

In recent years, several compilation and 'Companion' volumes relevant to Alexander's campaigns have been published. These provide useful essays on many aspects of the period, and also extensive bibliographies and notes to support further reading. The most useful for present purposes are Ogden, *The Cambridge Companion to Alexander the Great* (2024) (although the chapter on the army is very brief), Sabin, van Wees and Whitby, *The Cambridge History of Greek and Roman Warfare I: Greece, the Hellenistic World and the Rise of Rome* (2007), and Roisman and Worthington, *A Companion to Ancient Macedonia* (2010). The last two contain essays from Nicholas Sekunda on Macedonian and Hellenistic armies, which expand on his Osprey title.

The more in-depth scholarly debates concerning Alexander's army, which I have only touched on in the present volume, can be pursued via the notes and bibliographies to the works noted above (and those listed below), and most recently in the chapter by C. Willekes, 'Army and Warfare', in Ogden's *Cambridge Companion* referenced above. Another good starting point is A.B. Bosworth, *A Historical Commentary on Arrian's History of Alexander* (two volumes, 1980, 1995). The appendices to P.A. Brunt's translation of Arrian in the Loeb edition are also very useful. The most important English language scholar for Macedonian history is N.G.L. Hammond, some of whose many articles are listed below, and who was also co-author with G.T. Griffith and F.W. Walbank of the essential, three volume *History of Macedonia* (volume 3 covers the reign of Alexander).

Finally, Alexander has naturally made some inroads into popular culture, and there are other ways outside of academic studies and popular histories to explore Alexander's world. In literature, Mary Renault's Alexander trilogy (*Fire from Heaven*, *The Persian Boy*, and *Funeral Games*) remain unsurpassed both as historical novels and for their evocation of the times in which Alexander lived. However, they do not contain much material that is relevant specifically to the army. Alexander's impact on the cinema has been rather modest – the 1956 *Alexander the Great*, starring Richard Burton (with improbable hair),

FURTHER READING

a talky sword and sandal epic, might in some ways be preferred to Oliver Stone's disappointing *Alexander* (2004), but the latter does include better sets and costumes, and a visually striking and mostly historically accurate depiction of the battle of Gaugamela which is worth seeing in its own right (the film's travesty of Hydaspes however is best avoided). Needless to say, there are numerous wargames and computer games inspired by Alexander's battles, with varying degrees of historical accuracy, none better than Sabin's *Lost Battles*. Worth seeing also are the battles in *Rome: Total War* by The Creative Assembly and its expansion, *Rome: Total War: Alexander*, which perhaps give some feel for the chaos and confusion of the ancient battlefield.

Bibliography

Aldrete, G.S., Bartell, S. and Aldrete, A. (2013), *Reconstructing Ancient Linen Body Armour: Unravelling the Linothorax Mystery* (Baltimore: Johns Hopkins University Press, 2013)

Andronikos, M. (1970), 'Sarissa', *Bulletin de Correspondance Hellénique*, 94 vol 1 (1970), pp.91–107

Andronikos, M. (1989), *Vergina: The Royal Tombs and the Ancient City* (Athens: Ekdotike Athenon, 1989)

Anson, E.M. (1981), 'Alexander's Hypaspists and the Argyraspides', *Historia*, 30 (1981), pp.117–20

Anson, E.M. (1985), 'The Hypaspists: Macedonia's Professional Citizen-Soldiers', *Historia*, 34 (1985), pp.246–8

Anson, E.M. (2008), 'Philip II and the Transformation of Macedonia: a Reappraisal', in T Howe and J Reames (eds), *Macedonian Legacies: Studies in Ancient Macedonian History and Culture in Honour of Eugene N Borza* (Claremont: Regina Books, 2008), pp.17–30

Anson, E.M. (2010a), 'The Introduction of the "Sarisa" In Macedonian Warfare', *Ancient Society*, vol.40 (2010), pp.51–68

Anson, E.M. (2010b), 'The Asthetairoi: Macedonia's Hoplites', in E. Carney and D. Ogden (eds), *Philip II and Alexander the Great: Father and Son, Lives and Afterlives* (Oxford: Oxford University Press, 2010), pp.81–90

Aperghis, G.G. (1997), 'Alexander's Hipparchies', *Ancient World*, 28 (1997), pp.133–48

Baynham, E. J. (2003), 'The Ancient Evidence for Alexander the Great', in J. Roisman (ed.), *Brill's Companion to Alexander the Great* (Leiden: Brill, 2003), pp.3–29

Badian, E. (1965), 'Orientals in Alexander's Army', *The Journal of Hellenic Studies*, vol.85 (1965), pp.160–161

Badian, E. (1977), 'The Battle of the Granicus, a New Look', in *Ancient Macedonia II* (Thessaloniki: Institute for Balkan Studies, 1977), pp.271–93

Bernard, P. (1990), 'Nouvelle contribution de l'épigraphie cunéiforme à l'histoire hellénistique', *Bulletin de correspondance Hellénique*, 114 (1990), pp. 514–41

Best, J.G.P. (1969), *Thracian Peltasts and their Influence on Greek Warfare* (Groningen: Wolters-Noordhoff, 1969)

Billows, R.A. (2018), *Before and After Alexander: The Legend and Legacy of Alexander the Great* (New York: Abrams, 2018)

Bloedow, E.F. (2015), 'On 'wagons' and 'shields': Alexander's crossing of Mt. Haemus in 335 BC', *Ancient History Bulletin*, 10 (2015), pp.119–30

Bosworth, A.B. (1973), 'Asthetairoi', *Classical Quarterly*, 23 (1973), pp.245–53

Bosworth, A.B. (1980), *A Historical Commentary on Arrian's History of Alexander* (Oxford: Clarendon Press, 1980), vol.1

Bosworth, A.B. (1986), 'Alexander the Great and the Decline of Macedon', *Journal of Hellenic Studies*, 106 (1986), pp.1–12

Bosworth, A.B. (1988), *Conquest and Empire: The Reign of Alexander the Great* (Cambridge: Cambridge University Press, 1988)

Bosworth, A.B. (1995), *A Historical Commentary on Arrian's History of Alexander* (Oxford: Clarendon Press, 1995), vol.2

Bosworth, A.B. (1997), 'A Cut Too Many? Occam's Razor and Alexander's Footguards' *Ancient History Bulletin*, 11 (1997), pp.47–56

Bosworth, A.B. (2010), 'The Argeads and the Phalanx', in E. Carney and D. Ogden (eds), *Philip II and Alexander the Great: Father and Son, Lives and Afterlives* (Oxford: Oxford University Press, 2010), pp.91–102

Brunt, P.A. (1963), 'Alexander's Macedonian Cavalry', *Journal of Hellenic Studies*, 83 (1963), pp.42–5

Buckler, J. (1985), 'Epameinondas and the "Embolon"', *Phoenix*, 39, 2 (1985), pp.134–143

Carney, E.D. (1996), 'Macedonians and Mutiny: Discipline and Indiscipline in the Army of Philip and Alexander', *Classical Philology*, 91 (1996), pp.19–44

Campbell, D. B. (2003), *Greek and Roman Artillery 399 BC – AD 363* (Oxford: Osprey, 2003)

Cartledge P. (2005), *Alexander the Great: The Hunt for a New Past* (Woodstock: Overlook Press, 2005)

Cohen, A. (1997), *The Alexander Mosaic: Stories of Victory and Defeat* (Cambridge: Cambridge University Press, 1997)

Collins, A.W. (2001), 'The Office of the Chiliarch under Alexander and the Successors', *Phoenix*, 55 (2001), pp.259–83

Connolly, P. (1998), *Greece and Rome at War* (London: Greenhill Books, 1998)

Connolly, P. (2000), 'Experiments with the sarissa – the Macedonian pike and cavalry lance – a functional view', *Journal of Roman Military Equipment Studies*, 11, pp.103–12

Devine, A.M. (1983), 'Embolon: a study in tactical terminology', *Phoenix*, 37 (1983), pp.201–17

Devine, A.M. (1985a), 'The strategies of Alexander the Great and Darius III in the Issus campaign', *Ancient World*, 12 (1985), pp.25–38

Devine, A.M. (1985b), 'Grand tactics at the battle of Issus', *Ancient World*, 12 (1985), pp.39–59

Devine, A.M. (1986), 'The battle of Gaugamela: a tactical and source-critical study', *Ancient World*, 13 (1986), pp.87–115

Devine, A.M. (1987), 'The battle of the Hydaspes: a tactical and source-critical study', *Ancient World*, 16 (1987), pp.91–113

Devine, A.M. (1988), 'A pawn-sacrifice at the battle of the Granicus: the origins of a favourite stratagem of Alexander the Great', *Ancient World*, 18 (1988), pp.3–20

Devine, A.M. (1989a), 'The Macedonian army at Gaugamela: its strength and the length of its battle-line', *Ancient World*, 19 (1989), pp.77–80

Devine, A.M. (1989b), 'Alexander the Great', in J. Hackett (ed.), *Warfare in the Ancient World* (London: Sidgwick & Jackson, 1989), pp.104–29

Ellis, J.R. (1975), 'Alexander's Hypaspists Again', *Historia*, 24 (1975), pp.617–8

Ellis, J.R. (1976), *Philip II and Macedonian Imperialism* (Princeton: Princeton University Press, 1976)

Engels, D.W. (1978), *Alexander the Great and the Logistics of the Macedonian Army* (Berkeley: University of California Press, 1978)

English, S. (2009), *The Army of Alexander the Great* (Barnsley: Pen & Sword, 2009)

English, S. (2010), *The Sieges of Alexander the Great* (Barnsley: Pen & Sword, 2010)

English, S. (2011), *The Field Campaigns of Alexander the Great* (Barnsley: Pen & Sword, 2011)

Esposito, G. (2022), *The Macedonian Army of Philip II and Alexander the Great 359–323 BC* (Barnsley: Pen & Sword, 2022)

Faure, P. (1982), *La vie quotidienne des armées d'Alexandre* (Paris: Hachette, 1982)

Foss, C. (1977), 'The battle of the Granicus: a new look', in *Ancient Macedonia 2* (Thessaloniki: Institute for Balkan Studies, 1977), pp.495–502

Fuller, J.F.C. (1960), *The Generalship of Alexander the Great* (New Brunswick: Rutgers University Press, 1960)

Gauthier, P., and Hatzopoulos, M.B. (1993), *La loi gymnasiarchique de Béroia* (Athens, Paris: Diffusion de Boccard, 1993)

Goldsworthy, A. (2021), *Philip and Alexander: Kings and Conquerors* (London: Bloomsbury, 2021)

Green, P. (1991), *Alexander of Macedon* (second edition) (Berkeley: University of California Press, 1991)

Griffith, G.T. (1935), *The Mercenaries of the Hellenistic World* (Cambridge: University Press, 1935)

Griffith, G.T. (1963), 'A Note on the Hipparchies of Alexander', *Journal of Hellenic Studies*, 83 (1963), pp.68–74

Griffith, G.T. (1980), 'Philip as General and the Macedonian Army', in M.B. Hatzopoulos and L.D. Loukopulos (eds), *Philip of Macedon* (London: Heinemann, 1980), pp.58–77.

Griffith, G.T. (1981), 'Peltasts, and the Origins of the Macedonian Phalanx', in H.D. Dell and E.N. Borza (eds) (1981), *Ancient Macedonian Studies in honor of Charles F. Edson* (Thessaloniki: Institute for Balkan Studies, 1981), pp.161–179

Hamilton, J.R. (1956), 'The cavalry battle at the Hydaspes', *Journal of Hellenic Studies*, 76 (1956), pp.26–31

Hammond, N.G.L. (1978), 'Note on Argyraspides (Silver Shields) and Hypaspists (Shield Bearers)', *Classical Quarterly*, 28 (1978), p.135

Hammond, N.G.L. (1980a), 'Training in the use of the sarissa and its effects in battle 359–333 BC', *Antichthon*, 14 (1980), pp.53–63

Hammond, N.G.L. (1980b), 'The Battle of the Granicus river', *Journal of Hellenic Studies*, 100 (1980), pp.73–88

Hammond, N.G.L. (1983), 'Army Transport in the fifth and fourth centuries', *Greek, Roman and Byzantine Studies*, 24 (1983), pp.27–31

Hammond, N.G.L. 1989a), *The Macedonian State: the Origins, Institutions and History* (Oxford: Clarendon Press, 1989)

Hammond, N.G.L. (1989b), 'Casualties and reinforcements of citizen soldiers in Greece and Macedonia', *Journal of Hellenic Studies* 109 (1989), pp.56–68

Hammond, N.G.L. (1989c), *Alexander the Great: King Commander and Statesman* (2nd ed.) (London: Bloomsbury, 1989)

Hammond, N.G.L. (1991), 'The various guards of Philip II and Alexander III', *Historia*, 40 (1991), pp.396–418

Hammond, N.G.L. (1992), 'Alexander's charge at the battle of Issus in 333 BC', *Historia*, 41 (1992), pp.395–406

Hammond, N.G.L. (1995), 'Connotations of Macedonia and Macedones', *Classical Quarterly*, 45 (1995), pp.120–128

Hammond, N.G.L. (1996), 'Alexander's Non-European Troops and Ptolemy I's Use of Such Troops', *The Bulletin of the American Society of Papyrologists*, vol.33, no.1/4 (1996), pp.99–109

Hammond, N.G.L. (1997a), 'Arrian's Mentions of Infantry Guards', *Ancient History Bulletin*, 11 (1997), pp.20–4

Hammond, N.G.L. (1997b), 'What may Philip have learned as a hostage in Thebes?', *Greek, Roman and Byzantine Studies*, 38 (1997), pp. 355–72

Hammond, N.G.L. and Griffith G.T. (1979), *A History of Macedonia*, vol.2, 550-336 B.C. (Cambridge: University Press, 1979)

Hatzopoulos, M.B. (1996), *Macedonian Institutions under the Kings* (Athens: National Hellenic Research Foundation, 1996)

Hatzopoulos, M.B. (2001), *L'organisation de l'armée macédonienne sous les Antigonides. Problèmes anciens et documents nouveaux* (Paris: De Boccard, 2001)

Head, D. (1982), *Armies of the Macedonian and Punic Wars* (Worthing: Wargames Research Group, 1982)

Head, D. (1992), *The Achaemenid Persian Army* (Stockport: Montvert, 1992)

Heckel, W. (1986), 'Somataphylakia: A Macedonian Cursus Honorum', *Phoenix*, 40 (1986), pp.279–94

Heckel, W. (1992), *The Marshals of Alexander's Empire* (London: Routledge, 1992)

Heckel, W. (2003), 'King and "Companions": Observations on the Nature of Power in the Reign of Alexander', in J. Roisman (ed.), *Brill's Companion to Alexander the Great* (Leiden: Brill, 2003), pp.195–225

Heckel, W. (2005), 'Synaspismos, Sarissas and the Thracian Wagons', *Acta Classica*, 48 (2005), pp.189–194

Heckel, W. (2006), *Who's Who in the Age of Alexander the Great* (Hoboken: Wiley, 2006)

Heckel, W. (2009), 'The Asthetairoi: A Closer Look' in Wheatley and Hanna (eds), *Alexander and his Successors* (Dunedin: Regina Books, 2009), pp. 99–117

Heckel, W. (2012), 'The Royal Hypaspists in Battle: Macedonian Hamippoi', *Ancient History Bulletin*, 26 (2012), pp.16–20

Heckel, W., and Jones, R. (2006), *Macedonian Warrior: Alexander's Elite Infantryman* (Oxford: Osprey, 2007)

Heckel, W., Naiden, F. S., Garvin, E. E. and Vanderspoel, J. (eds) (2021), *A Companion To Greek Warfare* (Chichester: Wiley-Blackwell, 2021)

Heckel, W., Willekes, C., Wrightson, G. (2010), 'Scythed Chariots at Gaugamela: A Case Study', in Carney & D. Ogden (eds), *Philip II and Alexander the Great: Father and Son, Lives and Afterlives* (Oxford: Oxford University Press, 2010), pp.103–9

Holt, F.L. (2003), *Alexander the Great and the Mystery of the Elephant Medallions* (Berkeley: University of California Press, 2003)

Howe, T. (2015), 'Arrian and "Roman" military tactics: Alexander's campaign against the autonomous Thracians', in Howe, T., Garvin, E.E, and Wrightson, G. (eds) *Greece, Macedon and Persia: Studies in social, political and military history in honour of Waldemar Heckel* (Oxford: Oxbow Books, 2015), pp. 87–93

Howe, T., Garvin, E.E, and Wrightson, G. (eds) (2015), *Greece, Macedon and Persia: Studies in social, political and military history in honour of Waldemar Heckel* (Oxford: Oxbow Books, 2015)

Juhel, P. (2009), 'The Regulation Helmet of the Phalanx and the Introduction of the Concept of Uniform in the Macedonian Army at the end of the reign of Alexander the Great', *Klio*, 91 (2009), pp.342–55.

Juhel, P. (2017a), 'The rank insignia of the officers of the Macedonian phalanx: the lessons of iconography and an indirect reference in Vegetius', in Rance, P. and Sekunda, N.V., *Greek Taktika: Ancient Military Writing and its Heritage* (Gdańsk: Foundation for the Development of Gdańsk University, 2017), pp.167–179

Juhel, P. (2017b), *Autour de l'infanterie d'élite macédonienne à l'époque du royaume antigonide* (Oxford: Archaeopress, 2017)

Karunanithy, D. (2013), *The Macedonian War Machine* (Barnsley: Pen & Sword, 2013)

Keyser, P. (1994), 'The Use of Artillery by Philip II and Alexander the Great', *Ancient World*, 1994, pp.27–59

King, C.J. (2010), 'Macedonian kingship and other political institutions', in J. Roisman and I. Worthington (eds.), *A Companion to Ancient Macedonia* (Chichester: Wiley-Blackwell, 2010), pp.373–91

Lane Fox, R.J., (1973), *Alexander the Great* (London: Allen Lane, 1973)

Lane Fox, R.J. (2011), 'Philip's and Alexander's Macedon', in R.J. Lane Fox (ed), *Brill's Companion to Ancient Macedon* (Leiden: Brill, 2011), pp.367–91

Lee, J.W. (2001), 'Urban combat at Olynthos, 348 BC', in Freeman and Pollard (eds) *Fields of Conflict: Progress and Prospect in Battlefield Archaeology* (Oxford: British Archaeological Reports, 2001), pp.11–22

Liampi, K. (1998), *Der makedonische Schild* (Bonn: Deutsches Archäologisches Institut Athen, 1998)

Lloyd, A.B. (1996), 'Philip II and Alexander the Great: The Moulding of Macedon's Army', in A.B. Lloyd (ed.), *Battle in Antiquity* (London: Duckworth, 1996), pp.169–98

Lock, R.A. (1977), 'The Origins of the Argyraspids', *Historia*, 26 (1977), pp.373–8

Lush, D. (2007), 'Body Armour in the Phalanx of Alexander's Army', *Ancient World*, 38 (2007), pp.15–37

Manning, S. (2021), *Armed Force in the Teispid-Achaemenid Empire: Past approaches, Future Prospects* (Stuttgart: Franz Steiner Verlag, 2021)

Manti, P.A. (1983), 'The cavalry sarissa', *Ancient World*, 8 (1983), pp.73–80

Manti, P.A. (1992), 'The sarissa of the Macedonian infantry', *Ancient World*, 23.2 (1992), pp.31–42

Manti, P.A. (1994), 'The Macedonian sarissa, again', *Ancient World*, 25.1 (1994), pp.77–91

Markle, M.M. (1977), 'The Macedonian Sarissa, Spear, and Related Armor', *American Journal of Archaeology*, 81 (1977), pp.323–39.

Markle, M.M. (1978), 'Use of the Sarissa by Philip and Alexander of Macedon', *American Journal of Archaeology*, 82 (1978), pp.483–97

Markle, M.M. (1982), 'Macedonian Arms and Tactics under Alexander the Great', in Barr-Sharrar and Borza (eds), *Macedonia and Greece in Late Classical and Early Hellenistic Age* (Washington, National Gallery of Art, 1982), pp.87–111

Markle, M.M. (1999), 'A shield monument from Veria and the chronology of Macedonian shield types', *Hesperia*, 68, 2 (1999), pp.219–54

Marsden, E.W. (1964), *The Campaign of Gaugamela* (Liverpool: Liverpool University Press, 1964)

Marsden, E.W. (1977), 'Macedonian Military Machinery and its Designers under Philip II' *Ancient Macedonia* 2 (Thessaloniki: Institute for Balkan Studies, 1977), pp.211–23

Matthew, C. (2015), *An Invincible Beast: Understanding the Hellenistic Pike Phalanx at War* (Barnsley: Pen & Sword, 2015)

Millett, P. (2010), 'The political economy of Macedonia', in J. Roisman and I. Worthington (eds.), *A Companion to Ancient Macedonia* (Chichester: Wiley-Blackwell, 2010), pp.472–504

Milns, R.D. (1963), 'Alexander's Macedonian Cavalry and Diodorus xvii 17.4', *Journal of Hellenic Studies*, 86 (1966), pp.167–8

Milns, R.D. (1967), 'Philip II and the Hypaspists', *Historia*, 16 (1967), pp.509–12

Milns, R.D. (1971), 'The Hypaspists of Alexander III, Some Problems', *Historia*, 20 (1971), pp.186–95

Milns, R.D. (1976), 'The Army of Alexander the Great', in Badian (ed) *Alexander le Grand: Image et Réalité* (Geneva: Entretiens Hardt, 1976), pp.87–136

Milns, R.D. (1987), 'Army Pay and the Military Budget of Alexander the Great', in Will (ed), *Zu Alexander dem Grossen Festschrift G. Wirth* (Amsterdam: Verlag Adolf M. Hakkert, 1987), pp.233–56

Milns, R.D. (2003), 'Alexander's Seventh Phalanx Battalion', *Greek, Roman, And Byzantine Studies*, vol.7, no.2 (2003), pp.159–166

Nankov, E. (2021), 'Thracian Warfare', in Heckel, W., Naiden, F. S., Garvin, E. E. and Vanderspoel, J. (eds), *A Companion To Greek Warfare* (Chichester: Wiley-Blackwell, 2021), pp.214–224

Noguera Borel, A. (1999), 'L'évolution de la phalange macédonienne: le cas de la sarisse', *Ancient Macedonia 6* (Thessaloniki: Institute for Balkan Studies, 1999), pp.839–50

Noguera Borel, A. (2006), 'Le recrutement de l'armeé macédonienne sous le royauté' in A.-M. Guimier-Sorbets, M.B. Hatzopoulos and Y. Morizot (eds), *Rois, cités, nécropoles: Institutions, rites et monuments en Macédoine* (Athens: Centre de Recherche de l'Antiquité grecque et romaine, 2006), pp.227–37

Ogden, D. (2024), *The Cambridge Companion to Alexander the Great* (Cambridge: Cambridge University Press, 2024)

Papazoglu, F. (1978), *The Central Balkan Tribes in Pre-Roman Times: Triballi, Autariatae, Dardanians, Scordisci and Moesians* (trans. M. Stansfield-Popovic) (Amsterdam: Hakkert, 1978)

Parke, H.W. (1933), *Greek Mercenary Soldiers from the Earliest Times to the Battle of Ipsus* (Oxford: Clarendon Press, 1933)

Rance, P. and Sekunda, N.V. (2017), *Greek Taktika: Ancient Military Writing and its Heritage* (Gdańsk: Foundation for the Development of Gdańsk University, 2017)

Roisman, J. (ed.) (2003), *Brill's Companion to Alexander the Great* (Leiden: Brill, 2003)

Roisman, J. (2012), *Alexander's Veterans and the Early Wars of the Successors* (Austin: University of Texas Press, 2012)

Romane, P. (1987), 'Alexander's Siege of Tyre', *Ancient World*, 16 (1987), pp.79–90

Romane, P. (1988), 'Alexander's Siege of Gaza, 332 BC', *Ancient World*, 18 (1988), pp.21–30

Sabin, P. (2007), *Lost Battles: Reconstructing the Great Clashes of the Ancient World* (London: Hambledon Continuum, 2007)

Sawada, N. (2010), 'Social Customs and Institutions: Aspects of Macedonian Elite Society', in Roisman and Worthington (eds), *A Companion to Ancient Macedonia* (Chichester: Wiley-Blackwell, 2010), pp.392–408

Schefold, K. (1968), *Der Alexander-Sarkofag* (Frankfurt-Berlin: Propylien Verlag, 1968)

Sekunda, N.V. (1981), 'The Rhomphaia, a Thracian Weapon of the Hellenistic Period', in *Ancient Bulgaria: Papers presented to the International Symposium on the Ancient History and Archaeology of Bulgaria* (Nottingham: University of Nottingham, 1981), pp.275–88

Sekunda, N.V. (1984), (with A. McBride), *The Army of Alexander the Great* (Oxford: Osprey, 1984)

Sekunda, N.V. (1992), (with S. Chew), *The Persian Army 560-330 BC* (Stockport: Montvert, 1992)

Sekunda, N.V. (2001a), 'The Sarissa', *Acta Universitatis Lodziensis, Folia Archaeologica 23* (Lodz: The University of Lodz, 2001), pp.13–41

Sekunda, N.V. (2001b), 'Antigonid shield device on a stele of a Cretan from Demetrias', *Archaeologia*, 52 (2001), pp.19–22

Sekunda, N.V. (2007), 'Military Forces: A. Land Forces' in Sabin, van Wees and Whitby (eds), *The Cambridge History of Greek and Roman Warfare I, Greece, the Hellenistic World and the Rise of Rome* (Cambridge: Cambridge University Press, 2007), pp.326–9

Sekunda, N.V. (2010), 'The Macedonian Army', in Roisman and Worthington (eds), *A Companion to Ancient Macedonia* (Chichester: Wiley-Blackwell, 2010), pp.446–71

Sekunda, N.V. (2012), (with P. Dennis), *Macedonian Armies after Alexander 323–168 BC* (Oxford: Osprey, 2012)

Sekunda, N.V. (2013a), *The Antigonid Army* (Gdańsk: Foundation for the Development of University of Gdańsk, 2013)

Sekunda, N.V. (2013b), 'The Iphicratean Peltast Reform' in A. A. Sinitsyn and M. M. Kholod (ed.), *KOINON ΔΩPON. Studies and Essays in Honour of Valery P. Nikonorov on the Occasion of His Sixtieth Birthday Presented by His Friends and Colleagues* (St. Petersburg: St Petersburg State University, 2013)

BIBLIOGRAPHY

Sekunda, N.V. and Burliga, B. (eds.) (2014), *Iphicrates, Peltasts and Lechaeum* (Gdańsk: Foundation for the Development of Gdańsk University, 2014)

Sekunda, N.V. and Warry, J. (1998), *Alexander the Great: his armies and campaigns 334–323 BC* (Oxford: Osprey, 1998)

Speck, H. (2002), 'Alexander at the Persian Gates. A Study in Historiography and Topography', *American Journal of Ancient History*, 1.1 (2002), pp.15–234

Spence, I.G. (1993), *The Cavalry of Classical Greece: A Social and Military History* (Oxford: Clarendon Press, 1993)

Stoyanov, T. (2015), 'Warfare', in Valeva, J. (et. al, eds.), *A Companion to Ancient Thrace* (Hoboken: Wiley, 2015), pp.426–42

Strootman, R. (2011), 'Alexander's Thessalian cavalry', *Talanta*, 42/43 (2010–2011), pp.51–67

Tarn, W.W. (1948), *Alexander the Great* (Cambridge: Cambridge University Press, 1948)

Taylor, R. (2020), *The Macedonian Phalanx* (Barnsley: Pen & Sword, 2020)

Taylor, R. (2021), *The Greek Hoplite Phalanx* (Barnsley: Pen & Sword, 2021)

Ueda-Sarson, L. (2001), 'Macedonian Unit Organisations', *Slingshot*, 214, pp.35–38

Ueda-Sarson, L. (2002a), 'The Reforms of Iphikrates', *Slingshot*, 222, (2002), pp.30–6

Ueda-Sarson, L. (2002b), 'Infantry of the Successors', *Slingshot*, 223, (2002), pp.23–8

Valeva, J. (et. al, eds.) (2015), *A Companion to Ancient Thrace* (Hoboken: Wiley, 2015)

Webber, C. (2001) (with A. McBride), *The Thracians 700 BC–AD 46* (Oxford: Osprey, 2001)

Webber, C. (2003), *Odrysian Cavalry Arms, Equipment, and Tactics* (British Archaeology Reports International Series, 2003)

Webber, C. (2011), *The Gods of Battle: The Thracians at War, 1500 BC – 150 AD* (Barnsley: Casemate, 2011)

Whatley, N. (1964), 'On the possibility of reconstructing Marathon and other ancient battles', *Journal of Hellenic Studies*, 84 (1964), pp.119–39

Willekes, C. (2015), 'Equine aspects of Alexander the Great's Macedonian cavalry', in Howe, T., Garvin, E.E, and Wrightson, G. (eds), *Greece, Macedon and Persia: Studies in social, political and military history in honour of Waldemar Heckel* (Oxford: Oxbow Books, 2015), pp.47–58

Willekes, C. (2024), 'Army and Warfare', in Ogden, D. (ed.), *The Cambridge Companion to Alexander the Great* (Cambridge: Cambridge University Press, 2024) pp.243–55

Worthington, I. (2004), 'Alexander the Great and the Greeks in 336? Another Reading of "IG" II^2 329', *Zeitschrift für Papyrologie und Epigraphik*, Bd. 147 (2004), pp.59–71

Worthington, I. (2008), *Philip II of Macedonia* (New Haven: Yale University Press, 2008)

Wrightson, G. (2010), 'The Nature of Command in the Macedonian Sarissa Phalanx', *The Ancient History Bulletin*, 24 (2010), pp.71–92.

Index

Note that many topics (such as 'Companions') occur very frequently throughout the text - only the main discussion is referenced below.

Agrianians 85-88
Allied cavalry 88-93
Allied infantry 93-98
Archers 72-75
Argyraspides 56, 110, 118
    See also Hypaspists
Asthetairoi 52-72

Battle cry 143-144
Bodyguards 124-125
    See also Hypaspists
Boeotian helmet 32, 36, 78

Chaironeia, battle of 6, 20, 66, 90
Companion Cavalry 28-40, 108
    Asians in 120-1
    command of 124
Cretans 74, 95

Elephants 116-117, 197-206
Engineers 99-103
Epigonoi 117-121

Gaugamela, battle of 186-197
Gaza, siege of 160
Granicus, battle of 167-175
Greek cavalry 88-93
Greek infantry 93-99, 111-113

Haimos, mount 150
Halicarnassos, siege of 21, 156-157
Hamippoi
Hellenic League 6, 20, 77, 89-90, 104, 111, 141
Hipparchies 105-109
Hippakontistai 113-114

Hippotoxotai 114-115
Hydaspes, battle of 197-206
Hypaspists 44-52

Indian forces 115-117
Intelligence 136-138
Issus, battle of 176-186

Jaxartes 152-153

Kausia 32-33
Kopis 37-38, 88, 174

Languages 119
League of Corinth - see Hellenic League
Logistics 133-136
Lyginos River 151

Mallian cities 164-165
Massaga 153-154, 163
Melophoroi 119-120
Mercenaries 93-98. 111-113

Odrysians 80-81, 85
Opis mutiny 113, 118-120

Pages 125
Pay 144-146
Peltasts 45, 50, 61-2, 74, 81, 85-86, 95-98
Persian Gates 152
Pezhetairoi 19-20, 52-72
Prodromoi 40-43

Recruitment 139-142
Religion 148
River crossings 132-133